Heraldry and Armor
of the Middle Ages

SOLA VIRTUS INVICTA

NORFOLK

Premier Duke and Earl and Hereditary Earl Marshall

Heraldry and Armor of the Middle Ages

Marvin H. Pakula

South Brunswick and New York:
A. S. Barnes and Company
London: Thomas Yoseloff Ltd

A. S. Barnes and Co., Inc.
Cranbury, New Jersey 08512

Thomas Yoseloff Ltd
108 New Bond Street
London W1Y OQX, England

Library of Congress Cataloging in Publication Data

Pakula, Marvin H
   Heraldry and armor of the Middle Ages.

   Bibliography: p.
   1. Heraldry. 2. Heraldry—Gt. Brit. 3. Arms and armor.
I. Title.
CR21.P25   929.8′0942   74-146770
ISBN 0-498-07843-4

Printed in the United States of America

To my wife,
Barbara,
whose help
with this text
was invaluable.

Contents

Foreword

Heraldry, a science developed in England during the Middle Ages, was a happy blending of artistry and tradition that has also been called "the shorthand of history." With these credentials to speak for it, heraldry is surely a matter of wide appeal.

The text that follows will carefully outline the many components and practices of this science without any attempt to catalogue the families who bear heraldic arms. The College of Arms in England exists partly for this purpose and has ably handled this enormous task.

From time to time, however, actual arms will be introduced to illustrate each phase of heraldry as it is being dealt with. It is the hope of the author that the information presented will help to provide an understanding of this subject and enable those so disposed to further pursue its study on more solid footing.

MARVIN H. PAKULA

Acknowledgments

The author is deeply indebted to the following people and organizations for their part in providing material, advice, or assistance in the preparation of this book: British Museum, Ministry of Defence, London; Gunther Pohl, Chief of Local History and Geneology, New York Public Library, and his associates, Frank Bradley and Lilian Zwyns; Picture Collection, New York Public Library; British Information Service, New York; Stephen V. Grancsay, past Curator, Metropolitan Museum of Art, New York; Chester Stevens, United States Playing Card Company, Cincinnati, Ohio; Cincinnati Art Museum, Cincinnati; Nancy DeAngelo, New York.

Introduction

English heraldry, as far as it can be established, began in the year 1127. The seeds of its creation were planted, however, more than a half-century earlier in 1066 at the time of the Norman invasion. A brief account of the times that brought heraldry into being will give it greater perspective.

Eleventh-century England had been ruled by Saxon kings, descendants of Germanic tribesmen who had conquered the land hundreds of years earlier. Their reign was not an easy one, as the continuously invading Danes had eventually gained the central portion. A few years later the Saxon resistance in the North collapsed and Canute, son of the Danish king, became the ruler of northern England.

With the death of Canute in 1035, oddly the kingdom soon dissolved. Two of his three sons died after ruling briefly in his place. A Wessex (West Saxon) earl named Godwin, a leader of the Danes, brought Edward, the exiled son of defeated Saxon King Ethelred back from Normandy to rule. He had hoped that this move would gain the support of both factions as well as the confidence of the new king, thus making him a power behind the throne.

Edward, however, had been influenced by his Norman upbringing while in long exile and so the Normans, instead, gained favor in his court. Realizing Godwin's lofty ambitions, after nine years of intrigue and counter-intrigue, they drove him out of the country.

The following year Godwin, who was not content to remain in exile, recruited Flemish troops and, supported by his son Harold, returned to drive out the Norman agents. In so doing he established himself as the guiding force behind Edward.

England witnessed considerable religious and artistic development during the reign of the pious Edward, who came to be known as Edward the Confessor. Un-

Great Seal of Edward the Confessor

13

fortunately the country did not progress in other respects, including its military defenses.

Edward had promised his cousin William, Duke of Normandy, that the throne of England would be his when he died. William still held some doubts that Edward's wish would be granted with Harold the Dane in the way. Through a twist of fate, Harold fell into William's hands about two years before the king's death. A ship in which Harold was sailing the Channel was windswept onto the French coast. As William's eventual prisoner, he was forced to renounce any future claim to the throne in order to secure release.

When Edward died in 1066, he supposedly used his last breath to go back on his promise to William. His final wish was that Harold, who had provided good counsel to him, be proclaimed king. The news of Harold's accession caught angry ears both in Normandy and Norway. William, outraged at the turn of events in which two men had individually cheated him of the English Crown, quickly mounted an invasion force. At the same time, irate descendants of King Canute stood ready to reassert their claim to the throne.

In Norway, King Harold Hardrada was met by Tostig, the vengeful and exiled half-brother of the new English sovereign. Tostig, who was ousted from his Northumbrian earldom by Harold of England, informed the Norwegian king of the weakness in English defenses. Together, the two set out on a second invasion.

The Scandinavian force landed first and attacked, meeting early success against a small isolated force near York. Five days later King Harold of England marched toward York with his main body to confront the invaders. In the course of the battle of Stamford Bridge, decisively in favor of the English, both the King of Norway and Tostig were killed.

In October, the following month, William of Normandy landed in Pevensey Bay. The first attacks against Harold's forces at Hastings proved fruitless, but a feigned retreat drew the well-positioned English out into the open where the Norman cavalry cut them down. Left with just his force of bodyguards to fight and protect him, Harold watched the approach of twilight. The Norman archers aimed their arrows high to clear the tall shields of the bodyguards and struck the King a mortal wound in the right eye. The battle had been lost.

Although William was crowned King of England a month and a half later, he encountered armed resistance in north England for the next five years. Leaders in William's army took possession of land according to their rank, and made their jurisdictions secure by fortifications placed at strategic points.

Because of the extreme hostility of the population for 20 years after the Battle of Hastings, it was necessary for the Norman kings to grant titles, land, and authority to a great deal of their followers and thus obligate them to maintain order. Such feudal lords would in turn grant titles and entrust holdings to their lower-ranking comrades-at-arms in exchange for *their* support. Such was the pyramided feudal system that controlled England.

It was under these Norman rulers that heraldry sprung up in England, and the many lordships created at the onset of their reign would soon take up the dignity of shield insignia.

Heraldry and Armor
of the Middle Ages

1

Heraldry—Its Meaning and Its Origin

The word *heraldry* is an obvious derivation or extension of the term *herald*. A herald of the Middle Ages was originally a tournament "crier," a man who was hired as needed to announce contestants before each event, and also describe their personal marks of identity. He first served the nobles who sponsored such tournaments, but in time he served only the king in this capacity.

As the king's permanent retainer, it was natural that the herald was soon called upon to make *all* royal proclamations. The herald then became entrusted with royal dispatches to other courts, and consequently, he often acted with the authority of an ambassador. Some of his dispatches indeed bore a message of war or peace. When in his own court, he would announce official visitors whom he identified by their flag or shield insignia.

The use of symbols grew with the ensuing years and so did the herald's knowledge of them. By the year 1200, insignias had developed a complex system of styling and in the next century were governed by specific rules and terminology. In this new form it became a science, and the herald became its prime authority. Quite logically this new science was called heraldry.

In approaching heraldry as a science, it is wise to first understand the full meaning of the word. Those with just a passing interest in this field would be inclined to define it simply as "coats of arms." While there

is a strong connection between the two terms, the latter one is technically only a facet of this colorful subject.

An authoritative but terse definition of heraldry by a renowned present-day writer is: "The *systematic* use of *hereditary* devices centered upon the shield."[1]

Another authority describes it as: "That science which takes into account the rules and laws governing the use, display and knowledge of the pictured signs and emblems pertaining to the shield, helmet or banner."[2]

A third explanation to be presented is: "The art of arranging and explaining in proper terms all that relates or pertains to the bearing of arms, crests, quarterings and other hereditary marks of honour."[3]

Some of these terms employed may be strange to those newly introduced to heraldry, but each will be further clarified in due course. In the first definition, I have emphasized two key words (*systematic* and *hereditary*) that will also be dealt with shortly. In the same definition, the word *devices* also appears, which will now aptly serve as a focal point from which to begin a search into the origin of heraldry.

Devices, as applied to the subject at hand, refer to the symbols or insignia placed upon the battle shield.

---

1. Sir A. R. Wagner (Garter Principal King of Arms).
2. Arthur Fox-Davies (Barrister at Law).
3. Sir Bernard Burke, C.B., L.L.D. (Ulster King of Arms).

A herald proclaiming a tournament (15th Century)

Symbols have been used since the earliest civilization to express either general ideas or religious sentiment. In this regard, the lion and the cross have become the most prevalent. The cross needs no explanation as to its significance, and the lion was usually suggestive of the shield-bearer's courage or strength.

During the Crusades, the cross was also worn on the surcoat or tunic of the Christian knights and was symbolic of their mission. The lion eventually became associated with nobility, since it was adopted in battle by many of the English sovereigns and feudal lords. Symbolism, however, up to the middle of the 12th cen-

tury, was an unstable commodity and generally not prone to establishing personal identities.

Shield devices were constantly subject to the mood of the individual bearer, and it was not uncommon for many symbols to be successively adopted and discarded by one warrior within his lifetime. This transient use of symbolism is not considered to be heraldic in nature. With personal devices ever changing, they clearly lacked hereditary usage and were ungoverned by any sort of system. The system that was actually employed in heraldry will be outlined in future chapters.

Authorities of modern times draw little or no rela-

French heralds of the 15th century

tionship between early symbolism and what is presently regarded as heraldic. Certain writings of the 16th and 17th centuries on this subject have mistakenly linked the two symbolic forms or added mystery and complexities in interpreting them. The fact that some ancient symbols had been later adopted *solely* because of their decorative merit, falsely led writers to the assumption that the original symbolic *meaning* was embraced as well. They also falsely concluded that their reappearance was a continuance of an *unbroken* line of hereditary usage. We have since established that ancient symbolism was *not* hereditary, *not* systematic, and unrelated in significance to insignia later adopted from its time.

An official act by Henry II was the basis for the

Geoffrey, Count of Anjou; father of Henry II

innovation of heraldry in 1127. In knighting his son-in-law Geoffrey of Anjou, he presented him with a blue shield bearing six small golden lions, which became Geoffrey's distinctive insignia throughout his lifetime. Upon his death, the insignia was adopted by successive generations of his descendants. Because it was used specifically in this manner, it became the first known example of true heraldry.

Shortly after Geoffrey's attainment of knighthood, another insignia came into evidence that satisfied the requirements of a heraldic device. It was found in the personal seal of another noble, Gilbert of Clare, the Earl of Hertford. The imprint, affixed to a document dating somewhere between 1138–1146, showed three chevrons vertically aligned upon a shield. Just as the previous shield was perpetuated by future descendants, so too were the arms of the Earl of Hertford.

The word *arms* is the more commonly used expression for total heraldic bearings or *achievements*. Its derivation can be easily understood in that the shield was a *defensive arm* carrying the bearer's insignia. The words *arms* and *achievements* are two of many terms in the heraldic vocabulary that was soon to be formed.

Perhaps the greatest stimulants affecting the origin of heraldic devices were the tournaments—games or contests staged to develop skill in battle, similar to the more complex army maneuvers of modern times. These tournaments were carried out with much pomp and pageantry in the presence of an audience. In the way that athletes now wear identifying team colors and personal numbers, tournament contestants wore distinctive insignia upon their shields. The insignia chosen might have been once carried in battle with valor and distinction by the proud contestant's father.

If such a contestant proved continually triumphant in tournament games, his shield insignia would eventually be well known enough to identify him as a warrior of superior skill and strength. Under these circumstances he would be further bound by increased pride to retain the use of it. The subject of tournaments is widely detailed and, accordingly, is given much wider coverage in this book, but for the present it is being cited only for the great influence that it had upon the origin of heraldry.

At the time when the earliest insignia came into being, battle armor was undergoing some changes. Heretofore the face was little protected by anything more than a metal bar called a *nasal*, which dropped

The French King of Arms prepares for a tournament

down from the front of the iron *skull cap*. Some warriors even lacked *this* nose defense. Small metal helmets were developed that completely covered the face and head, and small breathing holes were provided along with narrow eye slits, or occularia. The negative effect of this headgear was seen in the loss of the identity of the wearer. In battle, who was friend and who was foe? It did not take long for the remedy to manifest itself. Distinctive shield insignias were the answer.

Once having made their appearance, these basically simple devices became more imaginative and complex. At first they were plain geometric shapes, but soon they encompassed every form of matter that came to mind. In certain early instances they also came close to duplicating one another, thus creating a need for a method of distinguishing between similar arms—*differencing*. By the end of the 12th century, heraldry had developed many specific patterns. In the next century, terminology to describe it and rules to govern it became necessary because of its widespread adoption.

Some shield symbols were selected because they suggested or played upon the bearer's family name. These were called *allusive arms*. (A large sampling of such names and related bearings is given separately

German heralds of the 16th century

in the text.) The shield annexed other accessories such as supporters and crests, which also have received separate detailing in the book.

By the end of the 16th century, heavy armor and heraldic pageantry were at the point of decline. Henry VIII ended the golden tournament age with a flourish.

His reign saw the most glittering armor and pageantry of the entire era. Heraldry, which to this point had a functional purpose, became self-defeating in its vanity. Families striving for impressiveness in their armorial bearings over-adorned or complicated them so as to destroy their distinctiveness and initial character.

A careful depiction of all of the elements and some of the classic arms of heraldry has been attempted in succeeding chapters, along with an explanatory text.

2

Anatomy of the Shield

Since the shield provided the surface on which most symbols were affixed, it became the focal point of heraldry. When these symbols became systematized, provisions were included for defining various parts of the shield in heraldic terms. This language established in the most concise terms exactly where on the shield a device was assigned.

Translated into heraldic language, the top edge of the shield became known as the *chief* and the bottom edge the "base." The left side, as you faced it, was called the *dexter side* and the right side was the *sinister side*. The center point on the shield was called the "fess point" and other points within the body of the shield were given names that fixed their position in relation to center, that is to say, above or below it.

There were still other points accounted for: the points where dexter or sinister sides joined chief or base, and where the mid-points were located on the chief or base. A term such as *dexter chief*, for instance, would immediately establish a location in the upper left-hand corner. *Middle chief* could mean but one thing—the center point on the top edge of the shield. The limited use of descriptive wording should be readily apparent by means of this heraldic system.

While these terms remained constant in meaning, the shield itself was subject to change at various times. The type of shield that was most commonly found in

heraldic bearings was the "heater-shape" of the 13th and 14th centuries. Its name originated from its resemblance to the laundry flatiron and it was closely proportioned to an equilateral triangle except that its sides were curved while its top (chief) was cut straight.

A variety of this shape shortly appeared that was a little longer than wider. Its sides were straight for about half of their length before curving together as sharply as its predecessor's did. Its proportions could be likened to an acorn cut off straight from its widening cap. Another adaptation of the "heater-shape" was one, again more equilateral, symmetrically curved on all *three* sides.

All of the aforementioned shields were preceded in history by the type that the Norman invaders carried into England in 1066. They were considerably longer, some running almost from toe to shoulder. In addition, they were sharply wider on the top where they protected the correspondingly wider part of the body. They generally curved laterally to encircle the bearer for maximum protection.

These early shields were usually made of wood, covered on each side with a layer of stiff leather, and reinforced with metal strips on the front. While the intent of these strips was to add durability to the shield, they were affixed in such a way as to form horizontal, crisscross, and radial ("wheel spoke") patterns. It has

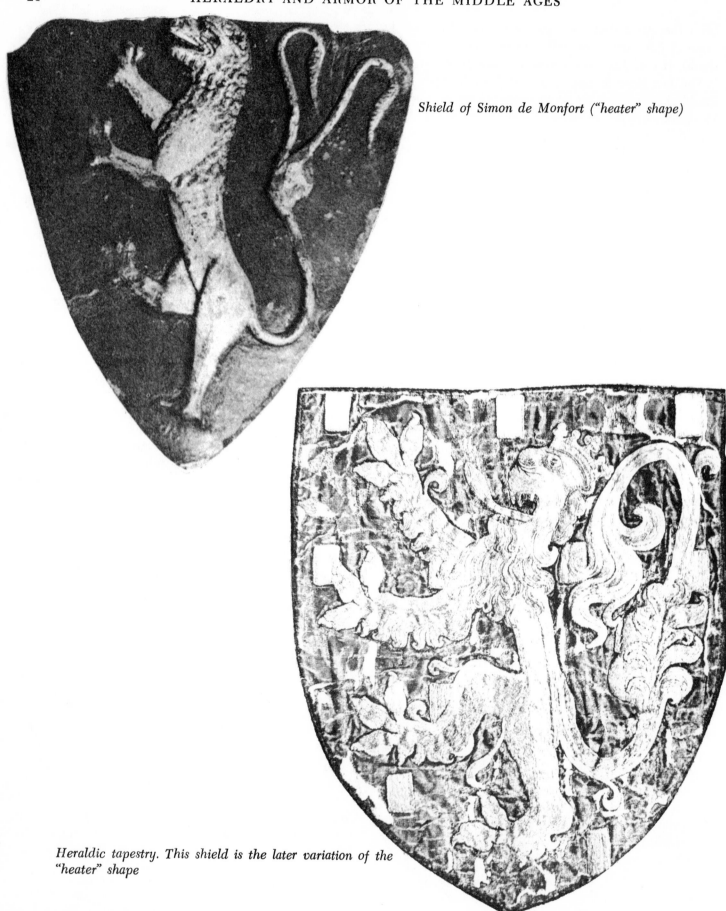

Shield of Simon de Monfort ("heater" shape)

*Heraldic tapestry. This shield is the later variation of the
"heater" shape*

been theorized that such patterns were the basis for some of the earliest heraldic devices created upon the shield. It may have been in some cases, but not in all.

The last form to appear in the Middle Ages was a shield smaller than all those used before it—a square-like plate designed primarily for tournament use. While shields heretofore curved convexly, or outwardly, this one favored an inward curve at its sides, though not quite as pronounced as the others. Another of its features was a circular notch in the dexter chief (upper left corner) that allowed for the bearer's lance to pass through. Defensewise, its front was curved outward to deter the opponent's lance point from glancing upward into the helmet. Some were also sloped on one side to draw the lance point entirely away from the vulnerable side of the body.

A more unusual vehicle for displaying arms was a shield in the form of a diamond or, as it was called, a lozenge. At its inception it was used by both men and woman, but presently it only bears the arms of an unmarried woman or widow. If such a woman was a *peeress* (possessor of arms) and she married or remarried, her arms would be transposed to her husband's shield. This system is called *marshalling of arms* and will be covered in more detail.

In the 19th century, heraldry, negating its basic functional purpose, went into a snobbish period of over-elaboration. Caught up in this pompousness, and apparently influenced by the recocco period of Louis XIV, shields changed drastically. They curved oddly and evidenced ornate borders that were akin to the gilt mirror frames of that earlier French period. In time, the trend reverted to the more traditional form. Some of the book's illustrations will reflect the rococco influence just described.

3

Basic Elements of Heraldry

Three factors serve as the essential elements of heraldry: tinctures, lines, and fields. In the matter of tinctures (colors), *or* and *argent,* represent the metals gold and silver respectively. The others—gules (red), azure (blue), vert (green), purpure (purple), and sable (black)—are flat colors that are used frequently.

Two other tinctures, tenne (orange) and sanguine (deep red), are uncommon and are occasionally found in livery colors. They have also controversially been described as "stains of dishonor." Authorities of the present time do not, however, acknowledge such past or present usage of these "stains" in arms.

Gold and silver (or and argent) can be represented by yellow and white. An 18th-century Italian writer, Father Silvester de Petra Sancta, developed the system of denoting specific color by varying line "hatchings" or dots as seen in the tincture plate. This of course made possible depictions of arms to be well executed even in line drawings.

The surface of the shield was called *the field.* If the field was divided horizontally, vertically, or diagonally by a single straight line and then a separate *and contrasting* tincture was applied to each side, the simplest of heraldic insignias would have thus been formed. This basic form was categorized as a party field, *party* alluding to the word *partitioned.*

You may recall the mention of the shield term *fess point.* It now comes to bear in describing the use of dividing lines. If a party field was formed by a horizontal line passing through the center of the shield, the line would of necessity pass through the fess point. The field, as a result, is heraldically termed *party per fess.* A vertical division through the center, now needing some term other than fess to describe it, was called, *party per pale.*

A diagonal division had two variations, hence two terms. If the line bisecting the shield started from the upper left or dexter chief, the field was *party per bend.* If the line started from the upper right or sinister chief, the field was *party per bend sinister.* The four fields just mentioned required only a single line in their creation. There are four other basic fields that need a second or third line.

These eight divisions are the "backbone" of heraldry, since they are the basis for the more complex fields that followed. They also entered into the origin of certain *charges* (symbols); another phase of this science. Additionally, *bendwise, palewise,* and *fesswise* are constant terms of heraldic reference.

What has been shown so far is the effect of a completely straight line in forming the basic fields. There are also ornamental lines of many variations that can be used in place of the straight line. They can be described as either notched, zig-zag, curved, or undulating in character. As the fields become more complex, the use of such ornate lines is not always applicable.

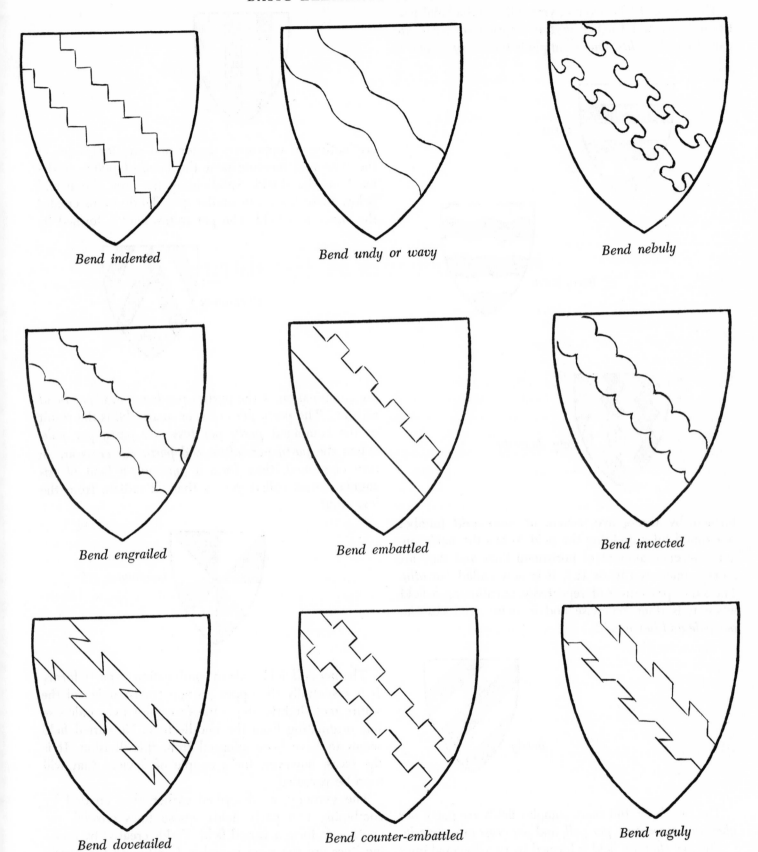

Bend indented

Bend undy or wavy

Bend nebuly

Bend engrailed

Bend embattled

Bend invected

Bend dovetailed

Bend counter-embattled

Bend raguly

Varied lines applied to an ordinary

The use of the horizontal, vertical, and diagonal partition is carried further in the creation of what are called *varied fields*. One example is the *barry*, which is

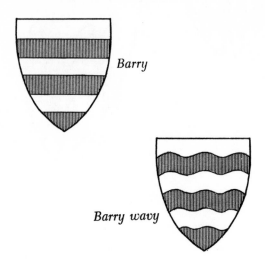

Barry

Barry wavy

Paly dancetty

formed by three, five, seven, or more *odd* number horizontal lines dividing the field. When the field contains an *even* amount of horizontal lines and they are more numerous (10 or 12), it is now called *barrully*. The same procedure of repeatedly partitioning a field when it is done palewise and fesswise produces the *per pale and barry* field.

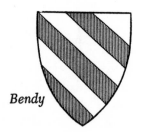

Bendy

The four basic but more complex fields are party *per chevron, per saltire, per pall*, and *per cross* or *quarterly*.

The *per chevron* field is formed by two diagonal lines

Paly

originating in opposite (dexter and sinister) sides of the base and meeting near the *nombril point*, as defined on the shield. Subdividing the area above and below these lines into similar, parallel divisions creates the *chevronny* field. The *per saltire* field is formed by

Chevronny

the combination of the parties *per bend* and "*per bend sinister*." The *party per cross*, or *quarterly*, is the result of the combined *party per fess* and *party per pale*. When the *party per saltire* and *party per cross* are in turn combined, they form a *gyronny*, a field of triangular forms called gyrons that all radiate from the *fess point*.

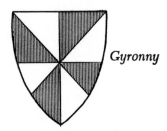

Gyronny

The *per pall* field is also a combination of party forms. It is essentially the upper portion (or triangle) of the saltire met slightly above the fess point by a palewise line originating from the middle base. No varied field seems to have been adopted from this division. It *is* the basis, however, for a couple of devices that will soon be revealed.

The gyronny, as described earlier, was created by combining two party fields whose lines crossed one another to form a varied field. Fields created by crossing lines are the most complex. Combining the bendy and the bendy-sinister creates the *lozengy,* a field of point-to-point connected diamond shapes. Combining

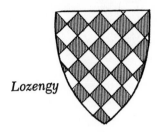

Lozengy

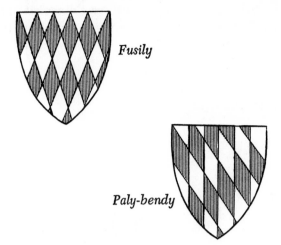

Fusily

Paly-bendy

the barry and paly results in the *checky,* a series of rows of connected small squares. The composition of other varied fields illustrated in this chapter should be easy enough to analyze from all that has just been outlined.

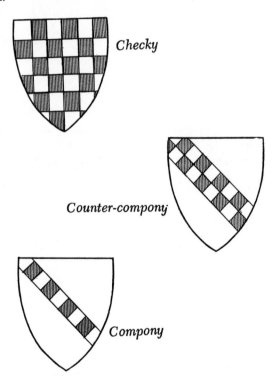

Checky

Counter-compony

Compony

It should become evident that certain of these more complex varied fields do not lend themselves to use with any of the varied lines. Those varied fields whose straight lines cross *frequently,* such as the checky, lozengy, barry-bendy, and fusily, are examples of fields to be *excluded* from the varied line treatment. A *simple* varied field crossed by only one line (horizontally, diagonally, or vertically) may have that line as a varied one. The use of the varied line is also applicable to all

the divisions in the *uncrossed* varied fields, such as the barry, bendy, and paly.

When a party field is combined with a varied field, the resulting field is one that is said to be *counter-changed.* That means that the horizontal, vertical, or diagonal bisection of the varied field created a situation, whereby the alternating tinctures on one side of the division are of necessity, *countered* by a *reverse* tincturing on the other side. This is seen in the per bend and barry field. The counter-changed fields are among the most striking bearings in heraldry and so I have devoted a separate plate to their depiction.

We have dealt to this point solely with linear patterns and fields. There are other types of fields that are created from repeating a symbol or *charge* often enough so as to form a pattern. These charges can take any form, and the fleur-de-lis is one of the classics to be used in this manner. In the case of the fleur-de-lis, the field that is created by its repetition is called a *powdered* field. It is so named because the pattern of charges suggests being scattered or strewn as powder.

There is actually some regularity in the way powdered charges are affixed since they *do* appear in *staggered* rows. To give the effect, however, of being casually strewn, some of the outer charges are allowed to reach and drift off the edges of the shield without being completed. This field, aside from being called powdered, is also called *semé* or *poudre* (terms for "strewn or scattered with small charges").

There are a number of common charges that are used so frequently in powdered fields that special terms are given to the specific fields in which they are used. The previously mentioned fleur-de-lis is one of these

Counter changes

HOLLAND ANCIENT.

Floretty

DE WASSINGSTONE.

Billety

Percy (1350)   *Robert de Vere (1298)*

De Warrenne (1350)   *De Warrenne (1390)*

Examples of diapering

charges. A field powdered with these flowers is termed *semé-de-lis*. A field of powdered crosslets is *crusily*, and bezants in a powdered field are *bezanty*. If the charge was not sufficiently used to merit special terminology, then the words *semé of* precede the standard name of the charge.

In citing the above types of powdered fields, a brief explanation of each might now be in good order. Crosslets are crosses whose limbs are crossed again near their outer extremes. Bezants are gold discs that along with *plates* (silver discs) form part of a larger series of circular devices called *roundles*. Bezants and plates, being discs, *must* obviously be represented as *flat* objects and only in the *single* tincture, which clearly defines each. The other distinctively named roundles may be depicted as balls, but again only in the specific tincture assigned to each. The tinctures are never mentioned *as such* in blazoning (heraldic descriptions of arms), so they had best be memorized beforehand. For this purpose, they are found in the plate on Essentials of Heraldry.

Another series of devices called *gouttes* are found in powdered fields in the semblance of liquid drops. As in roundles, each drop form has a specific tincture. When they appear as a powdered field, they are termed *goutté* or *gutté*. These tinctures *are* blazoned in arms where they exist, but quaint or fanciful terms are applied to them. In the case of the roundles, the quaint term was applied to the *device* instead. These last two series require study to learn both the device and tincture associated with it.

The *diapered field* is one inspired by the damask silks and brocades used in the vestments of the medieval clergy. These fabrics were created by the Byzantines and imported from them. The designs found in the cloth were copied into the stonework of early cathedrals. Later, the heralds adapted them as designs for shield surfaces. It is believed, however, that prior to this last use, they first appeared as an addition to simple shields depicted on stained-glass windows. Their purpose was to play upon or diffuse the light rays entering the buildings.

The diapered field was devised to merely embellish or decorate an otherwise flat shield surface. With this in mind, it is essential that the diapering be kept subordinate to the main basic partitions and/or symbols. At the same time, the diapering should not suggest a powdered field with spaces between its strewn symbols. A good method of keeping the diapering design subtle is to employ a contrasting value of the original field tincture in its execution. Black, silver, and gold are also effective general diapering tinctures since they are neutral hues.

Because of the subtle use of color necessary in the diapered field, it is the one system that is not governed by the usual laws of contrasting tincture. In all other cases, where maximum separation of color and form is the aim, the laws of tincture *do* apply. This is especially important as the shield becomes more and more complex. Charges placed over a party field or even another charge are considered to increase the level of the shield's surface with each element applied to it.

Conversely, while each area in a party or varied field should be distinct from its neighboring area, *none* should appear to rise in level *above* the other, since the entire field represents a completely flat surface. This purpose will be defeated if a shadow effect is evidenced between divisions by an overlay of tinctures. When the arms are depicted in what is called bas-relief, the level surface of party or varied field must be similarly maintained.

The depiction of furs in heraldry is bounded by prescribed tinctures, fields, and charges. The first fur to be emblazoned in arms was called *vair*. This was a

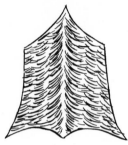 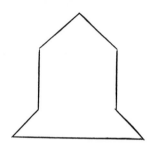

Origin of vair symbol

field of alternating blue and white pieces that depicted the back and belly skins of the squirrel. The pattern in which these skins were cut have been imitated, creating an easily recognized symbolism. In other representations of vair, the tinctures have remained the same, but the pieces have changed shape and placement.

In so far as a shape variance is concerned, this change is depicted in the piece called *potent*. The term is derived from *potence*, an old word for a crutch, to which this fur symbol is likened. In another case, the distinctive lines and points of the vair piece are softened with curved turns. The changes that remain in the vair or potent group are merely field pattern changes created by the different placements of the original symbols.

When ermine skins were depicted, they were illustrated by a powdered field. The symbol used for ermine was a representation of the ermine tail. These devices were called *spots* and appeared either in a black or white tincture. These spots themselves took on a considerable number of designs, the most typical being shown in an illustration within this chapter.

Much like the terminology used in connection with

powdered fields, the terms for fields are heraldically coded to be all-descriptive in the fewest words. Since

Ermine   *Ermines*

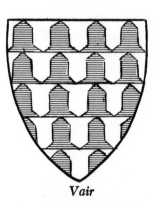 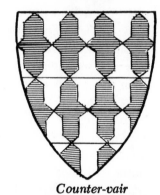

Vair   *Counter-vair*

Vair potent   *Vair counter-potent*

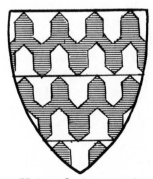

Vair urdy (en point)

Fur symbols

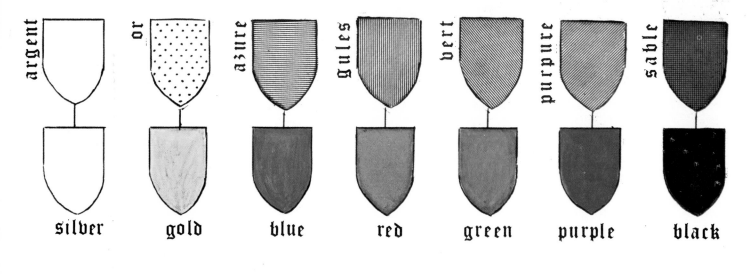

argent — silver
or — gold
azure — blue
gules — red
vert — green
purpure — purple
sable — black

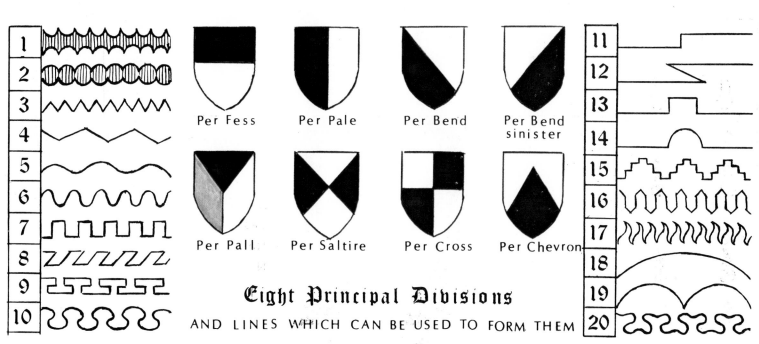

Per Fess	Per Pale	Per Bend	Per Bend sinister
Per Pall	Per Saltire	Per Cross	Per Chevron

1
2
3
4
5
6
7
8
9
10

11
12
13
14
15
16
17
18
19
20

Eight Principal Divisions
AND LINES WHICH CAN BE USED TO FORM THEM

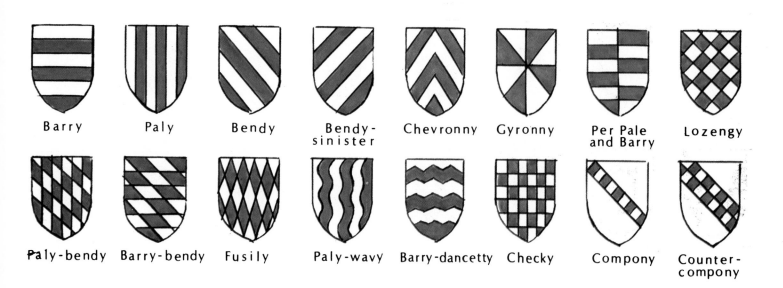

Barry · Paly · Bendy · Bendy-sinister · Chevronny · Gyronny · Per Pale and Barry · Lozengy

Paly-bendy · Barry-bendy · Fusily · Paly-wavy · Barry-dancetty · Checky · Compony · Counter-compony

ESSENTIALS OF HERALDRY: TINTURES, LINES & FIELDS

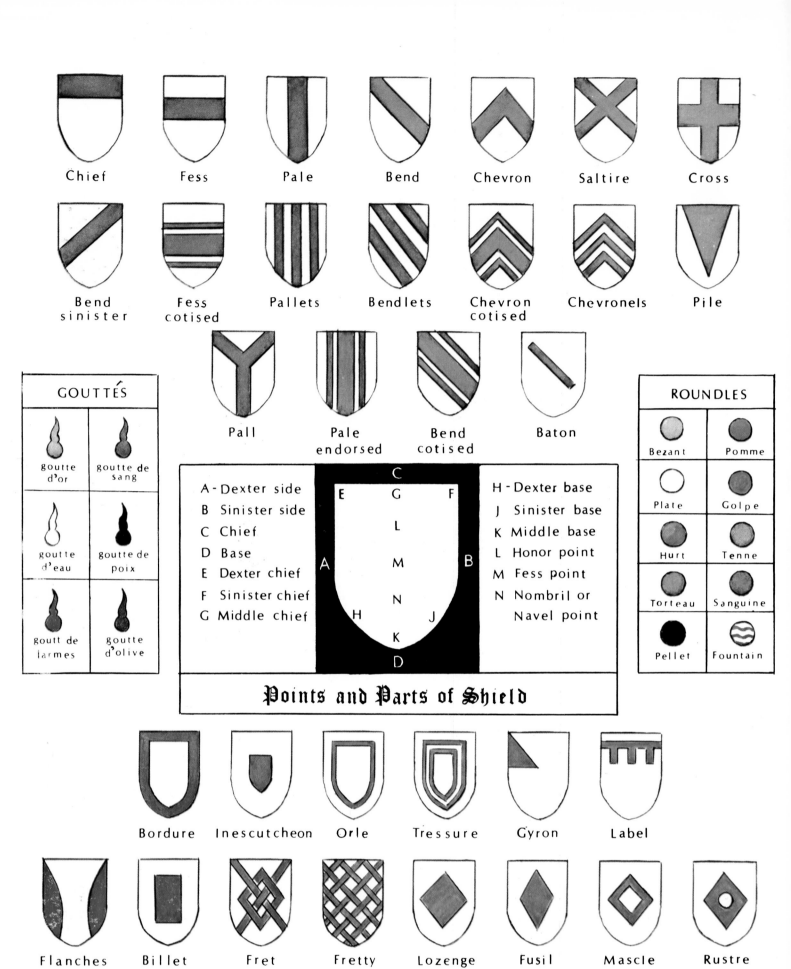

Chief · Fess · Pale · Bend · Chevron · Saltire · Cross

Bend sinister · Fess cotised · Pallets · Bendlets · Chevron cotised · Chevronels · Pile

Pall · Pale endorsed · Bend cotised · Baton

GOUTTÉS

goutte d'or	goutte de sang
goutte d'eau	goutte de poix
goutt de larmes	goutte d'olive

Points and Parts of Shield

A - Dexter side
B Sinister side
C Chief
D Base
E Dexter chief
F Sinister chief
G Middle chief

H - Dexter base
J Sinister base
K Middle base
L Honor point
M Fess point
N Nombril or Navel point

ROUNDLES

Bezant	Pomme
Plate	Golpe
Hurt	Tenne
Torteau	Sanguine
Pellet	Fountain

Bordure · Inescutcheon · Orle · Tressure · Gyron · Label

Flanches · Billet · Fret · Fretty · Lozenge · Fusil · Mascle · Rustre

THE ORDINARIES AND SUBORDINATES

Several types of ermine spots found in arms

the words are either fanciful or archaic in their majority, it is wise, as suggested earlier, to become fully knowledgeable in them. This way, a confrontation in blazoning will not necessitate continuous referral to other related text.

4

The Ordinaries

The ordinaries are the principal or most frequently occurring charges in heraldry. They are of a rectilinear nature, being a development of the eight party fields described in the previous chapter. The term *ordinary* arose in reference to common or ordinary usage. A difference of opinion exists as to how many charges are encompassed by this term. No fewer than eight have been cited, but as many as 11 have been classified as ordinaries. The widest range includes the chief, the fess, the bar, the pale, the bend, the bend sinister, the pile, the pall, the chevron, the saltire, and the cross.

The chief is a horizontal charge occupying the upper third of the shield. While specific fractions are men-

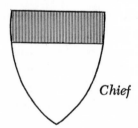

Chief

tioned in heraldry, they need not be that precise, as they are merely intended as a guide to general proportions. The chief is considered an outgrowth of the *fess*, another horizontal charge occupying the middle third of the shield. The fess is so named because of its location in regard to the fess point, or middle of the shield.

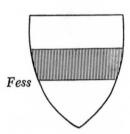

Fess

As the chief is a development of the fess, *the bar* is also a charge adopted from it. In the manner of the fess, the bar occupies the central portion of the shield but is a narrower device. It is generally about one-fifth of the shield's area as compared to the one-third width of the fess. The bar must never be placed so high in the top edge of the shield as to be taken for a chief.

A bar is generally repeated when used as a shield device or used in conjunction with another type of charge. When used alone, it may appear in a pair or in a series of three of more *evenly separated* charges. In the latter form it tends to be confused with the barry

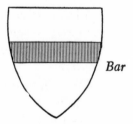

Bar

field described in the previous chapter. There is a distinct difference between the two.

To begin with, the barry or varied field is a completely *flat* field of an *odd* number of horizontal pieces as earlier stated. The bars on the other hand are *overlays* upon a flat field and are treated in a specific manner to show this surface rise. This is done by showing a strip of the field above and below each bar and in between them. If you will note the barry field with its odd number of pieces, the initial tincture in its alternation does *not* resolve itself, as does the bar with the field tincture, necessarily beginning and *ending* the pattern.

The bar is considered by some to be a *diminutive* of the fess rather than an independent charge. *Diminutive* means a scaled-down replica. Several of the ordinaries have such diminutives. In all instances, the basic diminutives have been further reduced to produce an even smaller version of the original charge. Treating the bar, for an example, as a diminutive, by reducing it in width, the *barrulet* is created.

The barrulets, when paired together on a shield, are called *bars gemelles*. When these *bars gemelles* appear on both sides of a fess, as they often do, the fess is termed *double cotised*. A *single* barrulet bracketing a fess top and bottom causes the charge to be termed *fess cotised*.

The pale is a vertical counterpart of the fess in that

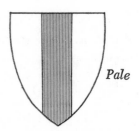

Pale

it also occupies a central portion of the shield in a similar one-third area. Like the fess, it has two diminutives —the pallet and the endorse. Just as the bar requires a strip of the field showing top and bottom when used repeatedly, so too does the multiple pallet require this. Otherwise it will be confused with the varied field called the paly. Most ordinaries, when placed between their *smallest* diminutives, are termed *cotised*. The pale, uniquely, is termed *endorsed*.

The bend is the last of the three ordinaries created from two lines running parallel to each other. Again, it might be said that it runs through the center of the

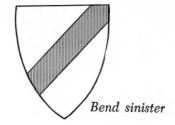

Bend   *Bend sinister*

field, but in a diagonal direction from dexter chief to sinister base. Its twin form, the bend sinister, varies only in that it runs from the sinister chief to dexter base. The bends' diminutives are the bendlet and the baton.

The baton differs from other narrow diminutives in that it is *couped* or cut short from the two edges of the shield. It is distinguished from its bend sinister counterpart only in name. The narrowest diminutive of the bend sinister is called a *scarp*.

The same principle is applied to the use of bendlets as was applied to the use of bars or pallets. This is the system where the field is shown on each side of the charges and between them. In this case, the bendlets must be distinguished from the bendy field.

The two diagonal sides of *the chevron* originate or

Chevron

issue from the dexter and sinister bases and meet at a point within the chief (upper third of the shield). This is the final charge possessing diminutives, which in this case are the chevronel and the couple-close. The chevron may be repeated once, but if this form is to be shown more times than this, it must be as a chevronel.

The chevron is termed cotised when placed between its couple-close diminutives. The chevronel, unlike any other ordinary, can be interlaced in a group of three. The chevron itself can appear in another unique form called *chevron rompu*, in which the diagonal sides are interrupted by the enhancement (elevation) of their upper halves.

The pile is a wedge shape whose point usually is in base. While the pile has no diminutives, this charge may

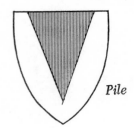

Pile

be more acutely angled, hence narrowed, so as to accommodate a series of them on one field. A lack of restriction uniquely connected with this charge is that it can issue from any of the four sides of the shield.

The pall is a charge easily recognized from its Y

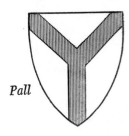

Pall

shape. It was adapted from the religious mantle of the same form and quite naturally appears as a form in ecclesiastical heraldry. The couped version of the pall is the shakefork. The limbs of this latter charge do not reach the edges of the shield as a consequence of the couping.

The cross is the most widely used symbol in heraldry.

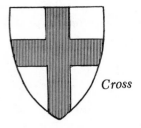

Cross

In its simple uncharged form it touches all four sides of the shield and has limbs occupying a fifth of it. When charged, the limb width is extended to one-third the area. The cross, however, had been the object of the most varied treatment. In many cases, the above standardization has been ignored. Because of its unique-

ness and its added religious significance, a chapter has been devoted to this one ordinary alone.

The saltire is a diagonal cross. Such a cross appeared in the flag of the Confederacy during the Civil War.

Saltire

The multiple crosses in the British flag are probably the earliest application of this form upon a flag. The width of saltire limbs are only about one-fifth of the shield's area, but they are to be widened to one-third when they in turn accommodate a secondary charge upon their surface.

When a single charge is placed upon a shield so that this charge occupies or falls into a position of an ordinary such as the pale, for example, the charge so placed is described as being palewise. Single charges may also be placed fesswise or bendwise upon a shield. When a series of charges rather than a single charge follows the line of a given ordinary, the series is said to be either *in fess, in* pale, or *in* bend, as the case may be. The two sets of terms are distinct from one another and yet can come into play at the same time in describing the position and nature of a charge.

An elongated *horizontal* figure in its normal position, such as a crawling serpent, when *vertically* aligned with two other crawling serpents, would be described when affixed to a shield as being *fesswise in pale*. Were they to be placed standing on their tails in a *horizontal* series then they would be described as *palewise in fess*.

A final point needs to be brought forward at this time. When charges are placed upon the diagonal limbs of a chevron or saltire, they are to slope or slant at the same angle of the limb unless the blazoning states otherwise. Any charge, however, that is placed in the point of the chevron or at the intersection of the saltire is always to be placed erectly.

5

The Cross

The cross is the predominant charge of heraldry. Its simple form is in close keeping with the desired heraldic image, but at the same time it has developed more variations than any other charge—including its rival forms, the lion and the eagle. Forty-six different crosses have been depicted herein and others can surely be found through research.

The religious significance of the cross, along with its suitability of form, has undoubtedly brought about its very frequent use. Perhaps some further impetus may have been given to its usage by returning Crusaders. Such men-at-arms wishing to identify themselves with past service in these religious campaigns could well have adopted the cross as their permanent device.

The cross that was in common usage in the early days of heraldry was a plain, straight, and relatively wide-bodied figure whose limbs extended to the edges of the shield. It most often appeared on a plain field. At first, changes of tincture and/or the addition of a simple charge were all that were necessary to vary or difference one cross device from another. Later its widespread adoption forced the creation of new forms to maintain such differences.

The forms that were created were mainly ornamental in nature. In order to obtain this effect, the cross had to first be couped, or cut short from the edges of the shield. With this done, distinctive or decorative treat-ment was applied to the shortened ends of the limbs. In some other instances, the sides of the limbs were *splayed* (gradually spread outward in straight or curved lines). In still other cases, the two procedures were jointly applied to the one cross.

Special heraldic terms defined each type of cross variety and a number of them are described as follows:

POMME—a cross whose limbs end in roundles or balls.

POTENT—a cross whose four limb endings each form a "T" or crutch (*potent*).

CROSSLET—a cross whose four limbs are individually recrossed near their endings.

FOURCHE—a cross whose endings are forked.

POINTED—a cross whose endings are pointed.

BOTONNY—a cross whose endings formed in the manner of a tre-foil or clover leaf.

FLORY—a cross whose endings are in the shape of a fleur-de-lis.

FLORETTY—a cross that varies from the flory only in that limb ends are first closed off; forming a partition between the cross and the fleur-de-lis.

PATONCE—a cross that is semi-flory or splayed into three points at its endings.

MOLINE—a cross whose endings each have short twin curls going in opposite directions. Said to be derived in name and form from the mill-rind.

RECERCELE OR CERCELE—a cross whose endings are

Latin	Pommé	Botonny	Pointed	Urdy	Double pitchee
Fourché	Patonce	Molineux	Cercelé	Potent	Potent engrailed
Flory	Floretty	Paty floretty	Botonny on besant	Crosslet	Paty or formy
Maltese	Fitchy at the foot	Fitchy	Fylfot	Tau	Double parted and fretty
Calvary	Lorraine	Besants-in-cross	Floretty engrailed	Entrailed	Ragulle

Crosses

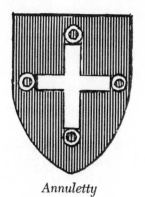

Annuletty

Barby

Elechee

Milrine

Paty with engrail

Anckered

Sarcele

Lambeaux

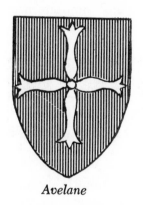

Avelane

Paty quadrate

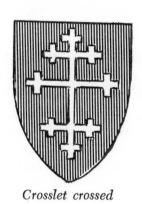

Crosslet crossed

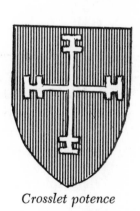

Crosslet potence

Crosslet fitched

Melton

Ermines-in-cross

Nowy

Crosses

curled as in the moline cross but are longer and more extreme in their curling.

FORMY OR PATY—a cross that has widely curving or splayed sides with straight ends.

MALTESE—a cross less splayed than the formy with semi-forked endings that come to short points. A total of eight points in all.

TAU CROSS—so called because of its Greek letter T shape with the absence of its upper limb. Also called the Cross of St. Anthony, or simply Tau.

ANCKERD—a cross similar to Maltese except that demi-forks or points are slightly curved.

BARBY—a plain cross that is barbed on its limb endings in the manner of arrowheads.

FITCHY—a cross whose lower limb tapers to a point.

CROSS-CROSSLET CROSSED—a cross crosslet re-crossed at the top and bottom limb.

SARCELE—a wide cross slightly splayed and completely open on the curled ends of all limbs.

AVELANE—a cross representing four filberts touching in cross.

MILRINE—a cross fourché whose forks take a reverse bend after first splaying outward.

ANNULLETTY—a plain cross with single annulets (rings) on each end.

PATY-FLORETTY—a cross that is a combination of two earlier forms having splayed limbs and a fleur-de-lis on each straight end.

CROSS-QUADRATE—a cross whose plain limbs issue out of a square center.

CROSS NOWY—a cross whose plain limbs issue out of a circle. If limbs are other than plain, the term describing them is added to the original term. Same rule applies for cross quadrate.

LAMBEAUX—a cross fitchy mounted on a label with three splayed points.

Many simple forms can be placed *in cross,* such as bezants, lozenges, ermine spots, and annulets. The cross can also be fashioned of variable lines, such as wavy, ragule, engrailed, and indented. Examples in particular family arms can be cited in most of the preceding cases.

Plain crosses can be varied by piercing their centers. They can be quarter-pierced, round-pierced, or lozenge-pierced. The plain cross can also be varied by being bordered by a narrow margin in a different tincture, which is called a *fimbriated* cross. When a cross appears to have the bulk of its inner area removed so as to reveal the tincture of the field beneath it, it is said to be *voided.* Unless tinctured exactly in this manner, it can be taken for the fimbriated cross or a smaller cross fixed upon a larger one.

Although the term *plain cross* generally applies to those wide-limbed forms that extend to edges of the shield, there are other forms that, although simple, vary from those just mentioned. The Latin or *long cross* is the prime example. This cross is mainly distinguished by its lower limb being about twice the length of the others. At the same time, its limbs are considerably narrower than the plain cross. A final variance is the fact that it is also couped. This long cross was originally regarded as the plain cross when the shields were correspondingly longer.

The Latin cross, when mounted on a platform of steps, is called the Calvary cross. Three steps are usually found but the exact number must always be stated. The long cross, when recrossed in its top limb, is called the Patriarchal cross.

An unusual cross is the Fylfot, one with limb endings that have clockwise, right-angled bends, a form similar to the German swastika (originally Greek). The bends in the latter form turn counter clockwise however. It is interesting to note that the American Indian once displayed a similar design on his tepee.

A plain cross that is extremely narrow is called a fillet. This fillet is often used as a differencing in quartered arms when placed centrally, touching all quarters as if to unite them.

6

The Subordinates

The ordinaries, or principal charges of heraldry, are supplemented by a second series of simple forms known as the *subordinates*. The subordinates were once considered to be of less importance than the ordinaries and so were categorized with the title that they presently possess. Opinions differ, as they did with the ordinaries, as to which number of charges comes under their scope.

The pale and the pall, herein established as ordinaries, have also been thought by some writers to be better listed as subordinates. It is actually of small consequence to which group such charges are affixed so long as the two-part breakdown aids in all of them being committed to memory. In-so-far as this text is concerned, the charges that will be treated as subordinates are the canton, gyron, flanches, lozenge, fusil, mascle, rustre, fret, fretty, roundle, annulet and gutte.

The canton, familiar as a flag element, is a square or rectangular device normally occupying about a ninth of the shield's area. It often appears charged with still another device within its boundaries. The canton is generally found in the dexter chief corner of the shield but can occur as a sinister canton in the opposite corner. It is said to originate from the banner honorably granted to a knight who provides and leads his own troops in allegiance to a feudal lord or sovereign.

When a canton appears upon a shield with a *bordure* or narrow margin around the edge of the shield, the canton is overlayed upon it. An exception to this rule occurs when the bordure has been introduced to the shield later than the canton as a mark of differencing (distinction from a similar shield). In this case the bordure is overlayed upon the canton, obscuring a portion of its left side.

The gyron is another charge commonly occurring

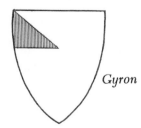

Gyron

in the dexter chief, although it too has its sinister counterpart. It is a triangular form originating from a piece found in a gyronny field. It is also termed the lower

Canton

half of a canton divided diagonally from the dexter chief to the fess point.

Flanches are twin curved forms occurring on both

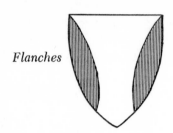

Flanches

*De Neville
Masculy*

sides of the shield. Their name is derived from the French word "flanc," meaning "side." The two lines that form them issue from opposite corners of the chief and curve downward to their respective bases. Flanches that are smaller or narrower because of their flatter curve upon the field are termed flasques or voiders.

The lozenge is the first of four diamond shapes that

Lozenge

follow, and each bears a small difference. The lozenge is composed of four equal sides that are not quite rectangular. The *fusil* is a form of this lozenge, which

Fusil

is more elongated. The *máscle* reverts to the original lozenge shape with its nearly square sides, but is voided

Mascle

through its center in such a way as to leave only a small border remaining. The *rustre* is also of the lozenge

Rustre

shape but contains circular piercing or void of smaller proportion than that of the mascle. It is interesting to note that the rustre is said to represent a screw nut and the mascle the fragment of early armor fastened to hard leather.

The fretty is somewhat unique as a subordinate,

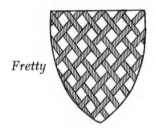

Fretty

since it is formed from two ordinaries. It contains a pattern of interlaced dexter and sinister bendlets covering the entire field. A modified form of the fretty is the *trellis*, which has the same bendlets crossing but *not*

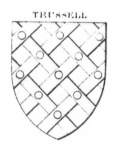

TRUSSELL

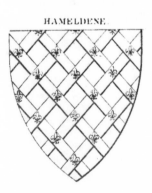

HAMELDENE

interlacing. Instead, at all points of crossing, a circular device representing a nail fastens them. In appearance this charge is truly suggestive of the garden ornamentation that bears its name. One existing form of the trellis incorporates a single ermine spot in all spaces formed by the crossing charges.

In a *fret*, a pair of bendlets in saltire are interlaced

Fret

with a mascle to form this charge. The fret is perhaps better expressed as coming from a single piece of fretty. The word *fret*, because of its heraldic reference to repeatedly crossing lines, has been applied to string instruments whose necks have lateral ridges crossing the strings at regular intervals.

The billet is a rectangular form placed upon a shield

Billet

in such a way as to resemble a brick on end. A field strewn with this charge is called *billetty*. The billet originated as a piece from a varied field once given the same name as the aforementioned powdered field now called billetty. This practice of adapting charges from single pieces of varied fields was also applied to the lozenge and fusil as it was to the fret, gyron, and billet.

The label is a *horizontal cotise* or riband *in chief*

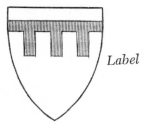

Label

with smaller vertical pieces pendant from it at regular intervals. These hanging pieces may assume one of several shapes and may be charged with another device. The original label was a mark of differencing between similar shields, but now it is confined to distinguishing the oldest son of a living father.

The bordure, as its name implies, is a margin around

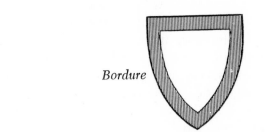

Bordure

the edges of the shield. Its original purpose was as a differencing in the manner of the early label. The bordure can be parted, varied, or charged.

The orle is a narrow margin following the contour

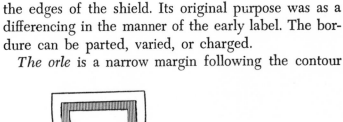

Orle

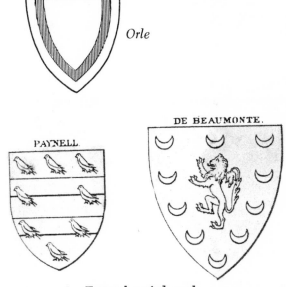

Examples of the orle

of the shield. However, it is half the width of the bordure and is set into the shield just beyond the area that normally would be occupied by the latter charge. It thus resembles a border *within* a border.

The tressure is a narrower border than the orle, being about half its width but occupying the same set-in position. Usually it appears in pairs ornamented with the

Tressure

fleur-de-lis in a form called flory and counter flory. This flory and counter flory pattern consists of fleur-de-lis alternately originating *and* pointing inwardly and outwardly across the two tressures. The flower is voided where it enters the narrow space between the twin charge. The Royal Arms of Scotland displays this charge so ornamented.

The inescutcheon is a small shield within the larger

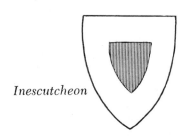

Inescutcheon

shield. It can appear singly or in groups. When borne singly and centrally placed, as it often is, it must be small enough so as not to create a narrow margin between it and the edge of the shield. If this narrow margin occurs, it can be mistaken for a bordure.

Roundles and *guttes* are usually found in powdered fields or groupings. They were dealt with in the earlier description of these fields. *The annulet* is a ring form sometimes described in blazon as a false roundle in lieu of its proper name. This charge may appear in linked pairs (gemel) or in three's, interlaced or independent of each other.

The annulet may be charged within its void, in which case it is termed a *chaplet*. The roundle, too, may be charged, but also parted or varied. One form of the varied roundles is the barry-wavy field called the fountain. This is a *heraldic* fountain form as distinguished from the *natural* fountain form that appears as a *common charge*.

7

The Lion

The lion, as a heraldic charge, rivals the cross in its frequency of use. In his symbolism the king of beasts has stood for strength, courage, and possibly magnanimity as in the case of the many sovereigns who have adopted it as their cognizance. Through its prevalence, it has developed many forms and many attitudes (body positions).

As a beast of prey, the special heraldic terms describing the lion in its attitudes are applicable to all beasts of prey depicted in armorial bearings. For this reason, the lion serves as an excellent example with which to delineate these various terms and forms. Three factors are considered in blazoning or describing the lion: a.) the attitude (position or action) of the body, b.) the position of the head, c.) the position or state of the tail *if* unusual.

There are eight basic attitudes that the lion variously assumes in shield devices:

a.) *Passant*—walking position with the head and the body facing the dexter and the dexter forepaw the only leg raised off the ground; the tail normally curved double over the back.

b.) *Statant*—a stationary or standing position varying only from the previous attitude (passant) in that all paws are grounded.

c.) *Rampant*—in an erect combat position with only one hind paw on the ground; the tail still following the line of the back is also erect.

d.) *Salient*—a leaping or springing position with the forepaws aligned with one another.

e.) *Sejant*°—a sitting position with the forepaws on the ground and the tail's end erect after passing between the rear legs.

f.) *Sejant Erect*°—a sitting position varying only from sejant in that the forepaws are raised in a posture resembling the forepaw position of the rampant lion.

g.) *Couchant*—a reclining or crouching position with all four legs and belly flush with the ground.

h.) *Dormant*—a sleeping position with the head lowered on the forepaws; similar to couchant except for the head position.

The facing of the head and body in the aforementioned attitudes are all to dexter or viewer's left side. The pose, however, in all cases except dormant, can be varied by a change in the head position. Such a change must be blazoned when it is other than to the dexter.

When the lion faces the viewer, he is said to be guardant. When he is also rampant, for example, and so facing, he is said to be rampant guardant. The face position is to be described secondarily as a definite rule of blazoning. Should the lion be looking backwards over

---

° A *Sejant* or *Sejant Erect* lion can be positioned bodywise and headwise toward the viewer, in which case he is termed sejant affronté or sejant erect affronté.

45

STATANT GUARDANT	PASSANT	PASSANT GUARDANT	PASSANT REGUARDANT
SEJANT	SEJANT AFFRONTE	SEJANT ERECT	SEJANT ERECT AFFRONTE
RAMPANT	RAMPANT GUARDANT	RAMPANT REGUARDANT	SALIANT
COUCHANT	DORMANT	STATANT REGUARDANT	STATANT

POSITIONS OF THE LION IN HERALDRY

Two-headed

Double-tailed

Nowed-tailed

Tail overhead

Tail extended

Dismembered (mutile)

Combatant (counter-rampant)

Addorsed

Counter-passant

Demi-lion

Bi-corporate

Tri-corporate

Positions of the lion in heraldry

his shoulder in a rampant position, he is said to rampant reguardant. If his head position is not specified in blazoning as either guardant or reguardant, it is understood to be facing dexterwise and no special term need be applied to it.

The tail passing through the legs in sejant or couchant positions is considered normal to these poses. In the dormant, the tail languishes along the ground alongside the legs. In all others, it follows the line of the back in whatever position the back assumes.

If the tail appears between the legs in the rampant, salient, statant, or passant attitudes, it is said to be *coward*. An infrequent position of the tail held straight to the rear is logically termed *extended*. More often it may appear in a knot and is termed *nowed*.

A tail may have another variance other than its position. This occurs when the lion is either forked tailed (*queue fourche*) or double tailed. Some armorists prefer to distinguish between these two terms, suggesting that the forked tail is only a half-length appendage attached to one of normal length and therefore *not* actually a double tail.

The prior descriptions of the lion have dealt with him as a solitary figure. There are also terms to describe his attitude or status in relation to a second lion. Again, be reminded that these terms apply to all beasts of prey:

Counter-Rampant—two lions rampant closely facing each other as in combat.

Addorsed—two lions rampant standing back to back.

Counter Passant—two lions passant in pale (vertically aligned) facing the opposite sides (dexter and sinister) of the shield.

Occasionally, the term *lioncels* appears in early blazoning. This refers to the grouping of more than four lions on one field. The term was used in describing the first hereditary device of Geoffrey of Anjou with its six lioncels. The term means "little lions;" which they necessarily would be in order to be accommodated upon a shield in any large number. Modern blazoning, however, has generally discarded the term.

There are further descriptive terms pertaining to the lion and other beasts:

Collared—wearing a ring around his neck and possibly chained as well.

Gorged—encircled about the throat with a coronet as if it were a collar.

Vorant—in the act of devouring his prey. He may also

be holding something in his paw or mouth other than prey.

Heraldic goat—collared and gorged

It has already been shown that double-tailed lions have appeared in heraldry. This is only one of several unusual animal forms occurring in the lion charge. Here are others:

Double Headed—in rampant position.

Bi-Corporate—two bodies sejant erect with one head affronté.

Tri-Corporate—three bodies rampant with one head.

Mutilé or Dechaussé—usually rampant, with head, limbs, and tail separated from body by a series of imaginary sword cuts.

The influence of the lion has manifested itself even beyond all these forms. The lion's head or body has been adopted to other animal parts to form imaginary figures called monsters. The griffin and the sea-lion are examples of this practice. The former has the lion's body and an eagle's face and wings; the latter has the lion's face and a fish's body. These forms mainly appear as supporters (devices *outside* the shield).

Parts of the lion may also appear independently. The lion's head or paw are often seen as charges in themselves. When this occurs, these figures are either *couped* or *erased. Couped* means cut off sharply as with a sword (found in mutilé lion forms); *erased* means torn off leaving ragged edges.

Although it does not apply to the lion, a third type of head separation exists with the depiction of other animal heads. This term is caboshed, which refers to a head affronté where the neck is entirely removed.

A lion may be charged with other devices such as fur spots, annulets, or varied fields. He may also be crossed (and hence partly covered) by an ordinary such as the bend or bar. When this condition prevails, he is said to be *debruised* by the ordinary. In some cases the upper part of a lion with tail erect appears rising out of a fess or bar. He is said to be *issuant* or *naissant* from it. This lion form called *demi-lion* may be issuant from either the center of the ordinary or may appear to be resting on the upper line of it.

When referring to beasts of prey, their claws are considered weapons and so they are termed *armed* with same. The lion is normally *armed gules* unless the field is of the same tincture, in which case he is *armed azure* or whatever. His tongue is tinctured under the same conditions as the claws and so he is normally described as being *langued gules.*

The heraldic lion has the quality of being easily recognized in all of its stylized treatments. These treat-

Example of a heraldic lion

ments play strongly upon the outline of the mane and ragged edges of hair on the legs and tail. The narrow, elongated, and intermittently shaggy tail is also distinctive with this animal.

Some of its body styling is a matter of circumstance. When a number of lions had to fit within the converging boundaries of the shield, certain *distortions* of the lion's normal form inevitably had to occur. The forced conformation of the lion to his limited space actually proved to be artistic rather than undesirable.

Even when later depictions of the lion were not necessarily bounded by space limitations they still embraced the styling dictated by the previous condition. Some of the primitive depictions have captured a quality that even skilled heraldic artists have since adhered to.

Here is a list of arms that bear the various lion attitudes and forms.

Lion rampant—Lord de la Warre; Lord Mowbray; Sir Thomas Percy; Richard, Lord Talbot; Stafford.

Lion rampant guardant—Fitz-Hammond; Halland, Earl of Kent.

Lion rampant reguardant—Cadogan, Sir John Pryce.

Lion salient—Worley, Felbridge.

Example of a heraldic lion

Lion passant—George, Earl of Guilford.

Lion passant guardant—Lord Hugh le Despencer; Ogilvie.

Lion couchant—Lynte.

Lion double-headed—Mason.

Lion double-tailed—Stokes; Wansford; Wells; Kingston; Brumball.

Lion bi-corporate—Attewater.

Lion tri-corporate—Nashe; Crouchback, Earl of Lancaster.

Lion queue-fourche—Sutton, Hastang.

Lion nowed tail—Bewes.

Lions counter rampant—Carter.

Lions counter passant—Clegg, Legge.

Three demi-lions—Herbert, Earl of Pembroke and Montgomery; Earl of Lankerville.

Lion dismembered (mutilé)—Maitland.

Lion issuant (naissant)—Chalmers, Esme.

Seven lioncels—Sir Thomas Danvers.

8

Common Charges

The figures that heraldry draws upon for its devices fall into three groups: the ordinaries, the subordinates, and the common charges. The common charges, which are almost unlimited in their number, have been subdivided in smaller categories for purposes of better examination.

The subdivisions to which common charges are usually assigned are as follows:

1. Divine and Human Beings
2. Living Animals
   a.) Beasts of Prey
   b.) Beasts of Chase
   c.) Miscellaneous Other Animals
   d.) Birds
   e.) Fish
   f.) Insects
3. Imaginary Animals (Monsters)
4. Natural Objects
   a.) Celestial
   b.) Trees and Plants
   c.) Flowers
5. Inanimate Objects
   a.) General
   b.) Canting (Allusive)

Figures of Divine beings are found mainly in ecclesiastical heraldry. The Almighty is represented in the armorial bearings of the See of Chichester. The Virgin Mary is depicted standing with the infant Christ in arm upon the shield of the Bishop of Salisbury.

More often such figures are represented by symbols long associated with them. Some examples are the Paschal Lamb for St. John the Baptist, the keys for St. Peter, the winged lion for St. Mark, and the winged bull for St. Luke. Roses and lilies are symbolic of the Virgin Mary.

Civic heraldry accounts for a number of figures of the saints and apostles themselves. St. Peter, St. Paul, St. Pancras, St. Andrew, and St. Mark appear in borough and city arms. Angelic figures are rare as figures within the shield but they can be found as supporters (shield accessories).

Human figures, like angelic figures, rarely appear as *charges* (devices placed upon a shield) but they do appear with some frequency as supporters. The wild man, savage, or man of the forest, as he is called, appears more often as a charge than any other single figure. Other popular figures are the Moor or African warrior (the heads of both are often depicted as separate charges) and the Saracen head.

The savage is found naked except for wreathing about the loins and temple, and he is normally armed with a primitive wooden club. The Moor is generally armed with spear or shield and wears a torse (braided silk band) around his forehead. He is also attired in short skirted apparel.

Plate-armored full figures occur mainly as supporters, but limbs of such figures do appear as charges. Such limbs are also found in crests (another shield acces-

Anchor	*Arm*	*Arrows*	*Antlers*	*Axe*	*Beacon*
Bells	*Boar*	*Bomb*	*Book*	*Bows*	*Bridge*
Buckles	*Bugle-horn*	*Bull*	*Caltrap*	*Carbuncle*	*Castle*
Catherine wheel	*Chess rook*	*Clarion*	*Crescent*	*Cup*	*Cushion*
Dolphin	*Eagle*	*Eagle's leg*	*Eagle, two-headed*	*Escallop*	*Estoile*

Common charges

sory). Uniformed figures sometimes appear dressed in the style contemporary to time that the arms were granted.

Imaginary or semi-human figures can be seen in heraldry, but almost always as supporters. The main figures in this category are those of Neptune as half man-half fish and the similar figures of mermaids. A harpy, or half woman-half cockatrice, is found only rarely. Neptune can also be represented in the full and normal figure of man, distinguished by his crown and trident.

When heads are represented, such as the previously mentioned savage, Saracen or Moor, their classification as such must be described. It must be further blazoned as being affronté or profile, couped or erased, as occurs also with animal heads. Anything adorning the head must be accounted for. If the hair coloring is to be conveyed, it is termed "crined" of whatever tincture is proper.

As the head is termed couped or erased, a human limb is also blazoned as such when it appears as a charge apart from the rest of the body. An arm may appear *embowed* (bent at the elbow), *vambranced* (encased in armor), or *habited, vested* or *cuffed* (dressed). Such dress tincture must be blazoned (described).

Legs can also be couped or erased either at the knee or thigh and flexed (bent at the knee). The hand itself may serve as a charge, and when it does the hand must be distinguished as being either dexter or sinister. If it is open with the palm exposed to the viewer, it is termed *appaume*. If it is closed, it is so described. Any object it holds in a grasping position must also be described as "the hand grasping a sword, etc."

The category of living animals immediately leads to its first subdivision, beasts of prey. The lion, of course, heads this classification. Other ravenous or fierce creatures generally considered in this grouping are the tiger, leopard, bear, boar, wolf, and wildcat. The terms describing the lion's various attitudes can be applied for the most part to the other beasts. Special terms are sometimes necessary to replace them. These substitutions occur most frequently in describing or blazoning beasts of chase or passive type animals.

As suggested in Chapter 7, claws of the lion are considered weapons and the lion is termed *armed* of them. If a beast possesses horns or tusks, he is deemed to be also armed of these. Animals such as deer are said to be *hoofed* or *unguled*. Any animal whose tongue appears is termed *langued* of it in its particular tincture.

The beasts of chase are mainly characterized by the deer and other members of the deer family. Smaller animals like the fox and rabbit should be included in the list of hunted or preyed-upon animals belonging to this group.

The stag and hart, depicted as the same figure in heraldry, generally appear fully antlered. The hind conversely is always shown without antlers. The buck is distinguished from the stag and hart by his broad and flat antlers. Other animals in the deer family are found mainly as supporters—the reindeer, antelope, and elk.

Deer are usually blazoned in a *springing* attitude in preference to the *rampant* (fiercer) attitude of the lion. The *rampant* term is permissible, however, although rarely used. The term *trippant* replaces *passant* when describing the walking deer. While *statant* is applicable in describing the standing deer, the animal is also said to be *at gaze* when the head is facing the viewer in what is normally termed the *guardant* position.

The deer and kindred animals appear in running attitudes unlike the lion and his fellow beasts of prey. Such running pose is termed *courant,* at speed or in *full chase.* When at rest, the deer is said to be *lodged* or *couchant.* Only the latter word is applicable to the lion.

The deer antlers are called *attires* and may appear in a different tincture than the rest of the head. When such is the case, the deer is said to be *attired* of said tincture. These attires often serve as a charge in themselves. Similarly, the heads of many of the animals appear more often as a charge than the full body.

The heads of the boar, bear, bull, ram, and deer are often seen as charges, and they can be couped, erased, or caboshed. The boar and bear heads, however, also appear in a fourth form called *couped-close.* In this form, the heads, which are always in dexter profile, are given a smooth vertical cut close to the ear at the back of the head. Additionally, the neck is removed by a close horizontal cut at a right angle to the first cut. This treatment of the head is common in Scottish arms.

A third group of animals depicted are miscellaneous creatures of a docile nature. Some of these are a domestic type such as the goat, the ram, the sheep, the lamb, the calf, the rabbit, the squirrel, the hedgehog, the beaver, the badger, the dog, and the horse. A few of these have particular terms for attitudes distinctive to them.

The horse, for instance, can be found in the common

rampant and *passant* attitudes and is so described. He is also found in *trotting* and *courant* attitudes. When in a rearing position with only his hindlegs grounded, he is termed *forcene* (enraged). Terms dealing with his riding equipment are also taken in account. He can be termed *bridled* or *furnished*. The latter term, along with *caparisoned,* means fully equipped with saddle and other fastenings.

The term *climant* is sometimes substituted for *rampant* when describing the goat. Of the few types of dogs encountered in arms, the greyhound is the most frequent. The talbot is another commonly seen dog. A rarely mentioned dog is the kenet, which occurs in the allusive arms of the Kent family. Since these are hunting dogs, the terms *in full chase* or *in full course* are often used in association with them. The *courant* term can also be applied in their case.

Other large yet docile animals such as the camel or elephant appear with some frequency. They may be seen as full figures or heads as with some of the other animals. While other animals exist in heraldic usage, their rarity in the form of charges is such that they need no further mention at this time. These animals are predominant as supporters and will be detailed later in the text.

Some animals seen in arms are adopted because their name is similar to the name of the arms bearer. These are called *allusive* arms because they allude to said similarity of names. Unfortunately, in a few cases, the early or archaic name of the animal is the one that is linked with the family name of the bearer. This being the case, the modern reader may be unfamiliar with such archaic names and so the motivation for its use escapes him.

The term *kenet,* mentioned previously in this chapter, is classic of this sort of wording. Kenet is a name for the small tracking dog. It is at present an uncommon word and though it was well used at the time of its origin, its significance as an allusive device is sometimes obscure. Modern writers have done much to clarify the meaning of an antiquated reference such as the above, but it is not always possible.

Dealing with the category of birds, the eagle immediately comes to the fore. This creature shares equal rank with the lion and the cross as a predominant symbol of heraldry. Like the lion it is a creature of prey, and so its beak and talons are considered weapons. Consequently, when these talons and beak differ in tincture

from the rest of the body the eagle is said to be *armed* of them in whatever tincture is specified.

Because of the conformation of their bodies as well as their function, eagle and other bird attitudes require entirely different terminology than the four-legged animals. Starting with stationary positions, if the bird is standing on the ground with folded wings, he is said to be *closed* or *trussed;* should he be atop some object he is *perched;* if he is about to take wing he is *rising* or *roussant.*

When poised in the act of taking flight, his wings can assume one of four positions:
1. Wings displayed and inverted (wings spread but with the tips pointed down).
2. Wings displayed and elevated (wings spread and pointed upward).
3. Wings elevated and addorsed (wings raised but back to back with one another).
4. Wings addorsed and inverted (wings back to back as the former but with the points down).

A number of these wing formations are found in supporters as well as in charges.

Once in flight, the bird is said to be either *soaring* (flying upwards) or *volant* (flying on a horizontal plane). An attitude closely associated with the eagle is the one termed *displayed.* This condition exists where the body is affronté, wings and legs are spread out to each side, and the head is turned (generally to the dexter). A variation of this attitude is one where all is the same except for the wing tips, which are inverted.

The eagle, unlike other birds, may be found crowned, gorged with collar or coronet, or charged upon the body or wings. Inasmuch as they are birds of prey they may appear with another creature in their beaks or standing upon one. The terms *preying* or *trussing* come into play in blazoning this condition of attitude.

The eagle is of such symbolic stature that his head, wings, and legs are also seen as charges. When the eagle head is used it is either couped or erased as in the leg. Certain terms or conditions apply to the use of wing charges, which may appear singly or in pairs. When joined in pairs and tipped downwards they are termed *in lure,* whereas if they are tipped upwards, they are deemed *a vol* (as in flight). The term *in lure* suggests the *hawks lure,* a device used for hawking. When one wing is used tipped upwards, it is sometimes termed *a demi-vol.*

The hawk can be mistaken for the eagle in heraldic

charges except for one factor that is not common between them. The eagle has a tufted head and neck, while the hawk, its fellow bird of prey, and the falcon are smooth crowned. To further distinguish them from the eagle, the falcon and hawk, which are depicted in the same form, are always shown in a *close* attitude, that is, with the wings folded.

In flight, the position of the falcon's wings are to be blazoned. It may appear hooded with a head mask or with bells tied to its legs as when used for sporting. If only one leg is tied, it is termed *belled,* but if two are tied, the term is *jessed and belled.* When the thongs to which the bells are tied are ringed at the end, the falcon is termed *vervelled* (the term *vervel* being the name of the ring).

The raven, crow, rook, and corbie are all depicted alike, just as the hawk and falcon are treated as one, and all are blazoned sable throughout. A similar looking bird, the Cornish chough, is distinguished from these other black birds by having a red beak and legs.

The pelican appears most frequently in a complex arrangement. It is found standing above its nest, nourishing its young with blood from a self-inflicted wound. The term "pelican in its piety" refers to this attitude. It has found its way into American heraldry in this form in the State Seal of Louisiana.

The ostrich is generally seen with a horseshoe held in its beak. Its feathers also serve as an important device both as a shield, a charge, and a badge of royalty and nobility. The three feathers of the Prince of Wales are among the prominent devices using the ostrich feather.

Other long-necked birds such as the swan, crane, heron, and stork occur in arms. The swan has precedence among this group, being adopted as a symbol by Henry V and De Bohun. This bird normally appears with its wings close but can assume all the rising attitudes outlined earlier.

The crane is depicted holding a stone in the one leg that is off the ground. It is supposed to prevent it from involuntarily falling asleep. The stone will drop and the sound will quickly awaken it. In this attitude, the crane is termed "in its vigilance."

The martlet is a heraldic swallow, usually depicted without legs. This is in symbolic support of an old theory that the swallow cannot perch on the ground. The marlet has the added distinction of being a mark of cadency (differencing within a family or its branches). Cadency and its symbols will be the subject of a separate chapter.

The rooster in heraldry is referred to as a cock. Its distinctive features, such as spurs, beak, whattles, and comb, must be blazoned in the appropriate tinctures. Consequently, in heraldically describing these tinctures, the rooster is said to be respectively armed, combed, and jelopped of them. In some cases, the rooster is termed *dunghill cock* to prevent it being confused with the game-cock or other varieties.

The peacock appears with tail close when in profile or with its tail displayed when affronté. The term "in its pride" describes the peacock in the latter attitude. This bird may be blazoned as *pawne.* The term *popinjay* may appear as a synonym for parrot and *colomb* can be found as a word for dove.

About a dozen types of fish have been blazoned in heraldry. Among these are the dolphin, whale, pike, salmon, trout, eel, lucy, herring, roach, and barbel. Added to these are the whelk-shell and escallop.

Three positions describe the attitudes of fish:
Naiant—swimming fesswise (horizontally).
Urinant—swimming palewise (head down or diving).
Hauriant—swimming head up palewise (or surfacing).

The term *embowed,* meaning "bent in a curve," is applied frequently to the dolphin but it also appears in blazoning the barbel and other fish on occasion. The tincture of the dolphin when blazoned *proper,* is green with red fins and tongue. The term *proper* in heraldry means "in natural color."

The reptiles and insects found in heraldry are few and far between. This is perhaps understandable since they generally lack the broad, distinguishable features favorable to heraldic charges. The snake or serpent, although it is one of the few reptiles encountered, possesses three attitudes. It can be knotted (*nowed*), coiled with the head erect, or crawling (*glissant*). In all cases the mouth is open and the fangs are projected. The lizard is the only other reptile appearing often enough to warrant mention. The lizard may alternately be described as a *scaly lizard* in blazoning.

The bee, because of its distinctive black and yellow body striping, may have found favor as one of the few insect forms adopted in arms. Added to this quality is its association with industriousness in the same spirit as the beaver.

The grasshopper, hornet, ant, butterfly, spider, stag-beetle, and scorpion are infrequently seen in achievements.

Monsters occupy another category of common charges. In past descriptions, they have been also defined as chimerical or imaginary animals. They are basically products of mythology embellished with a few hybrid creations of the heralds themselves.

The pegasus, unicorn, and griffin are perhaps names that are already familiar to readers even slightly versed in early mythology. The pegasus was of course the white-winged horse, and the unicorn was the horse with the single horn projecting from its forehead. Further distinguishing the unicorn is the lion's tail, cloven hoofs, tufted hocks, and beard. The griffin, in essence, is an eagle-lion, combining the head, breast, foreclaws, and wings of the former with the hindquarters and the tail of the latter.

Added to these creatures are the dragon, wyvern, cockatrice, opinicus, enfield, sea horse, and sea lion. The dragon, which constitutes the time-worn villain of the myths born of medieval chivalry, is a serpent-like animal that appears with bat-type wings, a horny mane, and an armored or laminated chest and belly. Its taloned legs and forked tail and tongue are also part of its distinctive but complex structure.

The wyvern is also a dragon but it varies from the original form in that it only has two legs. The cockatrice is also a two-legged dragon form but is further distinguished by a cock's head, comb, and wattles.

The opinicus is similar to the griffin in all but two details. The opinicus has a lion's forepaws and a bear's tail. The griffin has an eagle's foreclaws and a lion's tail. The griffin, incidentally, appears in another form that is identical to its original version except for the absence of wings. This version is termed a *male* griffin.

The enfield is a nebulous mixture of a fox's head and a wolf's body, hind legs, and tail. It also bears an eagle's shanks and talons forming its forelegs. It is the talons that prevent it from being taken for the wolf as seen in supporters. The enfield's fluffy tail also distinguishes it from the male griffin, which is also somewhat similar.

The heraldic antelope is noted by its horned nose, fierce tiger-like head, and serrated horns at variance with the horns of the natural antelope. Most heraldic or imaginary creatures possess the above-mentioned horn or tusk at the tip of the nose unlike their natural counterpart.

The heraldic tiger is probably the result of a misconception of the true appearance of the natural tiger.

The long pointed ears and again the beaked or horned nose set it apart from the natural beasts. In other respects it strongly resembles the lion. The blazoning of this creature sometimes has it spelled "tyger." It has been theorized that such spelling distinguishes it from the true tiger. This theory should be taken lightly inasmuch as such misspelling is typical of medieval writing under normal conditions.

The heraldic panther is a natural looking form except for the heavy flames pouring from its mouth and ears. This is a condition related to the dragon in medieval mythology. This attitude has been termed *incensed* (a decided understatement, if you will excuse the pun).

The sea lion and sea horse share the same feature of a fish's tail along with the upper parts of beasts. The sea lion shows the lion's face and chest but has narrow webbed forepaws. The sea horse has a horse's face and upper quarters but it too has webbed forepaws. These creatures have natural forms, the true sea lion being found as a supporter.

The figures of mermaids and mermen were introduced in the section on human figures. They are perhaps best properly classified as hybrids, thus belonging to the *monster* group. The figure of Neptune, the sea god, is pictured in this hybrid form but also as a human figure. This crowned and tridented figure should *not* be termed a triton. This title applies to lesser sea gods usually distinguished by their conch shell that they use for a trumpet.

Figures amid flames are the last two charges to be covered in this category. One is the salamander surrounded by fire and the other is the eagle, also amid fire. The eagle so depicted is termed the phoenix.

In the category of natural objects, we have those that deal with the sun, moon, stars, and sky. The sun may appear as a plain disc or display a human face. In either case, when surrounded by rays it is termed "in his splendor" or "in his glory." These rays are variable in number but are always alternately wavy and straight, respectively symbolic of heat and light. The sun may appear in less than its full circle in cases where it is partially hidden by a cloud, and the blazoning must specify this condition. Likewise, only a portion of the sun's rays may appear out of a cloud. This is called a sunburst. A single ray can also be depicted, which will issue from the edge of the shield in the manner of a wavy pile.

When a charge is placed directly over the sun "in

its splendor" so as to obscure all but its rays, the charge is said to be *en soleil*. Many badge charges have been given this treatment. It is also commonly seen in the metal insignias on the front of military headgear.

The moon, too, may be depicted with a human face. It is termed "in her complement" or "in her plenitude," when full. The different phases of the monthly cycle are also depicted by crescents facing in varying directions. When the horns of the crescent point upwards to the chief it is termed crescent, when pointed to the dexter it is increscent, and when pointed to the sinister it is decrescent. The heavenly star is called an estoile. It has six or more *wavy* rays and must not be mistaken for the molet, which has five *straight* rays. The molet *is* termed a star in Scottish heraldry, though not necessarily a heavenly star.

Clouds, rainbows, and thunderbolts all appear as individual charges in heraldry. The thunderbolt displays its symbolic jagged streaks in saltire between two conjoined and elevated wings. Clouds can be shown in their proper form or represented by a nebuly line. Sylvanus Morgan, in his 1661 treatise on heraldry, suggested the natural meaning or origin of many line forms such as those that have just been described (wavy and nebuly).

The oak is considered the predominant tree seen in armorial bearings. The tree category has its several special terms in blazoning as have the animal and bird classifications. An uprooted tree is described as eradicated. If only the chopped lower part of the trunk appears, it is said to be *couped* and that part is called a *stock* or *stump*. If on the other hand, the tree is rooted and bearing fruit it is termed *fructed*. With the oak tree, the appropriate term is *acorned*. A tree can be shown growing from the ground or rising from a mount.

The ragged branch of a tree is seen in the arms of Beauchamp and is the basis for the line form called ragully. Leaves and sprigs of leaves are seen in wreaths. If a leaf has a stem attached to it, such a leaf is termed *slipped*. The strawberry leaf is the one that is used for ornamentation on crowns and coronets.

The most famous of plant forms is the symbol of the Plantagenet dynasty, which ruled England for many years. This name was taken from the broom plant (planta genet), which also served as their badge of identity. The wheat garb is another symbol prevalent both in badge and shield devices. If a garb is of a grain other than wheat it must be specified.

Two flowers presently stand out in heraldic usage, the fleur-de-lis of France and the Tudor rose of England (the latter preceded by the gold rose of Edward I, the Yorkist white rose, and the red rose of the Lancastrians). Closely rivaling these flowers in importance is the Scottish thistle and the Irish trefoil.

The tincture of the rose has to be blazoned since it appears in the several colors as previously disclosed. This flower is also the cadency differencing of the seventh son in a family. The rose, in any color that it is blazoned, shows green sepals and a gold center. Termed *barbed and seeded*, it can be composed of two concentric five-petaled forms. In this state, it is usually tinctured gules and argent to represent the Tudor rose.

Another flower form that appears as a mark of cadency is the octofoil (or double quartrefoil). This is the cadency differencing of the ninth son in a family. The other flower forms commonly seen, other than this and the already mentioned trefoil, are the quatrefoil and cinquefoil. The thistle is slipped and leaved proper (in its normal colors) as is the trefoil when it symbolizes Ireland. The trefoil is representative of the clover, the quartrefoil, of the primrose, and the cinquefoil, of the pansy.

The widest category of common charges occurs in the grouping of inanimate objects and is the first part of this group of general nature with no overall premise in mind. The second series were all deliberately adopted because the name of each object played upon a similar sounding family name of the arms bearer.

The first or general grouping, while not specifically subdivided, does seem to fall into a handful of listings. Because of the militancy of the times, weapons were a favorite choice of symbols. Navigational symbols such as anchors and galleys were another group that were used as charges. Structures such as castles, gate towers, bridges, and arches were also frequently adopted.

Regardless of their classification, many of the objects provide an insight into the times. Some are interesting because of their present-day obsolescence; others because their early names are now archaic. These devices, which are listed below and described, have been depicted in a series of three plates without any attempt to affix their category.

ANCHOR—This device was called the emblem of hope. It was often granted to those who had distinguished themselves in naval expeditions. The anchor normally appeared without rope or chain. When this rope or chain is seen wound about the cross bar and shank, the charge is termed *cabled* or foul anchor.

ARROWS—The single arrow is always depicted palewise unless blazoned otherwise. However, the direction of the point, either up or down, must be stated. The tincture of the arrow point as well as its feathers, if different from the shaft, must always be stated in blazoning. Such blazoning will describe the points as being *armed* or *barbed* of such tincture and the feathers *flighted* or *feathered* of such tincture.

Three feathers usually form a *sheaf* with one arrow erect and the other two crossing it in saltire. The

term *band* applies to the horizontal tie through the middle of the sheaf.

AXE—Several types of axes are mentioned in bearings. The battle axe or broad axe is probably the most familiar. This is a short-handled or hafted axe with a spike on the haft end that joins with the curved blade. The pole axe is a long-hafted version of this form. The Danish axe has a short, *curved* haft but is otherwise similar to the battle axe. The Lochaber axe is straight hafted but has a hook on its top intended to catch the weapon of the enemy.

BATTERING RAM—This is a siege device used to smash down the gates of a fortress or castle. A ram's

Types of fleur-de-lis found in various heraldic periods (top row, left to right: 13th century, late 12th century, late 12th century, early 12th century; bottom row: 18th century, 15th century, 14th century)

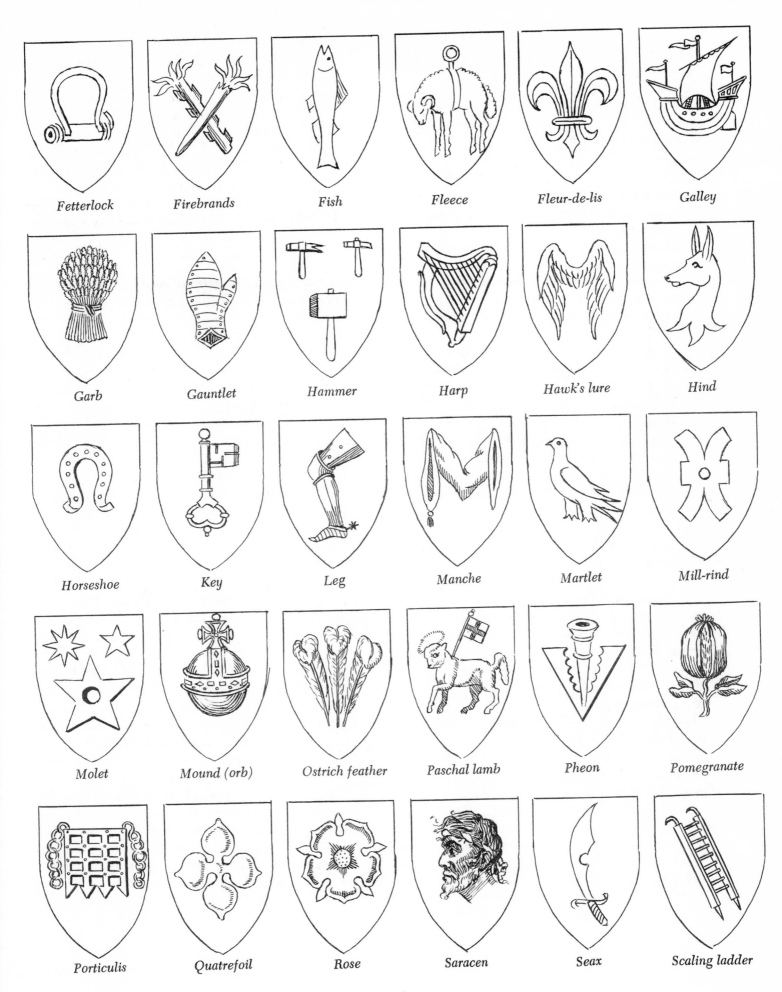

Fetterlock	*Firebrands*	*Fish*	*Fleece*	*Fleur-de-lis*	*Galley*
Garb	*Gauntlet*	*Hammer*	*Harp*	*Hawk's lure*	*Hind*
Horseshoe	*Key*	*Leg*	*Manche*	*Martlet*	*Mill-rind*
Molet	*Mound (orb)*	*Ostrich feather*	*Paschal lamb*	*Pheon*	*Pomegranate*
Porticulis	*Quatrefoil*	*Rose*	*Saracen*	*Seax*	*Scaling ladder*

Common charges

head normally appears on the battering end of this long form, with curved handles along its length to facilitate its being carried by several men.

BEACON—This is a device used to give warning of the approach of an enemy force. It was also used to direct mariners along dangerous coasts at night. It is in the form of an iron cage shaped like a basket. The cage is mounted on a high pole with a slanted ladder providing access to it. Material is then ignited in the basket, thus providing necessary illumination.

BELLS—Bells in heraldry take two forms—one is the common church bell, the other is the hawk's bell, which is the small round bell attached to its leg. Unless the blazoning distinctly specifies this latter bell, it is understood to mean the former when simply termed a bell.

BOMB—This appears as the familiar black ball with a hole or crack on top from which flames issue. British grenadiers, early American artillery, and the present-day Ordinance branch have all used this symbol.

BOOK—When blazoned, the book should be described as open or shut. Its furnishings, such as its clasp, bookmarks, page edgings, and leather bindings should be stated and their tinctures blazoned. Often oversized Latin phrases appear across the open book pages. These too must be detailed in blazoning. This charge is common to the arms of educational groups.

BOWS—Two types are found in arms: one is called the ancient type with a straight indented hand grasp in its center, the other is the plain curved type later used. It must be stated if the bow is drawn taut or unbent with the string wound or entwined about it. If this string is tinctured differently from the bow, it is blazoned as being "stringed" of this tincture.

The bow is understood to be the simple long bow. If the cross bow is intended it must be blazoned as such. In either case, the position (palewise, bendwise, or fesswise) should be stated.

BRIDGE—This charge is often used as an allusive device for families whose names have this word as a syllable of it. Such details as the number of arches should be given. Further description stating whether it is towered or embattled should also be blazoned.

BUCKLE—The buckle appears in seceral shapes and must be blazoned as being in one or the other of these forms. It can be round, square, oval, or lozenge-shaped. The position of the tongue in each of these forms should be stated.

It may be pendant (pointing down), point in chief, or fesswise (point in dexter or sinister). If the term "arming buckle" is blazoned, it is understood to be lozenge-shaped.

BUGLE HORN—This is also called the hunting horn and should not be taken for the instruments called the trumpet or bugle. It is a device in the shape of the old powder horn, which, like the bugle horn, is obtained from the natural horn of an animal. It commonly appears with banding—top, bottom, and center—as well as being suspended from strings. These bands and strings, if tinctured differently from the horn, must be blazoned. The term *stringed* has already been introduced with the bow as means of describing such different tincture. The bands on the other hand, are said to be *garnished* or *viroled* of their different tinctures.

CALTRAP—This is an obsolete device of four joined spikes spread outwardly from their point of juncture. Its purpose was to maim the horses of the enemy. Its design provided for one spike to always be erect while the others, spread out as they were, steadied it as a tripod would in this position.

CARBUNCLE—This charge resembles a rimless wheel with spokes radiating from its hub. It is said to be inspired by the design of a lady's brooch. The carbuncle is the subject of a myth that it is being guarded by a dragon. This charge is distinguished by the semi-flory tips on each extension or radiation.

CASTLE—The castle is shown with only two towers unless blazoned otherwise. It has its familiar arched gate in the wall that joins them. An iron grill called a portcullis may appear before this central archway. The castle may also have a third tower arising from the central wall in which case the castle will be blazoned as *triple towered*.

Castles may vary beyond these two forms with the addition of pyramiding extra tower sections and walls shown in perspective. The tower may be domed or pointed as in French castles. The gate and slits for firing arrows may vary in tincture from the castle itself. If the cemented portion is of a different tincture than the natural stones used in its construction, it will be blazoned as "masoned" of such tincture. The wall and tower tops are usually flat and embattled, although the earlier-described towers are occasionally found. When a single tower appears, it is called a *gate tower* and is not to be confused with a castle. Such towers guarded an approach to a castle.

CATHERINE WHEEL—This has the same structure as the common wagon wheel except that it has curved blades following each of its six or eight spokes. It has been named the Catherine wheel to symbolize its connection with the martyrdom of St. Catherine.

CLARION—This was an odd-looking wind instrument played like a harmonica. This charge found in numerous forms, was also called the claricord and sufflue.

CRESCENT—This form is thought to originate from the moon phase that it sometimes depicts. It has had other applications as a charge, one of which is its use as a mark of cadency for the second son. Its role as a moon symbol has been described earlier in this chapter.

CUP—The cup, when appearing with a stem and base, is called a *chalice* or *goblet*. If a cup has a domed cover, as is sometimes depicted, it is blazoned as a *covered cup*. Should it have handles, this too must be stated.

CUSHION—The cushion appears in arms in rectilinear forms with tassels on each corner. The significance of this charge has not been established. Perhaps the pillow alludes to the cushion on which the coronation crown is placed.

FETTERLOCK—This is a shackle and lock normally placed around a horse's leg. It appears on a falcon's leg in some of the badges of the Plantagenet clan.

FIREBALL—This was a siege weapon fired from catapults in besieging a castle. It appears as a ball with four flames issuing from it crosswise. This charge is not to be confused with the earlier mentioned bomb.

GALLEY—This ship normally appears with one mast. Should it appear as a three-masted galley, the difference must then be blazoned. Other details regarding the oars being in action, the flags flying, and the mast *furled* (rolled up) must be all stated. The galley is also termed a *lymphad*.

GAUNTLET—This is generally taken to mean the ar-mored glove. Some details that are required in blazoning the hand are also used in blazoning the gauntlet.

HALBERD—This weapon was one of the several long-hafted arms, such as the spear, the pole-axe, the glaive, and the bill, that were all used in the Middle Ages.
The halberd combines the spear and the axe. Its design lent itself also to ensnaring the weapon of the mounted adversary by a foot soldier.

HAMMER—The hammer shows several head forms sometimes suggestive of the particular craft for which it served. It is essential that they are depicted of such type that may be stated in blazoning. A difference in head and haft tincture must be stated.

HARP—This instrument is ornamented as personal taste dictates. Again, if the string tincture varies from the frame, it must be stated as stringed of such tincture. The Celtic harp has lately replaced the Irish harp with the winged woman which once appeared in Royal Arms.

HAWK'S LURE—This training decoy is always pictured with inverted wings. As its name implies, it lured the hawk back to the falconer after a chase. The wings in the lure were joined by a line and ring.

KEYS—Keys have been called the symbol of trust. In heraldic usage they often represent St. Peter and are frequently seen in ecclesiastical arms. When they appear in saltire, the notched part, or ward, is generally pointed upward and outward.

MANCH—This is a loose hanging sleeve of a woman's dress. It has taken some rather abstract but decorative forms as a charge. It has been theorized that this could have been one of the tokens of favor a damsel tore off from her clothing for a tournament knight to display on his lance or crest.

MILL-RIND—This is the distinctive iron retaining piece centered on the millstone. This charge has also been called mill-iron or, in French, *fer-de-moline*. One of its curved variations is said to have inspired the limb endings on the cross moline as well as supplying its name.

MOUND—This charge has also been called a globe or sphere which, in truth, it is. It represents the world and usually has dominant horizontal and vertical bar, representing latitude and longitude. This charge can be found atop the Royal Crown and

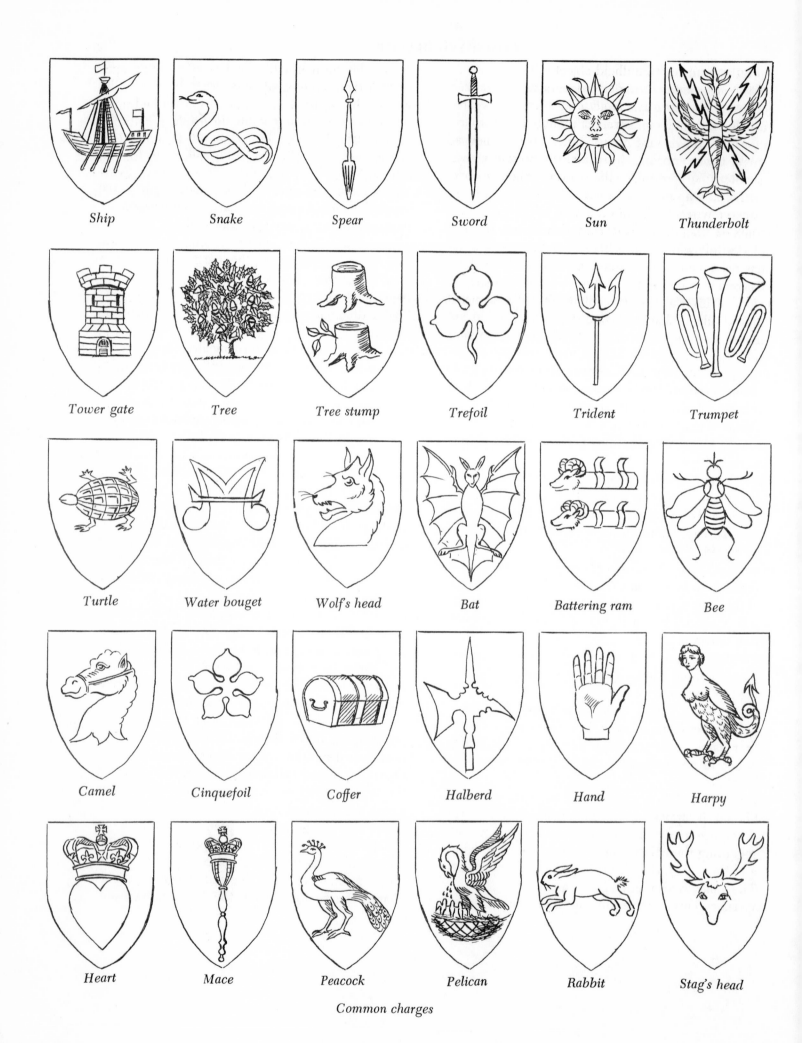

Ship	Snake	Spear	Sword	Sun	Thunderbolt
Tower gate	Tree	Tree stump	Trefoil	Trident	Trumpet
Turtle	Water bouget	Wolf's head	Bat	Battering ram	Bee
Camel	Cinquefoil	Coffer	Halberd	Hand	Harpy
Heart	Mace	Peacock	Pelican	Rabbit	Stag's head

Common charges

also appears as a handheld object.

MOLET—This is the form derived from the rowel (star) of a spur as its name *molette* in French indicates. It normally has five straight points or rays unless blazoned as having more. It has been confused with the estoile, which has six or more wavy rays. In Scottish heraldry the rowel, when pierced through the center, is also called a molet, while the unpierced molet is called a *star*.

PHEON—This is the barbed head of an arrow. It is distinguished from the charge sometimes called a *broad arrow* by the engrailing found on the inner edges of the pheon's barbs. Unless blazoned to the contrary, the pheon's point is faced downward.

PORTCULLIS—This is a rectangular metal gateway defense raised or lowered by chains attached to rings at its upper corners. It was made equally spaced of cross bars, the vertical ones all ending in barbs at the bottom. This device was also the well-known badge of the Beauforts, Henry VII, and Henry VIII.

SPEAR—This form usually appears as a tilting spear rather than the combat type.

SWORD—The sword always appears unsheathed unless stated otherwise and normally displays a straight blade. The hilt and the generally rounded knob on its end called the pommel may be of a different tincture than the blade. When this condition exists, the sword is blazoned *hilted and pommeled* of such tincture. It should be understood that the crosspiece of the sword is part of the hilt.

TOWER—This form is also called gate-tower or gateway, since it barred intruders from the castle. It can be triple towered or turreted as those towers in a castle are also depicted on occasion. It displays the same embattlements on top and arched doorway or port at the base. All rules of tincture involved with the larger castle apply to this form.

WATER-BOUGET—This was a water container composed of two hard leather bags joined by a wooden yoke so that they could be carried across the shoulders. Like the manche, some forms were very abstract.

9

𝕭𝖑𝖆𝖟𝖔𝖓𝖎𝖓𝖌 𝖆𝖓𝖉 𝕿𝖗𝖎𝖈𝖐𝖎𝖓𝖌

A heraldic description of the various bearings or devices within a shield and their relative placement is called a *blazon*. The act of providing such a description is therefore termed *blazoning*. A tournament herald was well versed in blazoning either in its oral or written form. As a tournament *crier*, he would describe the arms of the contestants to the spectators and later record them in manuscripts. (He would on occasion also record the arms of battle participants.)

It was not always convenient for the herald to actually paint facsimiles of the arms that he had announced, so he sometimes gave written blazons instead in the same heraldic terms that he had expressed verbally. At a later date, heralds might translate some of these written records of arms into painted representations.

When it was possible to do so, however, the herald would make his *original* entry of these tournament and battle arms in their painted form. These painted facsimilies were called *emblazonments* and should not be confused with blazons. At times, a compromise measure was adopted between these fully painted arms (emblazonments) and the blazon. This procedure was called *tricking* and will be spoken of shortly.

The early terms used in blazoning were direct and similar to the everyday language of the time. As heraldry became more complex, special terms were invented to describe a placement of a charge and its character. When such terms were applied to any charge or component of arms, none but a positive and singular interpretation could be derived from it. The terms invented for shield locations were the first unique terms introduced into heraldry that applied solely to this component of arms. The Normans, in their conquest of England, brought with them their own Norman-French heraldic terms, which in part have remained rooted in English heraldry. Some of their terms were replaced with English ones, thus creating a mixed jargon.

These changes were at first necessary to avoid any vagueness in descriptions. Later, armorists overzealous in their attempts to create synonyms for already acceptable words, encumbered the heraldic language with flourishy terms. Nonetheless, these later terms, like their predecessors, *did* convey a clear single meaning and so must be equally regarded.

Once the elements of heraldry are learned by a student of this subject, it is next necessary to learn how to either convey or interpret these essentials in a blazon. There are seven descriptions that have to be given in a proper order when blazoning a shield of arms.

1. The shield surface, its tincture(s), and then its field. (It should be stated if the field is parted, varied, or strewn with small charges.) If the field

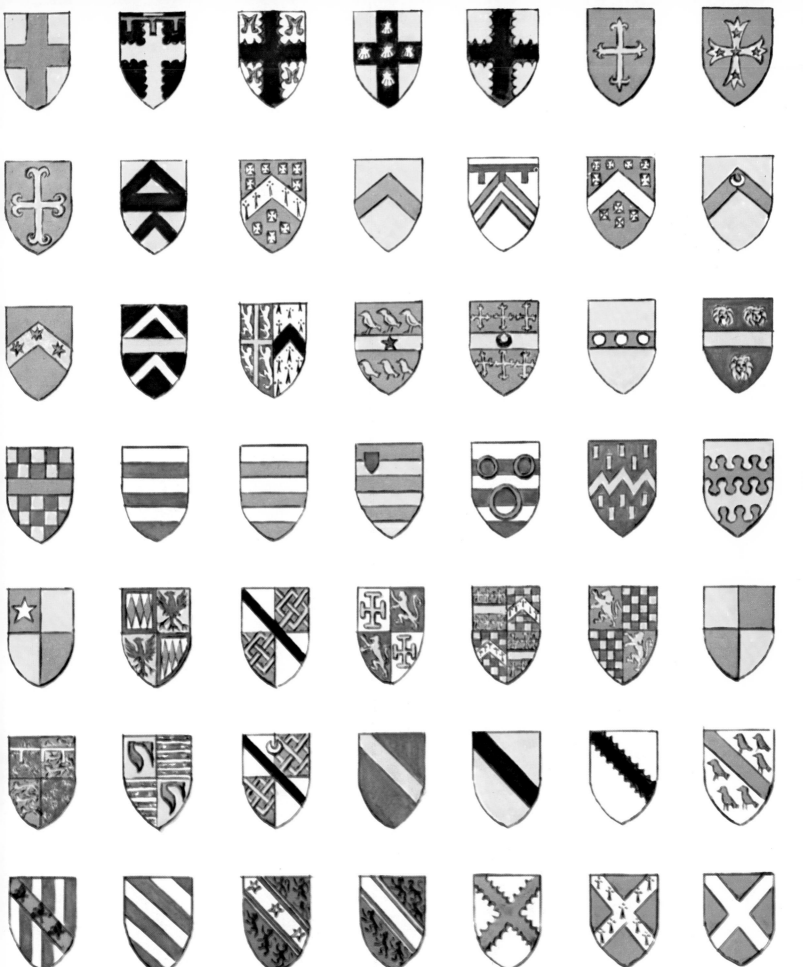

Arms of participants in the Battle of Crecy, first series. Top row, left to right: Sir Edmund de Burgh; Sir William Ufford; Lord Bouchier; Sir John de Grailly; John, Lord Mohun; Lord Latimer; Sir Thomas Ughted; second row: Lord Willoughby; Sir John de L'Isle; Lord Maurice de Berkely; Sir Ralph Stafford; Lord St. Maur; Lord Thomas Berkely; Sir Hugh Stafford; third row: Sir Reginald de Cobham; Sir William de Kildesby; Thomas Hatfield (Bishop of Durham); Sir Roger Beauchamp; Sir William Beauchamp (Lord Aberghvenny); Sir William Huntingfield; Sir Michael de la Pole; fourth row: Lord Thomas Clifford; Lord Grey; Lord Multon; Lord Geoffrey de Harcourt; Lord Greystoke; Sir William Deincourt; Lord Lovel; fifth row: Vere, Earl of Oxford; Sir John de Montague; Edward, Lord Le Despencer; Sir Richard Beaumont; Beauchamp, Earl of Warwick; Fitz-Alan, Earl of Arundel; Lord Saye; sixth row: Edward Plantagenet (Prince of Wales); Hastings, Earl of Pembroke; Lord Hugh de Despencer; Lord Scrope of Bolton; Lord Mauley; Sir John Radcliffe; Lord Furnival; seventh row: Sir Thomas Grandison; Sir John Philibert; Bohun, Earl of Northampton; Bohun, Earl of Hereford; Sir John Tiptoft; Sir John Neville; Sir Robert Neville

Arms of participants in the Battle of Crecy, second series. Top row, left to right: Lord Zouche; Lord Lascelles; Sir Guy de Bryan; Sir John Chandos; Sir Richard Fitz-Simon; Lord Lucy; Lord Ryther; second row: Lord Roos; Lord Darcy; Lord Scales; Richard, Lord Talbot; Courtenay, Earl of Devon; Sir Peter Courtnay; Lord Greystoke; third row: Sir Richard de la Vacha; Sir James Audley; Lord Ferrers; Montague, Earl of Salisbury; Lord Fitz-Hugh; Sir Roger Beauchamp; Sir Simon de Burley; fourth row: Clinton, Earl of Huntingdon; Sir Thomas Danvers; Lord Morley; Sir John Cornwall; Sir Edward de Monthermer; Lord Lewis Tufton; Halland, Earl of Kent; fifth row: Sir John Neville; Lord de la Waree; Lord Hugh le Despenser; Sir Thomas Percy; Lord Mowbray; Sir Walter de Wentway; A. Stafford; sixth row: Sir Miles Stapleton; Sir Roger Mortimer; Sir Richard Pembrugge; Sir Daniel Strabalge; Sir Thomas Felton; Sir John Hastings; Edward, King of England; seventh row: Sir Thomas Bradestone; Ralph, Lord Basset of Drayton; Ufford, Earl of Suffolk; Sir John Tiptoft; Lord Fitz-Payne; Henry Plantagenet (Duke of Lancaster); Sir Hugh de Hastings

*A roll of imaginary arms, those of non-existent sovereigns,
apparently created for the amusement of children.*

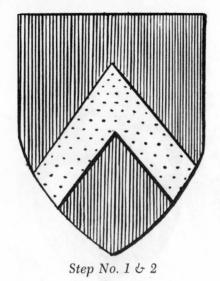

Step No. 1 & 2

Step No. 1.
The surface or field of the shield——

azure (blue)

Step No. 2.
The principal charge(s) resting on this surface and occupying a central or dominant position——

a chevron or (gold)

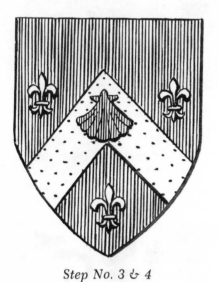

Step No. 3 & 4

Step No. 3.
Secondary charges also resting on the field of the shield——

three fleur-de-lis argent (silver)

Step No. 4.
Objects resting on this secondary and last-mentioned charge——

an escallop azure (blue)

Step No. 5 & 6

Step No. 5.
Important charges resting on the field but not in a central position——

a chief gules (red)

Step No. 6.
Any charges (objects) resting on last-mentioned charge——
a mollet argent (silver)
These six steps when joined in a single blazon thus become:
Azure, a chevron or,
three fleur-de-lis argent, an escallop azure, a chief gules and a mollet argent.

Argent

Azure

Gules

Or

Order of Blazoning in Arms

is plain, the naming of the tincture will suffice.

2. The principal charge (resting on the shield in the most prominent or central position).

3. The secondary charges, if any, resting on the field (shield surface).

4. Objects overlayed upon all the previous charges.

5. Important charges still resting on the shield but not in a central position. (The canton chief or bordure are examples of such positions.)

6. Objects placed in these last-mentioned charges.

7. Marks of cadency, if existent.

The glossary in the last pages of the book will give some good examples of the language of heraldry. Animal charges, as shown in Chapter 7, involve a special language not only to describe the position of animal, but also if it is collared or grasping any object. Such description would likely enter into the second step of the blazoning procedure.

Up to this point we have dealt with the contents of the shield. There is more than this to a complete display of arms, which, incidentally, is termed an *achievement*.

The shield itself has several accessories that are described in any blazoning.

1. The crest or ornamentation upon a helmet displayed above the shield.

2. The supporters—Figures that uphold the shield from each side.

3. The scroll—An extended horizontal roll below the shield that supports the supporters and serves as a vehicle to contain the motto.

4. The Motto—An inscription generally found in the scroll.

In the course of the text, the term "badge" will appear in a detailed description. For now let us say that it is a supplementary means of identity other than the shield or its accessories. It has, on many occasions, been the basis for some of the charges adopted in arms.

The term *tricking* meant sketching the outline of a coat of arms and blazoning its tinctures next to each form involved. The name of the field tincture normally was written upon the field itself, while most of the tinctures of overlayed charges were designated by terms written outside the shield. These tincture terms were then connected to the charges to which each alluded, by means of short straight lines.

Many individual arms had charges that appeared two or three times within the same coat. It was often the practice in tricking to eliminate drawing all but one

Trick of the arms of Howard, Earl of Surrey

of these. This single-drawn charge would be marked number one and the other charges simply suggested by successively higher numbers placed in the areas where duplicate charges would normally appear. This avoided time-consuming repetition in *tricking*.

Certain repetition was also avoided in blazoning, but for a different reason. When a shield contained two or more components that shared the same tincture, it was once considered awkward to continually repeat the tincture by name. The order in which each tincture was introduced was therefore noted and numbered. When a second charge was introduced in an already-used tincture, the charge was said to be "of the first" rather than of this tincture. A charge could be "of the second" or "of the third" as well.

Modern armorists do not all endorse the use of the terms "of the second" or " of the third," as it necessitates a constant re-check into the previous part of the blazon. Quite often the field tincture (always mentioned first) was a color that was used again in the arms. It is considered equally proper in this case to say "of the field" instead of mentioning the tincture by name. The term "of the field," since it is not sandwiched deep into the blazon, appears to be unobjectionable for this reason.

A good example of the confusion rather than simplicity caused by substituting numbers for repetition of tincture names is well illustrated in the blazon of the corporate arms of Central London Railway. These arms are described in Chapter 21, *Corporate Heraldry*.

Sometimes the preposition "and" would proceed or follow in blazoning the word *or* (the term for gold). In a case such as this, it is considered permissible to use the word *gold* in its place. In all cases, however, the tincture is always placed *after* the charge that it describes.

You will often find large principal charges repeated within the one coat of arms. Many times they will appear in groups of three. Because of the triangular shape of the shield, they will invariably appear in two rows (two charges above and one below). When they are smaller in size and hence able to be displayed in greater number, they are also able to take other row formations such as 3,2,1; 1,3,1; or 2,1,2; etc. These are called *dispositions*. Charges of this increased number must be blazoned to show the number in each row from top to bottom. In the case of only three identical charges, it is assumed that they run 2,1 and need not be stated as such unless disposed differently.

Dispositions

10

The Need for Differencing

In the early period of heraldry, obviously only a small percentage of individuals possessed arms. All that was therefore needed to give each man an unduplicated shield bearing was for him to choose from the few basic fields and ordinaries then in existence. These were later supplemented as needed by a limited group of common charges, among which were the lion, eagle, molet, crescent, boar's head, cinquefoil, and fleur-de-lis. Varying the tinctures would provide further distinctions where necessary between similar devices in arms.

Soon the increasing use of arms exhausted the supply of possible combinations that could be supplied from these forms and tinctures. The effect of these limitations became the inevitable appearance of many accidental similarities. The need to create additional heraldic forms in the manner of the ordinaries and common charges was now apparent. At the same time, the needs of heraldry were being further complicated by a developing trend.

Many men-at-arms chose to identify with their feudal

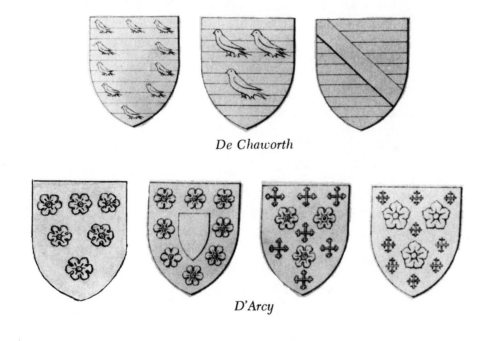

De Chaworth

D'Arcy

lords by adopting arms resembling those of their leaders. Men who were themselves leaders displayed their alliance with another leader by incorporating the latter's arms into their own. On one hand, there were those earlier-mentioned arms that were similar by chance (due to the narrow range of available forms), and on the other hand there were those last-mentioned bearings that were similar by choice.

Although the clear aim of heraldry was the establishment of distinctive personal devices for each arm bearer, similar arms once assumed were not readily surrendered. Cases tried in the still-existing Court of Chivalry testify to this. It therefore became necessary to establish a system of distinguishing between similar arms. This system was known as *differencing*.

Differencing in regard to the arms of those feudally allied was accomplished in several ways. If the feudal lord was known by a particular common charge, such

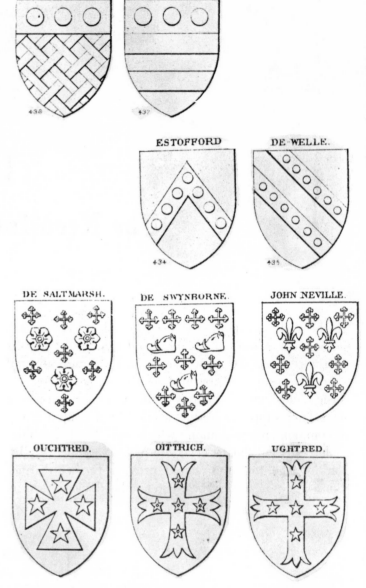

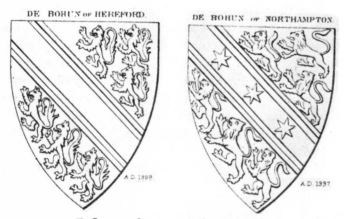

Differenced arms of the De Bohuns

as a garb of wheat, a cinquefoil, an escallop, or a fleur-de-lis, this common charge was *added* to the individual bearings of his allies. If the feudal leader was distinguished instead by the ordinary that he bore, his allies could adopt this form in one of three ways:

a. Assume the entire form of the bearing but simply reverse the tinctures of the field and ordinary.
b. Adopt the ordinary but apply a new (secondary) charge upon it.
c. Modify the ordinary by adding cotises or endorses

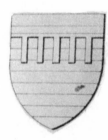

De Valence

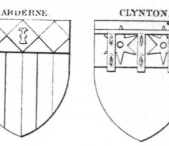

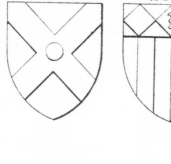

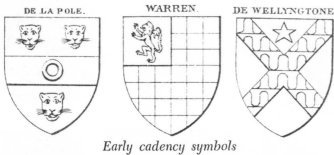

Early cadency symbols

to it or reduce the ordinary itself to a diminutive of its original form.

It can be theorized that the choice of methods depended on the particular adaptability of an adherent's bearing toward one procedure or another. The type of differencing that has thus been described deals with similar arms borne by unrelated individuals, this is to say, not of the same blood. There exists another type of differencing for distinguishing each member of the same family and also all of its branches. This system is called *differencing for cadency.*

The early procedures adopted in differencing for cadency were not unlike those previously outlined in many respects. The family bearings that had been passed down to the members of a family were individually treated with some separate addition or modification that, while not obscuring the main and distinctive features, added enough variation to create a new design.

A system closer to the present one was to introduce some fresh and minor charge, unrelated to the design of the original bearings and in no way modifying them. The charge, so affixed to the original bearing, would be subject to removal if the individual's position were to change.

In the first procedure, differencing was accomplished with changes in tincture, replacement of secondary charges, or the combination of these two actions. An-

other method employed for differencing was to add an ordinary, bordure, or label. The change in tincture might be made either in the field, ordinary, or secondary charge, or it could be made in all areas at once. Some new subordinate charge could be added rather than replacing the original one.

The original charge, however, as an alternative, could be modified to a small degree. In any event, no change should be so extreme as to affect the overall character. One clever approach was to change a plain argent field into an ermine one. This change would not infringe on the contours or tincture of any ordinary serving as the main feature of the arms.

When new charges were added, no apparent principle was involved in their choice except for a possible allusive reference. As shown by the use of ermine in place of argent, small repeated charges occurring as powdered fields were employed so as not to conflict with the dominant ordinary. Somehow, with time, these repeated charges became reduced in number but proportionately increased in size so as to now become secondary charges. Having reached this stage, they were often replaced with other charges of similiar stature. This last change was an indirect form of differencing since the previous charge had been established for a reasonable time before it too was finally replaced.

Certain ordinaries and subordinates were especially suitable as marks of cadency. The bordure and the canton were good because they did not obscure the greater portion of the shield and hence its distinctive features. They also served as a decorative field for further differencing in the form of powdered fields. This did not preclude the canton from also being used as background for a singular device.

The chevron and the bend, because of their diagonal lines, would stand out on an otherwise untouched rigidly horizontal or vertical party field and, in themselves, serve as a vehicle for secondary differencing with other charges. The label and the chief were effective in many

De Vere

De Hastings

De Cornwall

L'Estrange

De Umphraville

De Balliol

D'Arcy

Humphrey,
duke of Gloucester

John de
Beaufort

T. de Beaufort,
pre-1397

Edmund
Tudor

Jasper
Tudor

Thomas de
Beaufort

De Merley

Berkeley

John of Eltham

Courtenay

De Stapledon

Lenox

De Montbourchier

De Ferrers

De Vaus

Le Despencer

Bordures: for cadency and differencing

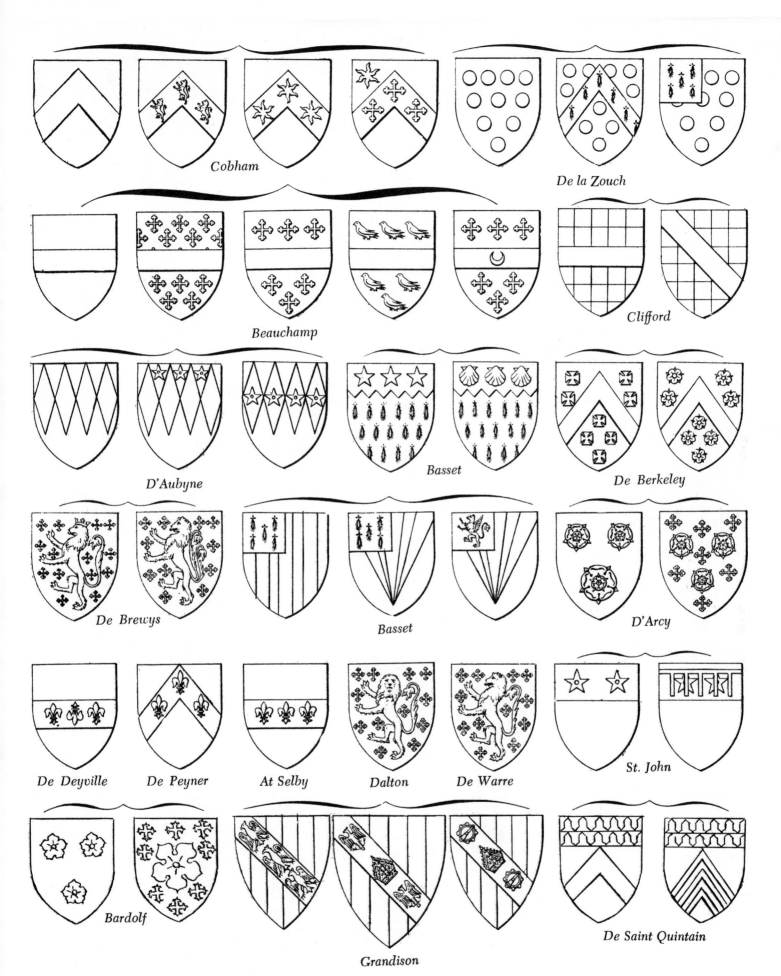

Cobham

De la Zouch

Beauchamp

Clifford

D'Aubyne

Basset

De Berkeley

De Brewys

Basset

D'Arcy

De Deyville   De Peyner   At Selby   Dalton   De Warre   St. John

Bardolf

Grandison

De Saint Quintain

Differencing: cadency and alliances

Cadency symbols for Neville of Raby

situations, allowing for the original and distinctive forms to be exhibited *below* them without change and, in the style of bordure and canton, present themselves for further differencing.

The symbols that were repeatedly used for secondary differencing seemed to evolve around some of the common charges that were mentioned earlier in the chapter. These were the crescent, molet, annulet and fleur-de-lis. Along with these later appeared the martlet, rose, label, cinquefoil and crosslets.

Neville, a noble of great standing, incorporated most of these charges as his own family's various cadency marks. His principal and distinctive device was a saltire with each member centering its individual common charges upon its intersection. It is perhaps his treatment that heralded the final form that was taken in differencing for cadency.

The earliest known use of the label is accredited to the first Earl of Winchester (circa 1200). It was said to have many more points than the three or five point labels commonly seen. Their early use was as an integral part of arms design rather than for differencing purposes. Some became hereditary, although this would prove to be in contradiction to their later use.

They became charged in time with other devices in each of their points. The points were made broader than the ribbon from which they hung, perhaps so that such secondary charges could be accommodated. This would be in the same manner that the bend, saltire, and cross were permissively widened to accommodate such charges. As will be shown later, the label figured prominently in royal cadency.

The first procedures in differencing proved unsatisfactory in the long run. The system of repeating charges in powdered fields, although unobtrusive, was vague as a cadency symbol. It was often taken for a basic element of the original arms and was even transmitted (passed to heirs) in this state. The small single charge while more desirable, was also ineffective at times since it often lacked distinctiveness and authority. It too fell into the pattern of becoming a permanent rather than a transient charge.

The final method of denoting cadency became a common practice near the end of the 15th century. The several marks of cadency that had been predominantly used in previous attempts at differencing were finally assigned to specific grades or seniority in the family line of inheritance or succession. They were also given

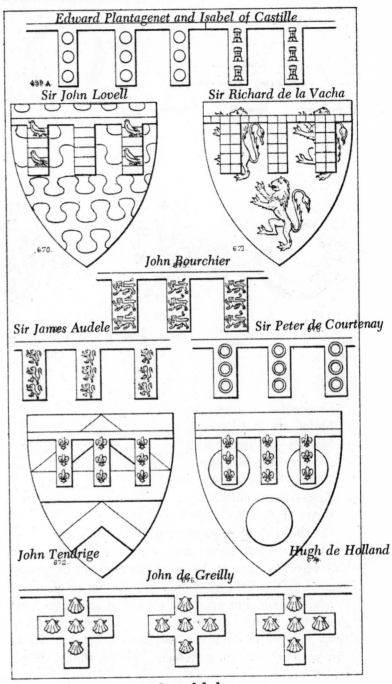

Cadency labels

definite points of placement on the shield, so that such a mark in such a position could mean only one thing.

The label became an exclusive mark of the eldest son, and among royalty it is the only cadency mark used in their arms. The mark in order of their seniority are listed below:

Label—the eldest son (during his father's lifetime)

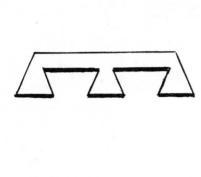   

The nine marks of cadency (top row, left to right: *label, crescent, mollet, martel;* bottom row: *annulet, fleur-de-lis, rose, cross flory, octofoil*)

Crescent—the second son
Molet—the third son
Martlet—the fourth son
Annulet—the fifth son
Fleur-de-lis—the sixth son
Rose—the seventh son
Cross Moline—the eighth son
Octofoil (Double Quartrefoil)—the ninth son

The next generation's arms can also be differenced this way for seniority by using the crescent or second symbol as the field on which to affix the original cadency symbols. For example, the eldest son in the next generation or next family in line of inheritance would show a label on crescent, the next oldest son would display a crescent on a crescent, and the third oldest a molet on a crescent.

These cadency marks, when used in unquartered arms, are normally placed in the chief. When the arms are quartered, the cadency mark is centered so that it touches each quarter. It may be of any tincture except argent. This tincture is reserved for the label in the arms of the Royal Family. The eldest son's mark of cadency is removed upon the death of his father but the others are kept as hereditary in all branches of the family.

Although junior marks of cadency are intended to be permanent, they can be removed if a subsequent marriage results in the arms of an heiress being added to the family bearings. Another instance where a mark of cadency is removed is when the son receives an augmentation, or new honor. Women do not carry cadency marks except for those borne by their father when they inherit his arms. This mark is also transmitted to their husbands' arms.

Marks of cadency are sometimes seen on animals that appear in crests or as supporters. In a crest this symbol can manifest itself as a collar around the neck of the animal. They can appear as a powdered field on supporters and on mantlings, and are also found in badges.

11

Allusive Arms

The pre-heraldic and early heraldic symbols found upon shields were mainly of an impersonal, objective, or even abstract nature. Religious or moral sentiments were usually expressed rather than the personal identity of the bearer. When it later became necessary to identify a comrade or leader-in-arms, heraldry provided the personal identification that was required.

As symbolism turned to the individual, men who bore arms became imaginative in their use of common charges. Often their choice of a shield symbol was a whimsical reference to their family name rather than a device borne of deep conviction. Such bearings were called "allusive arms" because they alluded to or suggested the bearer's name by their spelling or sound. Occasionally, rather than suggesting the family name, they played upon the name of an estate that the family held.

Not all the allusive devices were whimsical. Many were simple straightforward employments of symbols that ideally referred to the family name. Perhaps even in what seemed whimsy a serious attempt was being made to cope with a shortage of existing devices.

It has been difficult for modern armorists to recognize each and every case of allusive arms carried forth from the Middle Ages. This problem has come about through the fact that some of the early objects selected for symbols have long passed out of use or their original names have been changed with modern terminology.

Thanks to the research and knowledge of present-day heralds, the archaic names of many symbols have been uncovered and the connection between these devices and the family names are at once apparent. Below are listed a number of family names and the allusive device that their arms bore. Some of these symbols were also the basis for personal badges.

AMBESAS—three dice (to throw ambesace, three aces)
APPLEGARTH—apple tree
ARBLASTER—arblaster (cross-bow)
ARCHER—arrow
ASKEW—three asses
BACON—three pigs
BARLINGHAM—three white bears

Shelley.

BAYNES—two crossed bones
BERNAKE—horse barnacles
BILSBY—hammer (beal)
BORDOUN—burdon (pilgrim's staff)
BOSON—a boson (birding bolt-dulled dart)
BOWES—bows (archer's)

BUCKINGHAM—buck's heads
BULKELEY—three bulls' heads
CALVELEY—three calves
CHAMBERLEY—chamberlain's key (Lord Chamberlain)
CHEYNDUT—oak (cheyne) tree
COLFOX—three foxes' heads
CORBET—two corbies (crows)

GRIFFIN—griffin
HAREWELL—hares' heads
HARPESFIELD—three harps
HAUVILLE—three haws
HERON—three herons
HERTFORD—harts' heads
HORSELEY—horses' heads
KENT—kenets (small tracking dogs)
KILPEK—especk (thrusting sword)
LAMBTON—lambs
LUCY—three luces (fish)
MALET—mallets
MANGWALL—mangonel
MAULEVERER—leverers (greyhounds)
MOYLE—white mule
OTTER OF YORK—otters
PELHAM—three pelicans
PICOT—picks
PIPE—pipes (clarion)
PIRITON—pear tree
QUINCY—cinquefoil
ROKEBY—three rocks
ROKEWOOD—chess rook
RYE—three ears of rye
SAMON—three salmon
SHEFFIELD—wheat sheaves

Corbet.   Cockfield.   Rokeby.

COROUN—crowns
CRANESBY—three cranes
CUNLIFFE—conies (rabbits)
DALSTON—three daws (crows)
DOWNES—hart lodged (lying down)
DUFFELDE—three doves

Arundel.   Fauconer.   Pelham.

EADY—three old men's "eads"
FAUCONER—three falcons
FERRERS—horseshoes
FISHACRE—a dolphin
FORRESTER—hunting horns
GATES HEAD—goats' heads
GRAINDORGE—barley ears

Lucy.   Fishacre.   Roche.

DE TRUMPINGDON.

STURGEON—three sturgeon
TREMAYNE—three men's arms
TUCK—tuck (stabbing sword)
VEEL—calves
WAUNCY—wauns (gloves)
WHALLEY—three whales' heads

12

Augmentations

An augmentation is an addition made to a coat of arms as an honor granted by the sovereign. It can be given for services rendered to king or country, or merely as a mark of the sovereign's personal favor. These augmentations sometimes take the form of additional quarterings in the arms, but more commonly appear as a chief, canton, or escutcheon. Once granted, augmentations become an integral part of the hereditary arms and are transmitted with them.

One of the earliest augmentations was granted by Edward II circa 1320. Its recipient was Sir Alexander Seton, governor of Berwick. In recognition of his service, he was granted a sword palewise azure, supporting the Royal Crown proper.

Richard II granted the arms of Edward the Confessor to his kinsmen, the Hollands (Dukes of Surrey and Kent), as a mark of favor. Since these same arms were impaled with his own prior to this grant, it indicated a close tie with these two nobles. Richard II also made the same grant to Thomas Mowbray, Duke of Norfolk, again as a mark of favor.

Another example of a grant made by *mere grace* is the quartering granted to Robert de Vere, Duke of Ireland. These were the arms of St. Edmund, at that time considered the arms of Ireland. It consisted of azure, three crowns or, within a bordure argent.

The rivalry between Edward IV and the House of

Arms of Richard II

Lancaster was symbolized by grants of augmentations that Edward made to his Queen, Elizabeth Woodville. In order to have her arms equal to the Lancastrian peeress, Margaret of Anjou, he created a series of quarterings based on Elizabeth's maternal ancestry. The example that Edward IV set in granting wifely augmentations was followed by Henry VIII in honoring some of his consorts.

The arms of St. Edmund (Ireland) were also granted

Mowbray   Holland

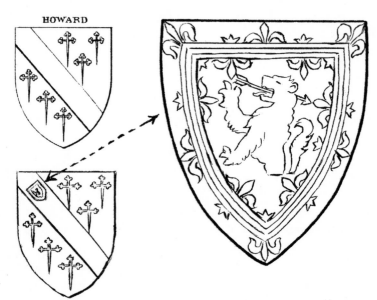

Arms of Howard, Duke of Norfolk (before and after augmentation)

to Sir John Pelham for his part in capturing King John of France at the battle of Poitiers in 1536. Sir William Pelham, in commemoration of this same event, was given an augmentation derived from a device appearing on the ornate sword belt of Richard II. This was azure, three pelicans argent, vulning themselves. It appeared in the second and third quartering of Pelham's arms.

Henry VIII granted several augmentations both for service in the field as well as for marks of grace or favor. For his victory at Flodden Field in 1513, Thomas Howard, Duke of Norfolk, received an escutcheon bearing the Royal Arms of Scotland. The augmentation dis-

plays a demi-lion pierced through the mouth by an arrow and in double tressure.

A month before the victory at Flodden, Sir John Clarke (Clerk) captured Louis, Duke of Longueville, at the battle of Therouenne (Battle of the Spurs). To his coat was added a sinister canton bearing devices taken from the arms of the captured duke. These appeared as azure, a demi-ram salient argent, armed or, in chief two fleurs-de-lis gold, and overall a baton dexter argent.

Henry VIII augmented the arms of Sir Thomas Manners, K.G.: Earl of Rutland as a mark of personal favor and in commemoration of a royal descent from Anne Plantagenet, a chief combining the arms of France and England with those of his descendents the Dukes of Rutland.

After the battle of Worcester, 1651, Charles II granted Colonel Newman an escutcheon gules, charged with a porticullis imperially crowned or, to be borne *en surtout* above the paternal coat in the first and fourth of his quartered arms. The porticullis signifies the gate that the colonel held until Charles made good his escape. Charles II also granted to "Mistress Jane Lane" a canton containing the arms of England for her part in this escape.

James I granted a lion of England to be borne in dexter chief to his favorite Robert Carr, Viscount Rochester. He also gave him an additional quartering to be borne in the first and fourth quarters.

The arms of Marlborough received two augmentations. The first was granted by Charles I to Sir Winston Churchill for services rendered. This took the form of a canton argent charged with a cross gules. Sir Winston's son John, Duke of Marlborough, was victorious at the Battle of Blenheim in 1704. For this victory he received an inescutcheon in chief bearing the cross of St. George super charged with another inescutcheon bearing the arms of France Modern.

For his victory at Waterloo, the Duke of Wellington received an inescutcheon in chief bearing the flag of the United Kingdom. Nelson, the famous victor at Trafalgar, received two augmentations for his naval successes. One was in a chief undy, a landscape displaying a palm tree, a disabled ship and a destroyed coastal battery. This commemorated his victory at the Battle of the Nile.

His second augmentation was a fess wavy azure charged with the word "Trafalgar" or. This last bearing, because it obliterated the horizontal limb of the cross flory in his original arms, was later removed from the coat by his descendant Earl Nelson.

13

Marshalling

The initial purpose of heraldry was to create personal cognizances and also to supply the rules that would govern their use. Such rules were fully formulated by the early part of the 13th century. In the latter part of the same century, a new heraldic practice came into being that broadened the original function of heraldry and thus created the need for additional rulings.

This new practice was called *marshalling*, the grouping together of two or more sets of arms into a single heraldic form. The purpose of these forms, in one instance, was to signify possession of two lordships by one individual. Another purpose was to depict the marital or feudal alliance of two people bearing hereditary arms. A third premise upon which arms were placed together on a single shield existed when a hereditary arms bearer displayed these arms next to the arms of some temporary office to which he was appointed.

Marshalling took on several forms in its development, some of which were discontinued with the passage of time. The first instance of what might be called marshalling was found in the early personal seals of the nobility. Here the various arms claimed by one person through inheritance and/or a marital alliance were displayed in ornate, symmetrical groupings within the circular area of the seal.

This method of grouping arms was adopted by several peeresses and princesses. Their seals displayed several individual lozenges or roundles each containing a separate heraldic bearing. These bearings usually displayed their personal arms, their husband's arms, and those of one or both of their parents. The arms of England would often be found among these devices.

The system of grouping several arms within one *seal* was later the basis for the grouping of such arms within one *shield*. This system, however, was preceded by another method of marshalling called "compounding arms."

This method combined the principal or dominant charges from two or more shields to form a new and separate coat of arms. Like the grouping of arms on a seal, it was a way of symbolizing personal, marital, and

Elizabeth D'Amori

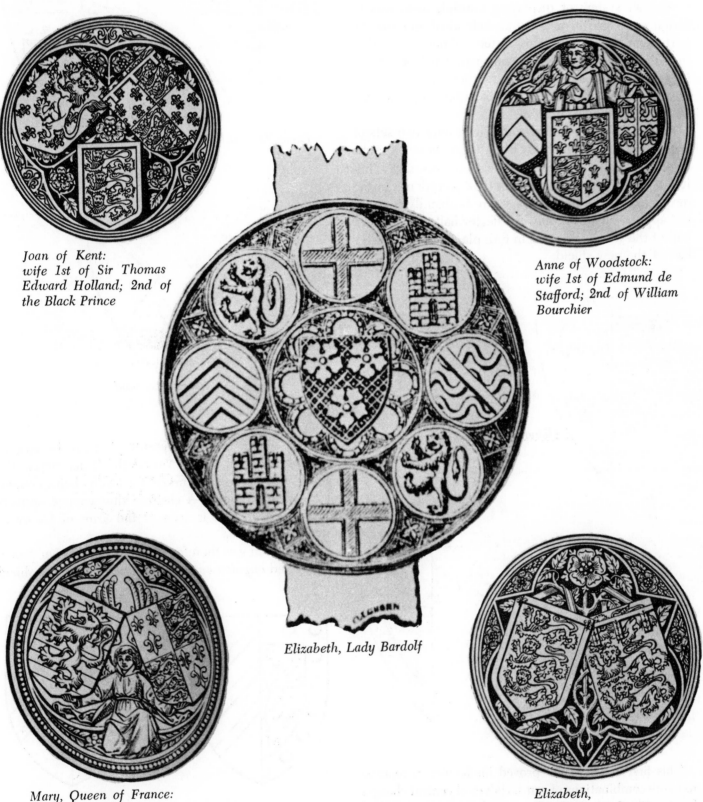

Joan of Kent:
wife 1st of Sir Thomas
Edward Holland; 2nd of
the Black Prince

Anne of Woodstock:
wife 1st of Edmund de
Stafford; 2nd of William
Bourchier

Elizabeth, Lady Bardolf

Mary, Queen of France:
daughter of Henry VII;
wife of Charles Brandon,
Duke of Suffolk

Marshalling of arms (grouping of separate shields)

Elizabeth,
daughter of John Gaunt;
wife of John Holland,
Duke of Exeter

parental arms, but it also expressed feudal alliances as well.

Another system of displaying multiple arms was to assign each coat of arms to an individual and specific portion of the shield. This system, alluded to earlier in the text, was akin to the manner in which seal bearings were displayed. Three different arrangements were employed with this form of marshalling: dimidiation, impalement, and quartering.

Dimidiation involved shields where only two sets of arms were displayed. Most often these were the arms of a marital alliance, but they were not necessarily limited to this. The husband's arms took precedence in the dexter half of the shield. The entire husbandly coat did not appear, however, only the dexter half. The sinister half of the wife's arms was in turn placed in the sinister half of the new shield.

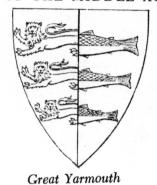

Great Yarmouth

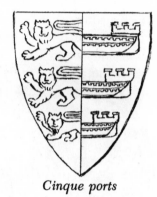

Cinque ports

Clare-Fitzgerald

Alianore Ferre

manner, creating strange hybrids. This can be seen in the civic arms of Great Yarmouth. Other times, the identity of a distinctive charge was lost by being couped at the halfway point. A chevron thus couped appears to be a bend. This is seen in the arms of Cornwall dimidiating Clare.

Dimidiation was therefore replaced by another procedure called *impalement*. In this arrangement, the shield

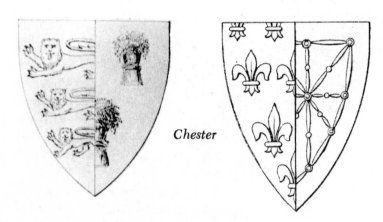

Chester

This first arrangement proved ineffective in relation to many combinations of arms. Halves of central charges from each arm often came together in an awkward

was again partitioned palewise, but now the entire coat of arms was displayed in each half. This new procedure was somewhat linked to its predecessor in that arms containing bordures or tressures would still have to display them in their *halved* condition.

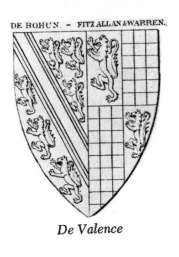

De Valence

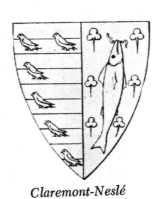

Claremont-Neslé

Examples of impaled arms

The matter of showing complete bordures or tressures was dealt with when *quartering* came into being. Here complete arms were displayed in each of four quarters formed by the fesswise and palewise partitions. When two coats of arms are involved in the quartered shield, the more important one is placed in the first quarter (upper left) and the fourth quarter (lower right).

Arms of Eleanor, wife of Edward I

In quartering, it is possible to display more than two sets of arms. When three coats of arms are to be displayed, the most important one again occupies the first and fourth quarters while the other two coats are placed

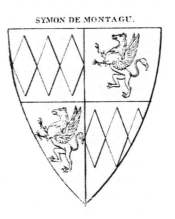

in the second and third quarters according to their remaining order of importance. When the importance of these coats are equal, the one that was acquired first is given priority in quartering.

A shield may be divided into smaller pieces (also

called "quarters") when more than four coats of arms are to be displayed. Such a shield may be divided quarterly of six, eight, or more. An individual quarter may be quartered again, thus becoming a *grand quarter*. A shield so subdivided is termed *quarterly quartered*.

The latter half of the 14th century saw impalement and quartering receive increasing usage. The system of impalement posed no particular problem in its genealogical interpretation, but quartering gave rise to unforeseen complexities. As a result, this latter system of marshalling today remains the most difficult phase of heraldry to fully grasp.

Aside from the involved rules that were developed to govern it, quartering was beset by a period of ostentation. When it was realized that a family as a result of quartering could display several coats of arms within one shield, many armigerous houses began a frantic search into their family histories. If a junior branch or past marital alliance produced other arms, these arms would be crowded into the original family shield. Of necessity, the shield might now be quarterly of eight, nine, or more divisions.

Heraldry, to such families, had become merely a status symbol. It was certainly no longer a reflection of the simple and distinctive symbolism upon which it was founded. It had instead fallen accessory to a prestige contest where the prominence of a family was judged solely by the number of quarterings in their arms. Later, some families reevaluated the confused state of their arms and returned them to their original form. A group of many-coated arms have nonetheless survived to evidence the bad taste of this period.

Frequently, marshalled arms had a legitimate reason for being so disposed. The basis for their existence was described early in the chapter. Accordingly, rules were provided for them which dictated the manner and conditions under which they might be displayed.

Marshalled arms are presently dealt with in two separate categories:

a. Temporary and non-hereditary combinations in effect only during the lifetime of the bearer.
b. Permanent and hereditary combinations.

In the first category, we have two types of arms that fit this description. The first type is one created by a union of the arms of husband and wife where the wife's arms are not hereditary. This occurs when her titled or armigerous father has sons who will inherit the arms that she temporarily displays in the sinister half of her husband's shield. Consequently, she possesses no right of transmission of these arms to her children. Upon the death of their parents, the children will inherit only their father's arms.

In the above situation, if the wife dies in advance of her husband, he will henceforth cease to impale her arms. He may however impale her arms in the funeral hatchment or memorial. Should he re-marry, and his second wife die, he would again impale her arms in a hatchment, but in this case, the arms of both deceased wives would share the sinister half of the shield. The sinister half would be parted either palewise or fesswise with the first wife represented in dexter portion or chief portion respectively.

A permanent and hereditary combination of arms exists when an arms-bearing man marries an heiress or coheiress and becomes a parent. In this case, the child or children of such a marriage inherit the arms of both parents. It is appropriate to emphasize at this point that the terms *heir* and *heiress* are applied in the heraldic sense of inheriting arms. For a woman to become an heiress, her father must have died, leaving no other sons or daughters with children of their own. The existence of another sister, however, would make her a co-heiress.

In order to perpetuate her paternal family arms, an heiress is permitted to carry these arms to her husband. The impaled arms thus formed would eventually be transmitted to her children. Children of a marriage where, as in the earlier case, the wife is not actually an heiress, may yet inherit her paternal arms if the last male member of the mother's family dies after her, without he or any other of the previous males leaving children.

Returning to temporary impalements of a different type, another instance where they occur is in official arms. Heads of colleges, town mayors or their equivalent, and churchmen (archbishops and bishops) may temporarily display the official symbols of their office impaled with their own hereditary devices. The temporary arms are placed on the *dexter* side of the shield. Note that this is in contrast to the previously mentioned temporary arms of the non-heiress that were placed in *sinister* impalement. The impalement ceases when the post is vacated by death or by conclusion of tenure of office.

To best illustrate how quartering is marshalled, an authentic genealogy table is now presented in two forms. The first table shows the actual arms of John Lord Hastings, father of the Earl of Pembroke, and his ancestors. This first-mentioned noble died in 1325. His ancestors are believed to be the first family of nobility to quarter arms.

The second table is a diagramatic treatment of the same genealogy table to simplify the explanation of the various marshallings. Letters in the alphabet are substituted for the family branches and their arms. The code letters are printed on each side of the final marshalling.

Using this code as a guide the following pattern occurs:

Hugh de Kevilioc, Earl of Chester circa 1150, bears arms that are here coded X. His daughter Maude, a coheiress, marries David, Earl of Huntingdon (A). Her

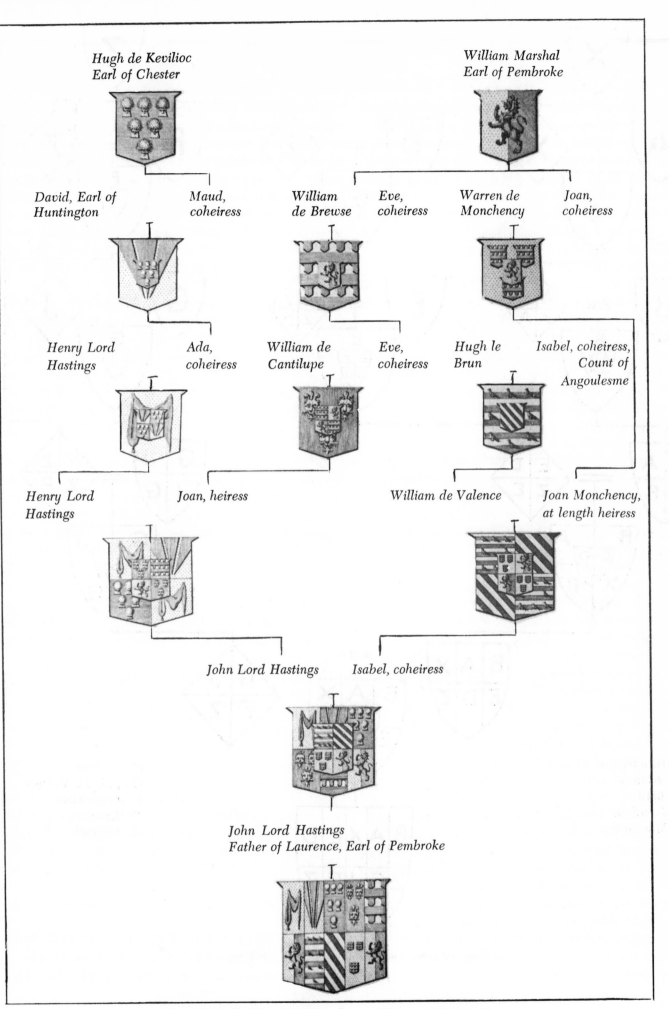

Hugh de Kevilioc
Earl of Chester

William Marshal
Earl of Pembroke

David, Earl of
Huntington

Maud,
coheiress

William
de Brewse

Eve,
coheiress

Warren de
Monchency

Joan,
coheiress

Henry Lord
Hastings

Ada,
coheiress

William de
Cantilupe

Eve,
coheiress

Hugh le
Brun

Isabel, coheiress,
Count of
Angoulesme

Henry Lord
Hastings

Joan, heiress

William de Valence

Joan Monchency,
at length heiress

John Lord Hastings

Isabel, coheiress

John Lord Hastings
Father of Laurence, Earl of Pembroke

Geneological table of quartered arms (House of Hastings)

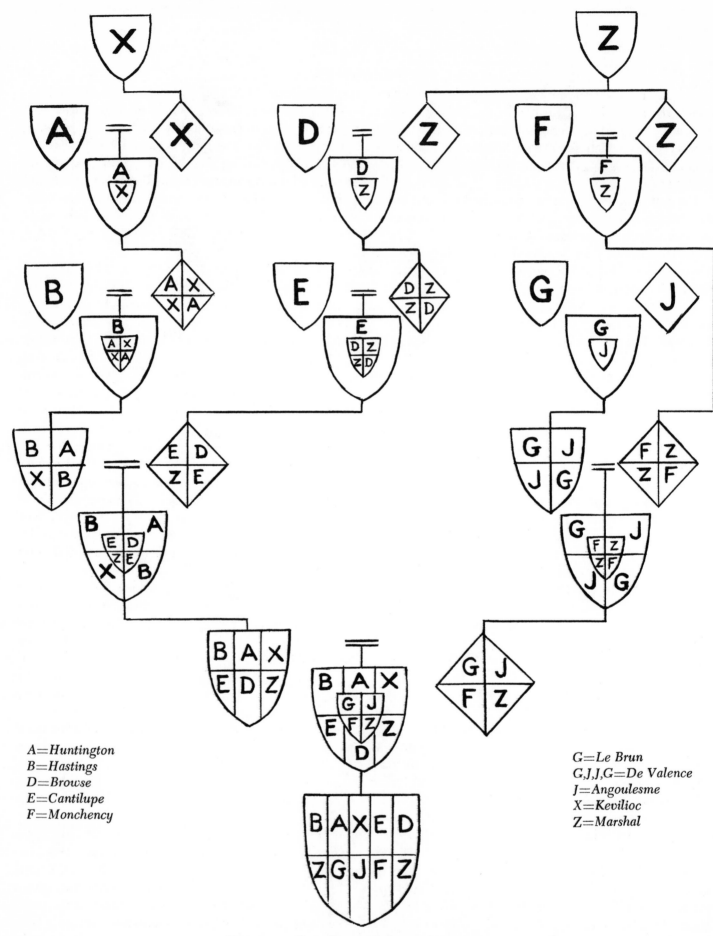

A=Huntington
B=Hastings
D=Browse
E=Cantilupe
F=Monchency

G=Le Brun
G,J,J,G=De Valence
J=Angoulesme
X=Kevilioc
Z=Marshal

Diagram and analysis of Hastings geneology

arms (X) are carried on an escutcheon of pretense within the shield of her husband (A). Their daughter Ada, also a coheiress, is entitled thereby to quarter her parents' arms, which she carries into an escutcheon of pretense (A,X,X,A) when she marries Henry, Lord Hastings (B).

The first male child appears with the birth of Henry, the third Lord Hastings (B,A,X,B), who also removes the escutcheon of pretense upon inheriting the family arms. He marries Joan de Cantilupe, daughter of Lord Abergavenny (E,D,Z,E), whose arms are also quartered. The origin of her arms will be dealt with shortly.

The Cantilupe arms (E,D,Z,E) are carried in an escutcheon within her husband's shield (B,A,X,B). Their son, John, the third Lord Hastings (B,A,X,E,D,Z), now bears his family arms quarterly of six upon inheriting them. He marries Isabel de Valence, coheiress daughter of the Earl of Pembroke who bears his arms (G,J,F,Z) in an escutcheon of pretense within her husband's shield. Their son John, Lord Hastings, becomes entitled to bear the combined arms in a shield quarterly of ten (B,A,X,E,D,Z,G,J,F,Z).

Returning to the arms of Joan de Cantilupe (E,D,Z,E), we next trace her right to these arms. Her grandfather William de Brewse (D) married Eve Marshall, coheiress daughter of William Marshall, Earl of Pembroke (Z). Her arms were carried in an escutcheon of pretense (Z) within her husband's shield (D).

Their daughter, a coheiress also named Eve, marries William de Cantilupe, Lord Abergavenny (E). His daughter, Joan, bears the Cantilupe arms in the quartering (E,D,Z,E) encountered earlier when her marriage to Henry, the second Lord Hastings is mentioned.

Farther down the ancestral chain we see the marriage of John, the third Lord Hastings to Isabel de Valence, coheiress and daughter of William de Valence of Pembroke. Her arms began with her great-grandfather William Marshall, the same Earl of Pembroke (Z) whose daughter Eve married William de Brewse. The earl had a second daughter and coheiress, Joan, who married William de Monchency (F). The Pembroke arms thus became carried in an escutcheon of pretense (Z) within her husband's arms (F).

Their daughter Joan Monchency married William de Valence (G,J,J,G). His arms were derived from his father, Hugh Le Brun, the Earl of March (G), and his mother, Isabel, coheiress of Aymer, Count of Angoulesme. Joan Monchency carries her arms in an escutch-

eon of pretense (F,Z,Z,F) within his arms (G,J,J,G).

Upon the death of her father, no heirs other than herself survived to carry his title. It therefore passed to her husband. Her own father gained the title in the same manner, having had it passed to him by her mother, who was the first Earl of Pembroke's daughter. Isabel, the daughter of the new Earl, and Joan Monchency carried their joint arms (G,J,F,Z) into an escutcheon with John, the third Lord Hastings (B,A,X, E,D,Z).

Though the diagram does not show the subsequent development, John, the fourth Lord Hastings, also became Earl of Pembroke through the right of his wife.

The tables just illustrated and described do not cover, of course, all the situations encountered in marshalling. Some quartered coats of arms may not be broken up and requartered after inheritance for either of two reasons: they have existed for so long a time as to acquire a status as a single and indivisible coat, or they were quartered originally by Royal License, where as condition of inheritance they must remain unseparated.

An official who impales the arms of his temporary office next to his own personal arms may not marshall his wife's arms in the same coat. It is permissible to create a second shield placed next to his own. One shield will bear the arms of his office impaled with his own; the other, the arms of his wife impaled with his own.

Knights of the Garter and members of like orders who display the insignia of their order with their arms are also prohibited from marshalling the arms of their wives within the same shield. Again, as with the case of the office holder, a second shield may be employed for the impalement of the marital arms. To balance the insignia-encircled arms of the husband, the wife may adopt a conventional wreath to encircle her arms.

A man who possesses no personal coat of arms upon marriage to an heiress can not display her arms nor can his children of the marriage do so. It is, however, permissible to petition for a grant of arms for himself in order to preserve and transmit his wife's arms to their children.

If an arms-bearing man marries an heiress and has a daughter by the marriage, and then marries a non-heiress who bears him a son, the daughter inherits the arms of both parents while the son only inherits the father's arms. The daughter, however, cannot transmit the quartered arms as such to her husband. She may only bear

Sir Sidney Smith K.

Arms of Knight Bachelor. Note display of decoration below shield

The Marquis of Wellington.

Arms of Knight of the Garter (order's motto encircles shield)

Sir Thos. Graham.

Arms of Knight of the Bath (order's motto encircles shield)

an escutcheon of pretense of her mother's arms charged with a canton of her father's arms.

Unmarried women officials who bear personal arms may impale the arms of office with their own, as do the men. Women's arms are borne on lozenges, a shield form going back to the 15th century. Because of the space limitations placed on charges through the acute angles of this diamond shape, the substitution of an oval is permitted.

Married men may use their own arms separately for business purposes but married women may not. For business reasons, women may unofficially use a shield marshalling their marital arms. The lozenge is not used for marital arms in this case, as it implies widowhood.

A peeress in her own right bears no supporters or crest with her lozenge. If she should marry a peer, his supporters and crest are incorporated with her arms into a single achievement.

A peeress marrying a commoner ensigns his arms with her coronet in pretense. She, however, bears her arms separately in a complete achievement next to her husband. Since the man's arms are normally to the dexter in marital arms, this practice again prevails.

The lozenge, although presently associated with the arms of woman, was at one time used to display the shield and arms of a deceased person of either sex. These lozenge panels of wood or canvas were called funeral hatchments and were seen during the period of mourning. If the person had been married the arms of

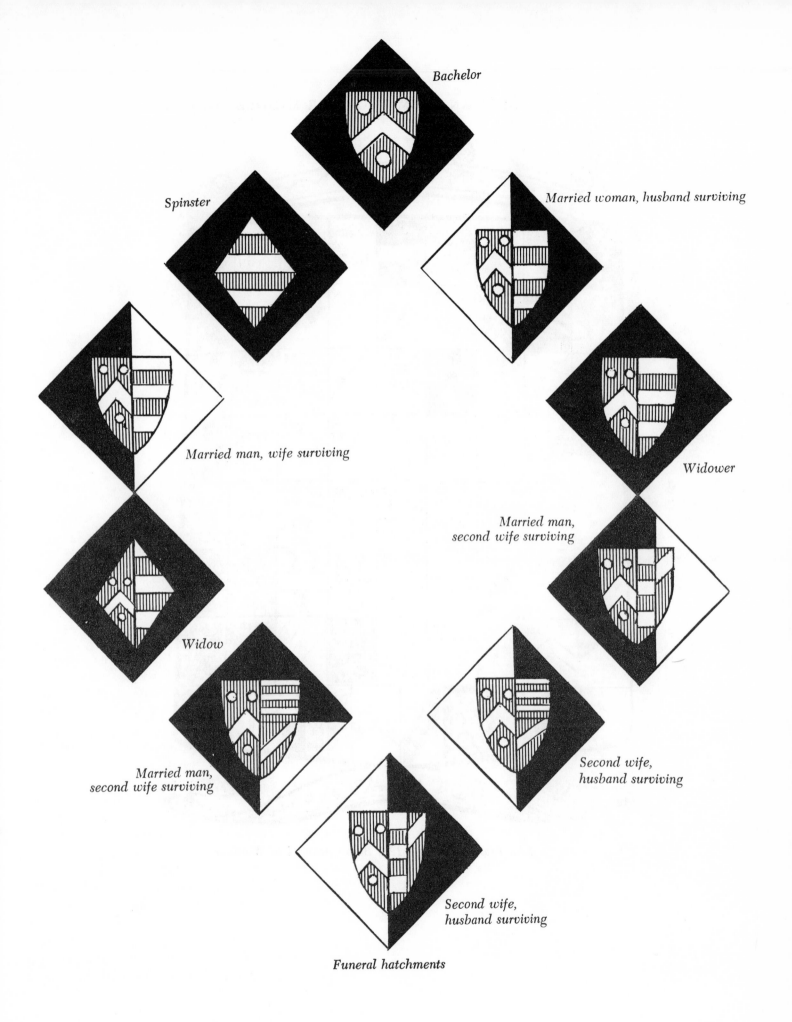

Bachelor

Spinster

Married woman, husband surviving

Married man, wife surviving

Widower

Married man,
second wife surviving

Widow

Married man,
second wife surviving

Second wife,
husband surviving

Second wife,
husband surviving

Funeral hatchments

John Francis Arundel, 12th Baron Arundel of Wardour

his or her spouse were impaled in the same lozenge.

To distinguish between the arms of the dead and the surviving, their lozenge halves were respectively painted black and white. As with regular impalements, the husband's arms were placed in the dexter half of the lozenge. It was customary to replace the motto with a Latin phrase expressing an appropriate sentiment such as "Rest in Peace." By using a shield within the lozenge when a married man died to impale his marital arms, and a lozenge within the lozenge to impale a deceased wife's marital arms, it was readily apparent which mate was being mourned.

Hatchments existed to denote, in addition to the usual marital arms, conditions of bachelorhood, spinsterhood, and second marriages. In the case of single persons, the lozenge field would, of course, be all black. Where a man had a second wife, she could share her portion of the impalement with the first wife. This impalement half would be again divided palewise or fesswise (depending on the character of the arms) to accommodate both coats.

The crest of a wife was omitted from funeral hatchments and occasionally a cherub was shown where a man's crest might have been placed. If a family line ended with the death of the arms bearer, a "death's head" would sometimes substitute for the crest.

14

The Crest

At its beginning, heraldry was primarily involved with the shield and the various symbols that it displayed. In time, the shield was supplemented by other components of arms that were called *accessories*. The crest was one such accessory, its name being derived from the Latin word *crista*, meaning *cock's comb*.

The crest was a decorative device affixed to the top of the battle or tournament helmet. Both the helmet and the crest eventually became a regular part of the achievement or total display of arms. The crest was derived from a simpler helmet fixture that at first had some defensive value.

The first crests, or their equivalents, were metal plates set upon their edges into the top of the helmet. In such a position they were effective in absorbing the impact of a sword's sweeping blow. These fan-like protrusions were relatively plain at first, but with the increasing pageantry of the tournament, crests became almost purely ornamentation.

Although it was no longer functional defensively, the crest in its new decorative role served still another purpose. The animal charges that it adopted were often personal badge or shield symbols that further helped to identify the joust contestant. Where the original crest was of metal, the tournament crest was mostly wood or boiled leather. They were no longer flat, as were the plates that proceeded them. Instead, they were modeled figures of infinite variety.

An attempt was often made to duplicate in a crest a charge found in the shield. As a result, the same animal, bird, and monster figures that were predominant as shield charges were also predominant as crest devices. Some substitutions for the shield charge had to be made in cases where its design was impractical as a crest. When the crest became a shield accessory, it was usually apparent to the viewer which arms were adaptable by comparing the shield with its new component.

The term *crest* is generally regarded today as the entire portion above the shield. As evidenced from the preceding text, it is technically only a segment of the several devices that may be found there. To start with, there is first the helmet.

Because of constant changes in armor defenses, the helmet took on successively different forms in achievements. The pot-helm and bascinet were the early helmets upon which crests were affixed, and were later replaced by the armet. Head defenses such as these are described and illustrated in Chapter 29. The jousting helmet is frequently seen since it is closely associated with the crest itself. Both it and the crest are generally regarded as developments of the tournament. In heraldry it is considered in good taste to display a helmet contemporary with the time of the original arms grant. Helmets are not usually shown where a crest was not created. This would be most likely where an arms-bearer was not a tournament participant.

*Sir Geoffrey Luttrell, from the 14-century Luttrell Psalter
British Museum. Note helm crest, pavon (or pennon), and
ailettes*

In the reign of James I (1603–1625), a series of helmets were adopted to denote the rank of the arms bearer.

Sovereign (and Royal Princes)	A gold armet, affronté with six vertical bars or more across the visor.
Peers	A silver armet of the same type, sideways, with five gold bars showing.
Knights and Baronets	A steel armet affronté etched with silver, visor up.
Esquires and Gentlemen	A steel armet, sideways, visor down.

The helmets with the open visors displayed a red or blue interior representing the silk padding of these closely fitting armets.

The use of these helmets brought about a problem in properly presenting the crest above them. Since the crest was normally shown in profile, the adoption of two helmets affronté created an unnatural situation when the crest continued to be shown sideways on the sovereign's and knight's helmets. The reverse problem arose when helmets displayed sideways continued

Helmets and crests

England

Prince Edward

Prince Arthur

Scotland

Ireland

Ireland

The Heir Apparent

Tudors

Tower of London guard with badge of United Kingdom

Stafford

Bourchier

Wake

Anne of Bohemia

Bowen

Heneage

Lacy

Hastings and Hungerford

Wheathamstede

Dacre

Harrington

Badges and Knots

Heir Apparent

Sovereign's sons

Sovereign and grandchildren

Duke

Marquess

Earl

Viscount

Baron

Sovereign

Knight

Noble

Esquire

Crowns, Coronets and Helms

to show human heads generally placed affronté. The affronté-placed helmets were the greater evil since most crests were presented in profile.

The early crest was joined to the helmet in a crude bolting or lacing. Various ideas were tried to conceal the awkward bond, for example a ribbon or a scarf (termed a "contoise"), which often was a gift of favor from a lady.

At first the scarf was fastened so as to leave the two

Helm of Thomas, Earl of Lancaster

ends flowing to the wind. This may have proved hazardous to the vision of the jouster since it was then fashioned into a turban-like crest-wreath called a *torse* (a contraction of *contoise*). This form of ornamentation lastly gave rise to a similar circlet called the crest-coronet. There are achievements in existence where both the torse and the crest-coronet above it are borne together, although this was not intended as a general practice.

The torse, when seen in arms, appears at the bottom of the crest, running in a horizontal line. It displays six twists in two tinctures, the tinctures alternating

with each turn or twist of the scarf. The torse follows the tincture plan of the shield, using the parted field colors or the single field color and that of the principal charge. If fur is used as a principal tincture, the dominant color of the fur is used. This could be blue for vair, white for ermine, or sable for erminois. In any event, the rule states that the first twist of the torse has to be of the metal tincture and then alternated with the color until the full six turns are accounted for.

The crest-wreath or torse is related to the orle. The orle originally served as a circular ring of cloth padding between the bascinet and the great helm when it was over it. It helped to keep the outer helmet steady and reduce the vibrations from a blow. When the helm was discarded, the orle remained as a decorative concealment for the crest joint. The orle, in some cases, was arrayed with fine weaving and bedecked with jewels.

The heat from a helmet long exposed to the sun

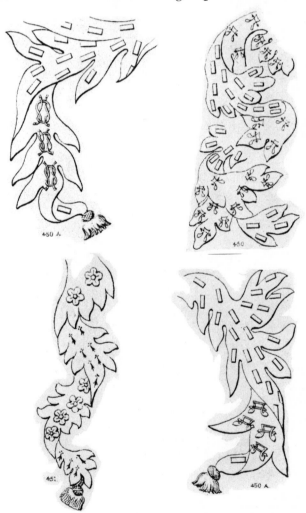

Examples of mantling

would have been almost unbearable for the wearer were it not for the mantling that covered a part of it. This mantling, or lambrequin, was usually a cloth material that was attached to the crown and extended down the back and sides of the helmet. It had a scalloped or fluted edging common to the attire of that time. These edges were later misconceived by heraldic writers to have originated from sword thrusts received in battle. Their colorful interpretation remains the basis

for the appearance that is evident in present-day arms mantlings.

The modern-day mantling, as an accessory to the crest, is double-tinctured, the lining being of a metal tincture. Generally, this tincture and the color on the outer surface repeat the principal tinctures of the arms. In rare instances, early mantling was formed from a continuation of the crest coloring or texture. In some cases, that texture happened to be a fur. In modern heraldic practice, only the sovereign and his male heir enjoy the privilege of an ermine lining in the mantling.

Two crests are sometimes found with one shield. This situation arises when an arms bearer possesses two titles and, hence, two coats of arms. He may, if he chooses, display a crest for each. These helmets can both face the dexter or else face each other. If they do face each other, the crest in the dexter helmet must be reversed to face the sinister. Multiple crests are common in German arms.

The reign of Richard I witnessed the first appearance of a crest worn by a sovereign. This was shown in the fan-like plating upon the helm of his equestrian figure in his Great Seal. Edward III, however, created the first crest above the Royal Arms, which remained in effect until the reign of Henry VIII. It was on a chapeau gules turned up ermine, a lion statant crowned or. Among the Plantagenets, Edward V and Richard III alone encircled the chapeau with a coronet. Edward III also bore an eagle as a second crest.

The House of Tudor retained the Royal Crest of the Plantagenets, but like Edward V and Richard III, the Tudors added the coronet encircling the chapeau. The helmet mantling of this and the previous Royal House was gules and ermine until Elizabeth I changed it to gold and ermine. The Stuarts changed the Royal Crest to be on the Royal Crown proper, a lion statant guardant or, regally crowned proper. Again the mantling was gold and ermine.

The Commonwealth retained the Royal Crest, although the arms themselves were changed. The House of Hanover continued the Royal Crest of the Stuarts as did the House of Saxe-Coburg and the House of Windsor.

Among the devices used to decorate the helmet, the lion is by far the most widely used. The Dukes of Norfolk, Grafton, St. Albans, Northumberland, and Richard all display this beast upon their helms. The Earls of Shrewsbury, Carlisle, Talbot, and Beverly are

629.

Garter Plate of Humphrey de Bohun K.G.
last Earl of Hereford, Essex & Northampton, died A.D. 1361
Date of the Garter Plate, about 1440.

Garter plate of Humphrey de Bohun

some who bear this same charge. The Viscount Faucon-berg and Barons Suffield, Southampton, and Foley complete a representation of peers who also use lion figures.

The boar's head of Lord Basset of Drayton issuing out of a crest-coronet was a familiar sight at the tournament. The swan's head also issuing out of a crest-coronet of Humphrey, Earl of Stafford, and Beauchamp,

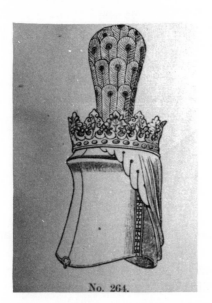

No. 264.

Earl of Warwick, were other crests seen at this event. The bull's head of Neville, Earl of Westmoreland, and the griffin's head issuing out of a crest-coronet of Richard, Earl of Arundel, were examples of other beasts that found favor as crests. Montagu, Earl of Salisbury, chose to include the wings in his griffin crest issuing from the crown-coronet.

The eagle, another popular device, was found in the crest of the Earls of Radnor and Denbigh, Viscount Bolingbroke, and Baron Gambier. A panache of blue feathers issuing out of a crest-coronet distinguished the Mortimers, Earls of March. Hugh de Courtenay, Earl of Devon, used white feathers in the panache, while Sir Edward de Thorpe's panache was made of peacock feathers.

Vere, Earl of Oxford, had a gold panache that matched the crest-coronet. William de Clinton, Earl of Huntingdon used a gold Saracen's head, Sir Robert Agilon a gold griffin's head, and Sir Thomas Grandison a gold phoenix.

While the boar was more usual as a crest, Sir Ralph Spigurnel, in allusion to his name, chose a pig's head for a crest. The dragon, the badge of Wales, was an obvious choice among Welsh knights and nobles.

15

Supporters

The arms of hereditary peers are distinguished by figures standing on each side of the shield that appear to uphold or support it. Living and imaginary animals constitute the greater percentage of the figures chosen as supporters but large numbers of human and angelic figures are not uncommon. Early arms generally displayed a matching pair of figures, such as two lions or two stags, but in the last two centuries, unlike figures occurred more frequently.

These devices first appeared as shield accessories at the end of the 14th century or more likely at the beginning of the 15th, as nearly as can be determined. The basis for their introduction is uncertain, but specific motivations or influences may have been involved. These are:

1. The desire to include badge symbols in the arms, which would not otherwise appear, according to the Laws of Arms.
2. A continuation of the already familiar animal figures found in personal seals, which filled the large and otherwise void space between the shield facsimile and the circular border.

Since it is known that seals and badges were in existence prior to heraldic arms, these two points have considerable merit. Firsthand knowledge of individual badges and seals might easily confirm or deny the likelihood of these motivations in certain individual cases.

A much less likely story exists that these figures were representations of the attendants of tournament contestants. It is said that these attendants who dressed in various animal skins guarded the shields, pennons, and lances of their master while these arms were displayed prior to each tournament. It would be more logical that their attire, if these stories be true, was merely an imitation of those figures already in the master's seal or badge.

Some of the seals of the peers show the animal figures supporting the *helm* rather than the shield below it, which is placed bendwise. Examples of such seals are those of John, Earl of Arundel, Edmund, Earl of March, and William de Wyndsore. The Earl of Arundel's seal shows two lions, as does that of the Earl of March, while the seal of Wyndsore displays two eagles. The bendwise shield in each case supports the supporters rather than the other way around. In any event, it was a step toward the ultimate use of these figures as they are presently found in arms.

In some cases seals displayed arms that were held by the shield strap (guige) in the beak of an eagle or rested against the breast of this bird. Thomas Holland, Earl of Kent, displays his arms supported by the neck or shoulder of a lodged stag. These figures also were the forebears of the present supporters.

Among the figures chosen for supporters, the lion is by far the most predominant one. Eagles appear to be second in popularity, while greyhounds, griffins, horses,

Elephant   Boar   Parrot   Tiger

Ram   Dragon   Fox   Stork

Monkey   Swan   Ostrich   Antelope

Supporters

Lion   Horse   Eagle   Leopard

Greyhound   Bull   Unicorn   Stag

Pegasus   Griffin   Talbot   Wyvern

Supporters

deer, unicorns, and talbots rank equally after these. The lion appears several times in paired supporters but a single one may appear in consort with a horse, unicorn, antelope, dragon, panther, leopard, bull, stag, and winged sea horse.

Scottish supporters once called *bearers* were developed in the same way about the same time as the English devices but were mostly found singularly. Savages or wild men are a predominant supporter in the Scottish arms. The Irish supporters generally follow the same pattern of choice as the English devices.

Animal figures that support French arms are called *supports* and human figures are called *tenants*. This latter term is the basis for the tournament term *tenants* or *tenans;* those contestants who upheld the honor of their arms by their participation.

The right to display supporters is as mentioned earlier a granted privilege of hereditary peers of the realm. This grant is transferable to their descendants. Where Knights of the Garter, Thistle, and St. Patrick are already members of the peerage, they too may display supporters along with their knightly insignia. Other few orders of knighthood may be granted supporters during the extent of their lifetime but these may not be transmitted to their descendants. Civic councils and certain corporations of service to the Crown may also be granted supporters.

The scroll, normally seen below the shield, was devised to provide a platform on which the supporters could be affixed. The Scottish heralds refer to this as a *compartment*. It also bears the not so elegant term of *gas bracket*. A mound or suggestion of turf is infrequently found as a substitute for the scroll.

Supporters do not definitely appear in Royal Arms until the middle of the Plantagenet Dynasty, Henry VI being the first positive bearer. Since it has been found that known badge devices (in this case animals) have often been the same figures found in the crest, there is some evidence for the attributed supporters listed below with the known supporters. The dexter supporter in each case is mentioned first:

Edward III (attributed) — a lion and falcon.
Richard II (attributed) — two white harts.
Henry IV (attributed) — a lion and an antelope; antelope and swan.
Henry V (attributed) — a lion and an antelope.
Henry IV — two antelopes argent, lion and panther, lion and antelope, lion and tiger (heraldic).
Edward IV — a lion or and bull sable; a lion argent and hart argent, two lions argent.

Edward V — a lion argent and a hart argent, gorged and chained or.
Richard III — a lion or and boar argent; two boars argent.

The dragon made its appearance as a Royal Supporter during the reign of the Tudors. Edward VI was the only one of the Tudors who did not have a second set of supporters. This monster figure was found in the Royal Arms of all the sovereigns of this house.

Henry VII — a dragon gules and a greyhound argent; two greyhounds argent; a lion or and a dragon gules.
Henry VIII — a lion or and a dragon gules; a dragon gules and a bull sable, or greyhound argent, or cock argent.
Edward VI — a lion or and a dragon gules.
Mary I — a lion or and a dragon gules; a lion or and a greyhound argent. Mary's arms when impaled with Philip of Spain featured as supporters, an eagle and lion.
Elizabeth I — a lion or and a dragon or; a lion or and a greyhound argent.

The House of Stuart displayed the supporters presently found in Royal Arms: a lion rampant guardant or, regally crowned proper for England, and a unicorn argent, armed, unguled and crined or, gorged with a coronet composed of crosses paty and fleur-de-lis and reflexed over the back.

In Scotland, the position of the supporters were reversed with the unicorn instead of the lion regally crowned and gorged. The dexter placed unicorn was found in this instance supporting between its forelegs the banner of St. Andrew, while the sinister lion supports similarly the banner of St. George.

SUPPORTERS

Dukes

Duke of Norfolk	— Lion and Horse
Duke of Somerset	— Unicorn and Bull
Duke of Grafton	— Lion and Greyhound
Duke of Beaufort	— Panther and Wyvern
Duke of St. Albans	— Antelope and Greyhound
Duke of Leeds	— Griffin and Wer Wolf
Duke of Bedford	— Lion and Heraldic Antelope
Duke of Marlborough	— Griffin and Wyvern
Duke of Northumberland	— 2 Lions
Duke of Devonshire	— 2 Antelopes
Duke of Portland	— 2 Lions
Duke of Newcastle	— 2 Greyhounds
Duke of Dorset	— 2 Panthers
Duke of Rutland	— 2 Unicorns
Duke of Manchester	— Heraldic Antelope and Griffin
Duke of Buckingham	— Lion and Horse
Duke of Bath	— Reindeer and Lion
Duke of Bute	— Horse and Stag
Duke of Cornwalles	— 2 Deer

Vultures

Cockatrice

Wildcat

Owl

Neptune

Sea horse

Savage

Mermaid

Bear

Wolf

Moor

Sea lion

Supporters

Marquesses

Marquess of Lansdowne	— 2 Pegasus
Marquess of Hertford	— 2 Moors
Marquess of Stafford	— 2 Wolves
Marquess of Exeter	— 2 Lions

Earls

Earl of Shrewsbury	— 2 Talbots
Earl of Peterborough	— 2 Eagles
Earl of Suffolk	— 2 Lions
Earl of Macclesfield	— 2 Leopards
Earl of Derby	— Griffin and Stag
Earl of Chesterfield	— Wolf and Talbot
Earl of Westmoreland	— Griffin and Bull
Earl of Pembroke	— Panther and Lion
Earl of Cardigan	— Stag and Horse
Earl of Shaftesbury	— Bull and Talbot
Earl of Abingdon	— Old Man and Savage
Earl of Carlisle	— Lion and Bull
Earl Ferrers	— Talbot and Reindeer
Earl of Aylesford	— Griffin and Lion
Earl of Cholmondeley	— Griffin and Wolf
Earl of Stanhope	— Talbot and Wolf
Earl of Harrington	— Talbot and Wolf
Earl Delawarr	— Wolf and Cockatrice
Earl of Spencer	— Griffin and Wyvern
Earl of Hardwicke	— Lion and Stag
Earl of Darlington	— Griffin and Antelope
Earl of Carnavon	— Panther and Lion
Earl of Beverley	— Lion and Unicorn
Earl of Mount	— 2 Greyhounds
Earl of Grosvenor	— 2 Talbots
Earl of Abergavenny	— 2 Bulls
Earl of Scarborough	— 2 Parrots
Earl of Rochford	— 2 Lions
Earl of Berkeley	— 2 Lions
Earl of Essex	— 2 Lions
Earl of Albemarle	— 2 Lions
Earl of Oxford	— 2 Angels
Earl of Bristol	— 2 Panthers
Earl Cowper	— 2 Horses
Earl of Jersey	— 2 Lions
Earl of Coventry	— 2 Eagles
Earl of Harborough	— 2 Rams
Earl Fitzwilliam	— 2 Savages
Earl of Ashburham	— 2 Greyhounds
Earl of Waldegrave	— 2 Talbots
Earl of Warwick	— 2 Swans
Earl of Brooke	— 2 Swans
Earl Harcourt	— 2 Lions
Earl of Guilford	— 2 Dragons
Earl of Radnor	— 2 Eagles
Earl of Ailesbury	— 2 Savages
Earl of Mansfield	— 2 Lions
Earl Fortescue	— 2 Greyhounds
Earl Talbot	— 2 Talbots
Earl Digby	— 2 Monkeys
Earl of Onslow	— 2 Hawks or Falcons
Earl of Romney	— 2 Lions
Earl of Effingham	— 2 Lions
Earl of Pomfret	— 2 Lions
Earl Camden	— Griffin and Lion
Earl Cadogan	— Lion and Dragon
Earl of Powis	— Elephant and Griffin
Earl Nelson	— Sailor and Lion
Earl of Chichester	— Horse and Bear

Earl of Malmesbury	— Eagle and Reindeer

Viscounts

Viscount Hereford	— Talbot and Reindeer
Viscount Grey	— Lion and Panther
Viscount Torrington	— Heraldic Antelope and Heraldic Sea Horse
Viscount Hood	— Merman and Mermaid
Viscount Fauconberg	— Stag and Unicorn
Viscount Duncan	— Angel and Sailor
Viscount Falmouth	— 2 Heraldic Sea Lions
Viscount Courtney	— 2 Boars
Viscount Hampden	— 2 Dragons
Viscount Saeville	— 2 Panthers
Viscount Lonsdale	— 2 Horses
Viscount Harrowby	— 2 Griffin
Viscount Bolingbroke	— 2 Eagles
Viscount Manvers	— 2 Lions

Barons

Baron DeClifford	— Wyvern and Monkey
Baron Grey de Ruthyn	— Wyvern and Lion
Baron Arundel of Wardour	— Lion and Owl
Baron Montfort	— Unicorn and Horse
Baron Leyham	— Stag—Heraldic Wolf
Baron Sondes	— Griffin and Bear
Baron Rivers	— Hawk and Unicorn
Baron Hawke	— Neptune and Winged Sea Horse
Baron Carteret	— 2 Winged Stags
Baron Boringdon	— Stag and Greyhound
Baron Berwick	— Pegasus and Stag
Baron Suffield	— Lion and Leopard
Baron Southampton	— Lion and Greyhound
Baron Grantley	— Griffin and Lion
Baron Douglas	— Savage and Stag
Baron Yarborough	— Horse and Talbot
Baron Rous	— Lion and Winged Horse
Baron Harewood	— Bear and Bull
Baron Bayning	— Stag and Panther
Baron Minto	— Ram and Hind
Baron Bolton	— Hind and Hawk
Baron Seaforth	— Greyhound and Savage
Baron Lofford	— Farmer and Soldier
Baron Keith	— Savage and Stag
Baron Barham	— Angel and Winged Sea Horse
Baron Collingwood	— Eagle and Lion
Baron Sheffield	— Lion and Horse
Baron Beauchamp	— Bear and Swan
Baron Le Despencer	— 2 Greyhounds
Baron Northwick	— 2 Angels
Baron Petre	— 2 Lions
Baron Spencer	— 2 Griffins
Baron Stourton	— 2 Sea Dogs (Beavers)
Baron Saye & Sele	— 2 Wolves
Baron Clinton	— 2 Greyhounds
Baron St. John	— 2 Monkeys
Baron Audley	— 2 Dragons
Baron Grantham	— 2 Greyhounds
Baron Holland	— 2 Foxes
Baron Ducie	— 2 Unicorns
Baron Harrowby	— 2 Griffins
Baron Boston	— 2 Antelope
Baron Foley	— 2 Lions
Baron Walsingham	— 2 Dragons
Baron Bagot	— 2 Goats

16

Badges and Knots

Along with his shield, crest, and tunic displaying heraldic devices, every noble in the 14th and 15th century bore still another mark of identity—the badge, which was often found in his banner (pennon) or personal seal. Such badges were actually known and used before the shield became the main cognizance. Badges have remained an independent device since the advent of the shield bearings, but in many instances they have also been incorporated into shield devices. In continuing their existence, badges have also been known to *conversely* adopt a shield symbol into *their* design.

Unlike the shield bearings that were personal and exclusive to their owner, badges were found suitable

John de Warrenne, Earl of Surrey

William Lord Clinton

to identifying the nobleman's followers and retainers. The same principles that prompted the adoption of a heraldic shield device were applied to the selection of a badge. The earliest use of badges, however, had no fixed form or hereditary usage like the early pre-heraldic shield symbols. It was not until the reign of Edward III that they gained importance, and not until the time of Henry VIII that any recorded heraldic control was placed upon them.

Several factors could motivate the selection of a badge device: an accomplishment in battle, the recognition of a family or feudal alliance, or the pretense or claim to territorial control. These symbols, once established, not only marked the nobleman, his adherents, and retainers, but also his battle gear and household goods.

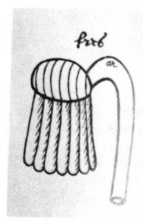

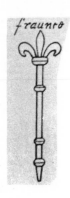

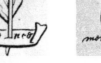

Badges

Bat wings of Daubney

carbuncle — John de Warenne (Earl of Surrey)
chamfron argent — Sir Ralph Hastings
cinquefoil gules — Darcy, Essex
cornish chough — Scrope
coudière — Sir John Ratcliffe
crescent argent — Percy
dunbull — Nevelle
escallop — Lord Dacre
falcon argent — La Zouche (Duke of York)
fleur-de-lis or — Sir Simon Montford
galley sable — Nevill
garb — Peverell
greyhound — Mauleverer
griffin's claw or — Earl of Derby
heart gules — Douglas
lion argent — Howard
lion azure — Percy (Earl of Northumberland)
Molet — Clinton
moor's head — Lord Willoughby
mulberry tree — Mowbray
peach — Peché
planta genista — Geoffrey of Anjou
porticulles — Beaufort
rudder — Willoughby
sallent argent — Duke of Norfolk
scabbard, crampet — De La Warr
swan — Toesni, Bohun, and Lancaster
talbot — Earl of Shrewsbury
tree stock — Duke of Gloucester
water bouget argent — Roos
unicorn — Thomas Grey (Marquess of Dorset)

Many sovereigns became as well known through their badges as their shields. The white hart of Richard II, the tree stump of Edward III, the ostrich feathers of the Prince of Wales, and the imperial crown of Henry V are just a few examples of famous badges. The most important historical reference to badges comes to us via the War of the Roses, fought between the Houses

Although the badge was shared with others, the tinctures of the nobleman's badge varied from those assigned to his subordinates. The obvious need to single himself out from his followers and retainers was satisfied by this color variance. It is likely that the tinctures of tenne and sanguine come into use here. Retainers often wore badges in the form of neck pendants called *livery collars*.

Below are listed a number of badge devices and the nobles and knights that are identified with them:

ape's clog argent — Duke of Suffolk
ass's head — Askew
bear and ragged staff — Beauchamp, Neville of Warwick, and Dudley of Northumberland
bear's head muzzled — Lord Morley
boar argent — Courtney (Earl of Devon)
boar azure — Vere (Earl of Oxford)
bucket and chain — Welles
buckle — Pelham
bugle horn azure — Northumberland
bull's head — Ratcliffe

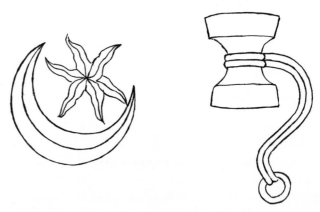

Left, *Estoile (star) and Crescent of Richard I;* right, *Ape's Clog of Suffolk*

Bottle badge of de Vere, Earl of Oxford

kings in England. Henry I is believed to have borne a single lion passant guardant as a badge, while Henry II is believed to have borne two lions in this attitude. The very basis for the origin of heraldry is in Henry I's gift of a shield bearing six golden lioncels.

The Arms of the Duchy of Normandy were later established as being gules, two lions passant guardant or. It would seem natural that such arms would be assigned to the rulers of this dukedom and their sons.

Henry II adopted a new badge symbol—the broomplant; a genet between two sprigs of broom whose Latin name was *plantagenista*. This symbol, adopted

of York and Lancaster for the throne of England. The Yorkists were known by their white rose badge and the Lancastrians by their red rose. The Lancastrians were defeated in 1471 in the Battle of Barnet and it is said that a mixup in two similar badges of hostile camps contributed to the defeat. This incident graphically stated the importance of such identification in battle. Another badge was developed from the two roses when Henry VII united them into the two-tinctured rose of the House of Tudor, thus signifying his marriage to Elizabeth of York.

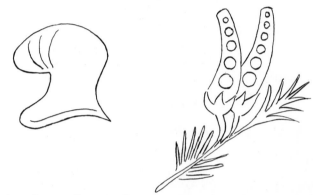

Left, silver sallet of Thomas Howard, Duke of Norfolk; right, broom plant of the Plantagenets

by the succeeding generations of this family who ruled, gave this dynasty its name, the House of Plantagenets. Other symbols were chosen as well by members of this house:

Early royal badge of England and Scotland

The use of the badge was not always just for cognizance. In fact, nobles at times bore badges of different devices so as to remain incognito at public fetes or in tournament participations. With much intrigue afoot at times, such a measure might have been a wise one.

Since badges existed before heraldic shields, there is evidence of them going back in time to the Norman

The House of Plantagenets

Henry II	— Planta genista; an escarbuncle; a sword and an olive branch.
Richard I	— Planta genista; a star above a crescent; a mailed arm and hand grasping a broken lance, with motto, "Christo Duce"; a sun over two anchors.
John and Henry III	— Planta genista; a star above a crescent.
Edward I	— Planta genista; a golden rose with a green stalk.
Edward II	— a castle.
Edward III	— a sunburst; or rays issuing from a cloud; the stock of a tree eradicated and couped; a falcon; a griffin; an ostrich feather; a sword; a sword erect on a chapeau, the sword blade enfiled with three crowns; a boar.
Richard II	— a sunburst; a sun in its splendor; an ostrich feather; a white hart lodged, ducally gorged and chained or; the stock of a tree erased

and couped or; a white falcon; a sprig of broom with empty and open cods; the sun clouded.

Henry IV — the monogram SS; a crescent; a fox tail; a tree stock; an ermine or genet between two sprigs of broom; a crowned eagle; an eagle displayed; a crowned panther; an ostrich feather encircled by a scroll inscribed "Sovereygne"; a columbine flower; the red Lancastrian rose; a sun in splendor; a rose en soleil; a white swan; a white antelope.

Henry V — an ostrich feather argent; a chained antelope with the motto "Dieu et mon Droyt"; a red Lancastrian rose; a fox tail.

Henry VI — a chain antelope; a spotted panther; two ostrich feathers in saltire (one silver and the other gold).

Edward IV — a black bull; a black dragon; a white wolf; a white lion; a white hart; the sun in splendor; a white rose; a white rose en soleil; and a red and white rose combined en soleil.

Edward V — a white rose; a falcon within a fetterlock.

Richard III — a white rose; a sun in splendor; a white boar; a falcon with a virgin's face holding a white rose.

The House of Tudor

Henry VIII — a porticullis; a fleur-de-lis; a Tudor rose; a white cock; a white greyhound courant.

Edward VI — a Tudor rose; a sun in splendor.

Mary I — a pomegranate; a pomegranate and rose cojoined; the Tudor rose impaling a sheaf of arrows ensigned with a crown and encompassed by rays.

Elizabeth I — a crowned falcon with a sceptre; a crowned Tudor rose with the motto: "Rosa sine spina"; a sieve; a gold crowned harp, stringed argent; a phoenix; a gold crowned fleur-de-lis.

The House of Stuart

James I — the Tudor rose; the thistle; the cojoined red and white rose demediated with a thistle and ensigned with the Royal Crown, with the motto "Beate Pacifici"; a harp; a fleur-de-lis.

Charles I — same as above without motto.

Charles II — same as above.

James II — same as above.

Anne — a rose branch and thistle issuing from a single stalk and crowned.

A special form of badge was created with interlaced cords called "knots," which by their individuality of design distingushed the bearer. In some cases they were physically tied to other symbols for further individuality. A number of these knots are named below:

1.) The Stafford Knot borne by the Earls of Stafford and Dukes of Buckingham.

Suffolk knot

2.) The Bourchier Knot.

3.) The Heneage Knot.

4.) The Wake Knot.

5.) The Lacy Knot, allusive to the name of Roger de Lasci.

6.) The Bowen Knot.

7.) The Harrington Knot, possibly allusive to a herring net.

8.) The Dacre Knot (gules) combined with the silver escallop from the shield of Lord Dacre.

9.) The Hastings and Hungerford Knot signifying an alliance between the Hungerford sickle and the wheat garb of the Reverels.

10.) The Anne of Bohemia Knot (from her effigy).

Presently only a handful of noblemen still mark their retainer's garb with the badge. As for identification of property, the broad arrow distinguishing government

Merchant's mark of Robert Pagge, 1440

stores is one of the few badges still used for this purpose. Certain government liveries still show badges on buttons or epaulettes. Perhaps one of the best known

Merchant's mark of Henry Garstang, 1464

and classic examples of badges surviving with time is that of the Yeoman of the Guard or "Beefeaters." These Tower of London guardians of the royal jewels still dress as in Henry the Eighth's time with the badge of the United Kingdom upon their chests.

The Royal Family, from the time of Queen Anne to the present, have gradually abandoned the use of personal badges in favor of the territorial type badge found

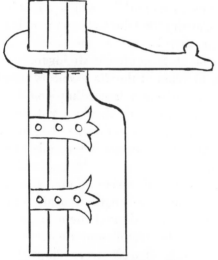

Rudder badge of Willoughby

on the uniform of the aforementioned Beefeaters. Badges such as the rose of England, the thistle of Scotland, and the shamrock of Ireland have become more representative of English sovereignty.

As stated earlier, the formation of a standing army in England brought about an end to the feudal lord's badge being worn by men-at-arms. In its stead, unit badges appeared, which in some cases were traceable to the earliest days of this regular army. These badges received considerable usage with the advent of World War I.

It became advisable during the 1914–1918 period to use badges that would identify military units and transports without such identity being properly interpreted by the enemy. Many of the insignias drew upon heraldry in their origin and character for inspiration. These symbols were employed at every unit level such as regiment, division, corps, and army.

The Royal Air Force and Royal Navy also adopted this use of badges during the period of the first World War. Prior to their official sanction, several units in each of the two branches had acted independently in creating such devices. When approval was officially requested by the R.A.F. unit commanders, the Air Ministry decided to make it a standard practice subject to their control. The Royal Navy similarly approved the use of badges after establishing a commission to consider suitability from among badges that they themselves would create.

The panels applying to the Royal Navy badges had

Capital Ship Badge of Royal Navy (1918–1942)

an interesting code attached to them. The capital ships were represented by badge panels of a circular form. Pentagon forms symbolized light cruisers, shield-shaped panels denoted destroyers, and lozenges stood for small craft. Each form in a nautical vein had a rope border.

The symbolism within each panel was of an illusive nature, playing upon the ship's name. An example is a human eye surrounded by rays suggesting the ship "Wakeful." This was typically heraldic, as was the naval crown or crest appearing atop all panels. During World War II, all ships became represented exclusively by round panels.

The Royal Air Force badges generally express a wider significance. They can be commemorative or symbolic

A squadron badge of the Royal Air Force. The crown displayed is the St. Edward crown. It is used when a queen reigns in England. When a king reigns, the Tudor crown with the depressed arches is used instead. This rule applies to all devices surmounted by a royal crown. The gauntlet symbolizes a challenge to all comers. The motto of the 17th squadron is: "Strive to excell"

of qualities, aims, or functions of the Force. They each have their motto in scroll below their round panel. These panels by the leaf depicted within the frame reveal the geographical origin or placement of each unit.

In America, the Civil War gave impetus to the devising of unit badges. Prior to the war, cap ornaments *did* distinguish branches (infantry from artillery, etc.) but made no provisions for numbered units such as regiments and higher echelon. At this time, both metal and cloth insignias appeared for numbered units, elite groups, and, in some cases, branches or corps. Battle flags also became widely used.

The Signal Corps's badge with its now-familiar crossed flags and torch came into evidence. The Engineers Corps's castle device was incorporated into a device with crossed oars and an anchor. Wilson's, Sheridan's, and Hancock's Corps displayed metallic badges. The Wilson and Hancock badges featured the sunburst; long used in military symbolism. Many numbered units headquarters had flags featuring an eagle in canton, or an ammunition pouch centered upon it.

General George Custer designed a divisional insignia for his cavalry that they all wore upon a red cravat or neckpiece. Its form was a gold cross paty with the number seven in its middle, which symbolized the 7th Michigan Cavalry that he first commanded as a brigadier. In a margin below the cross was inscribed "Tuebor," the state motto of Michigan.

The World Wars of the 20th century also stimulated American inventiveness regarding unit badges. They appeared either as cloth shoulder patches or metallic forms seen earlier. These devices, beginning with the second World War, became commonly worn with the dress uniform.

The knot badges also were an influence in decorative treatments applied to modern army uniforms. The French in particular adopted them in their hussar and Zouave attire. The trefoil and quatrefoil, already regarded as heraldic charges, were adopted as interlaced knots on breeches, jacket, or cap top.

The use of knots as decoration rather than badges was copied from the French by American forces at the time of the Civil War. The officers' overcoats displayed them around the button holes while the various Zouave units, in imitation of French Moroccan troops, featured them both on jacket and trousers. Confederate officers' grades were distinguished by the number of parallel trefoil knots displayed on their sleeves. Late 19th-century fatigue jackets of officers had button holes treated similarly to the Civil War overcoats. Presently, the Marine Corps officer's dress cap bears the quatrefoil knot atop the flat crown.

17

Mottoes

"Motto" is a term of combined Italian and French derivation that literally means "word." The motto is said to have its origin in the war cries of the early barbaric nations. Whether these phrases were intended to invoke the protection of their gods or to instill panic in the enemy is surely difficult to establish. It is safe to assume that with the passing of time the war cry was less designed to produce panic in enemy lines but more to create unity (*esprit de corps*) within one's own ranks.

This fact is evidenced in the medieval battle cry shouted by the English—"Montjoie Notre Dame, St. George!" and "Montjoie St. Dennis!" the exaltation of the French. The Dukes of Brittany placed the words "a ma vie" on their banner. The House of Montmorency used the words "unerring," "steady;" alluding to the north star, which they claimed as their emblem of cognizance. Richard the Lion Hearted's cry, "Dieu et mon Droit" (God and my Right), remains the motto of Royal Arms.

As suggested by the above phrases, mottoes were generally expressions of loyalty, virtuous thoughts, or admonitions to an unseen foe. From the shouted phrases they soon became a part of the banner and the badge. Inevitably, they found their way into the achievement as the message carried on the scroll or escroll below the shield. This was quite understandable, since certain such war phrases were obviously steeped in historical significance and tradition in the same manner as the symbols themselves.

Just as the badge and the common charge were often allusive in character, so too was the motto. Latin terms often provided words that primarily played upon the family name of the arms bearer and yet at the same time could be manipulated to provide a clever thought. Many of these, of course, had no relation to the early war cry but received their origin solely from the fact that combat phrases *did* become the first mottoes. Some examples of name-allusive mottoes follow.

Torte scutum salas ducum—"A strong shield is a leader's safety"—Fortescue

Cavendo tutus—"Secure safe by caution"—Cavendish

Ne vile fano—"Disgrace not the altar"—Fano, Earl of Westmoreland

Manus justa nardus—"The just hand is like a precious ointment"—Viscount Maynard

Ne cede malis—"Yield not to misfortunes"—Earl of Albemarle

Ne vile velis—"Form no mean wish"—Neville

Not all allusive mottoes refer to the bearer's family name. Some refer to a badge device, a crest, or a common charge by which he was known:

Duke of Richmond—*En la rouse je fleuris*—"I flourish in the rose." A reference to the fact that his arms are within a bordure charged with rose gules (the Royal Symbol of his time).

Earl of Thanet—*Ales volet propriis*—"The bird flies to its own." A reference to his principal charge, the eagle affronté or.

Viscount Maynard—*Manus justa nardus*—"The just hand is like a precious ointment." A reference to the hand (main) gules appearing as a charge in his arms (as well as to his family name).

Earl of Jersey—*Fidei corticula crux*—"The cross is the test of faith." A reference to the principal charge of his arms.

Some mottoes suggest an event in the history of the family:

Earl Delaware—*Jour de ma vie*—"Day of my life." This phrase alluded to the day that he captured the French King John.

Earl of Bristol—*Je n' oublierai jamais*—"I shall never forget." Possibly referring to a title that his ancestors once held in the Irish peerage. This title later became extinct when the Baron of Ross died in 1642. The symbolic clover leaf in his arms as a major charge would seem to validate this theory.

Le Despencer—*Pro magna charta*—"For the Magna Carta." A reference to his presence at the signing of this document by King John.

Many mottoes' significance, if not obviously allusive, are difficult to determine. The passing of time and the private subtlety of some phrases have obscured their full and true meaning. It is fortunate, therefore, that such allusive mottoes such as those exemplified in the text exist to give us something positive of the spirit of the Middle Ages.

Mottoes are unique in the total achievement in that they require no authority to be assumed. They can be constantly changed or entirely abandoned at the pleasure of the arms bearer. These latter alternatives generally are not acted upon since, as indicated, many mottoes are born of the same degree of honor as the hereditary arms themselves.

While the College of Arms places no restriction on the assumption of a motto, there are certain taboos in the way they might be displayed. The motto must *not* be incorporated into the shield itself. It is usually placed below the shield in the scroll but may also be placed above or behind it.

The Earl of Malmesbury, for instance, placed over the crest: *Je maintaindrai* ("I will support"). Below the shield he incribed: *Ubique patriam reminisci* ("In all situations, remember your country"). The Earl of Roslyn placed over the crest: *Renace Plu Gloriosa,* and below the shield he inscribed: *Illeso Lumine Solem* ("View with sight unhurt the meridian sun").

The motto and scroll may in rare instances encircle the shield. If this be the case, care must be exercised to delineate or differ it from the look of the garter, which symbolizes knighthood. It must in the same sense be unlike any other badge pertaining to another order.

As a final reflection on the choice of mottoes encountered in arms, many of the more interesting ones are outlined below:

Duke of Norfolk—
Sola virtus invicta
"Virtue alone is invincible."

Duke of Somerset—
Foy pour devoir
"Faith for my duty."

Duke of Grafton—
Et decus et praetium recti
"At once the ornament and reward of virtue."

Duke of St. Albans—
Auspicium melioris aevi
"A pledge of better times."

Duke of Beaufort—
Mutare vel timere sperno
"I scorn to change or to fear."

Duke of Bedford—
Che sara sara
"What will be, will be."

Duke of Leeds—
Pax in bello
"Peace in war."

Duke of Marlborough—
Dieu defend le droit
"God defends the right."

Duke of Rutland—
Pour y parvenir
"In order to attain it."

Duke of Ancaster—
Loyaulte me oblige
"Bound by loyalty."

Duke of Portland—
Craignez honte
"Fear disgrace."

Duke of Manchester—
Disponendo me, non mutando me
"Appointing me, not changing me."
Duke of Dorset—
Aut nanquam tentes, aut perfice
"Either not attempt, or accomplish."
Duke of Northumberland—
Esperance en Dieu
"Hope in God."
Duke of Newcastle—
Loyalte n'a honte
"Loyalty is never ashamed."
Marquess of Winchester—
Aymez loyaulte
"Love loyalty."
Marquess of Buckingham—
Templa quam dilecta!
"How delightful are thy temples!"
Marquess of Stafford—
Frangas, non flectes
"You may break, but shall not bend me."
Marquess of Lansdowne—
Virtute, non verbus
"By courage, not men."
Marquess Townshend—
Haec generi incrementa fides
"Ennobled for fidelity."
Marquess of Bath—
J' ai bonne cause
"I have a good cause."
Marquess Cornwallis—
Virtus vincit invidiam
"Virtue overcometh envy."
Marquess of Hertford—
Fide et amore
"By faith and love."
Marquess of Bute—
Avito viret honore
"He flourishes through his ancestors."
Marquis of Exeter—
Cor unum, via una
"One heart, one way."
Earl of Shrewsbury—
Prest d' accomplir
"Ready to perform."
Earl of Derby—
Sans changer
"Without changing."

Earl of Pembroke—
Ung je serverai
"One will I serve"
Earl of Suffolk—
Non quo, sed quomodo
"Not by whom, but by what means."
Earl of Bridgewater—
Sic donec
"Thus until."
Earl of Northhampton—
Je ne cherche que ung
"I seek but one."
Earl of Peterborough—
Nec placida contenta quiete est
"No content in soft repose."
Earl of Stamford—
A ma puissance
"According to my power."
Earl of Winchilsea—
Nil conscire sibi
"Conscious of no guilt."
Earl of Chesterfield—
A deo et rege
"From God and the king."
Earl of Sandwich—
Post tot naufragia portum
"After so many dangers I find a port."
Earl of Essex—
Fide et fortitudine
"By faith and fortitude."
Earl of Cardigan—
En grace affie
"On grace depend."
Earl of Carlisle—
Volo non valeo
"Willing, but not able."
Earl of Scarborough—
Murus aeneus conscientia fana
"A found conscience is a wall of brass."
Earl of Rochford—
Spes durat avorum
"The hope of my ancestors subsists."
Earl of Coventry—
Candide et constanter
"Sincere and constant."
Earl Poulet—
Gardez ta foy
"Keep the faith."

Earl of Cholmondeley—
Virtus tutissima caffis
"Virtue is the surest helmet."
Earl of Oxford—
Virtute et fide
"By virtue and faith."
Earl Ferrers—
Honor virtutis praemium
"Honour is the reward of virtue."
Earl of Dartmouth—
Gaudet tentamine virtus
"Virtue rejoices in trial."
Earl of Tankerville—
De bon vouloir servir le roi
"To serve the king with good will."
Earl of Aylesford—
Aperto vivere voto
"To live without guile."
Earl Cowper—
Tuum est
"It is your own."
Earl Stanhope—
A deo et rege
"From God and king."
Earl of Harborough—
Hostis honori invidia
"An enemy's envy is an honor."
Earl of Macclesfield—
Sapere aude
"Dare to be wise."
Earl of Pomfret—
Hora et semper
"Now and always."
Earl Waldegrave—
Coelum non animum
"You may change your climate but not your mind."
Earl of Ashburnham—
Le roi et l'estat
"The king and the state."
Earl of Effingham—
Virtus mille scuta
"Valour is equal to a thousand shields."
Earl of Harrington—
A Deo et rege
"From God and the king."
Earl of Portsmouth—
En suivant la verite
"In following truth."

Earl of Buckinghamshire—
Auctor preciosa facit
"The founder makes it more valuable."
Earl of Warwick—
Vix ea nostra voco
"I can scarcely call these things our own."
Earl of Egrement—
Au bon droit
"To the best right."
Earl of Harcourt—
Le bons temps viendra
"Good times will come."
Earl of Guildford—
Animo et fide
"By courage and faith."
Earl of Hardwicke—
Nec cupias nec metuas
"Neither desire nor fear."
Earl of Darlington—
Nec temere nec timide
"Neither rash nor dissident."
Earl of Ilchester—
Faire sans dire
"Act without ostentation."
Earl of Radnor—
Patria cara, carior libertas
"My country is dear, but my liberty dearer."
Earl Spencer—
Dieu defend le droit
"God defends the right."
Earl of Chatham—
Benigno numine
"By God's blessing."
Earl Bathurst—
Tien ta foy
"Keep the faith."
Earl of Clarendon—
Fidei coticula crux
"The cross is the test of faith."
Earl of Camden—
Judicium parium, aut leges terrae
"The judgement of our pens, or the law of the land."
Earl of Mount-Edgecumbe—
Au plaisir fort de Dieu
"At the all powerful disposal of God."
Earl Digby—
Deo, non fortuna

"From God, not from fortune."

Earl Talbot—
Humani nihil alienum
"Nothing is foreign to me that pertains to man."

Earl Grosvenor—
Nobilitatis virtus non stemma character
"Virtue, not pedigree, characterizes nobility."

Earl of Malmesbury—
Je maintiendrai
"I will support."

Earl Manvers—
Pie repone te
"In pious confidence."

Earl of Orford—
Fari quae sentiat
"Speak as you think."

Baron De Clifford—
Le roy le veut
"The king will have it so."

Baron Audley—
Je le tiens
"I will hold it."

Baron Grey—
Foy en tout
"Faith in all things."

Baron Saye and Sele—
Fortem posce vanimum
"Fortified with a strong mind."

Baron Stourton—
Loyal je serai ma vie
"Loyal will I be while I live."

Baron Willoughby De Brooke—
Vertue vaunceth
"Virtue prevails."

Baron Vernon—
Ver non semper viret
"The spring does not always flourish."

Baron Ducie—
Perseverando
"By perseverance."

Baron Brownlow—
Opera illus mea sunt
"His works are my works."

Baron Harrowby—
Servata sides cineri
"The promise made is the promise kept."

Baron Foley—
Ut profim

"That I may do good."

Baron Dynevor—
Secret et hardi
"Secret and bold."

Baron Bagot—
Antiquum obtinens
"Possessing antiquity."

Baron Southhampton—
Et decus et pretium recti
"At once the ornament and reward of virtue."

Baron Grantley—
Avi numerantur avorum
"I follow a long train of ancestors."

Baron Rodney—
Non generant aquilae columbas
"Eagles do not bring forth doves."

Baron Carteret—
Loyal devoir
"Loyal duty."

Baron Eliot—
Occurent nubes
"Clouds will intervene."

Baron Somers—
Prodesse quam conspici
"Utility without ostentation."

Baron Berwick—
Qui uti scit ei bona
"Nobility is an honor to him who does what he ought."

Baron St. John—
Data fata secutus
"Complying with his declared fate."

Baron Howard of Walden—
Vincit qui se vincit
"He is conqueror who subdues himself."

Baron Arundel—
Deo data
"Devoted to God."

Baron Dormer—
Cio che Dio vuole io voglio
"What God wills I will."

Baron Teynham—
Spes mea in Deo
"My hope is in God."

Baron Petre—
Sans Dieu rien
"We are nothing without God."

Baron Byron—

Crede Byron
"Trust Byron."
Baron Clifford—
Semper paratus
"Always ready."
Baron Ashburnham—
Le roy et l'estat
"The king and the constitution."
Baron Middleton—
Verite sans peur
"Truth without fear."
Baron King—
Labor ipse voluptas
"Labor itself is but pleasure."
Baron Monson—
Pret pour mon pays
"Ready for my country."
Baron Montfort—
Non inferiora secutus
"Despite mean pursuits."
Baron Stawell—
En parole je vis
"By the word I live."
Baron Sondes—
Esto quod esse videris
"Be what you seem to be."
Baron Scarsdale—
Recte et suaviter
"Justly and mildly."
Baron Delaval—
Dieu me conduise
"God be my conductor."
Baron Suffield—
Equanimiter
"Equanimity of mind."
Baron Dorchester—
Quondam his vicimus armis
"With these arms we formerly conquered."
Baron Heathfield—
Fortiter et recte
"Courageous and faithfully."
Baron Kenyon—
Magnanimiter crucem sustine
"Bear afflictions with magnanimity."
Baron Amherst—
Victoria concordia crescit
"Concord insures victory."

Baron Douglas—
Jamais arriere
"Never behind."
Baron Thurlow—
Justitiae soror fides
"Truth is sister to justice."
Baron Mulgrave—
Virtute quies
"Content in virtue."
Baron Lyttleton—
Ung Dieu, et ung roy
"One God, One king."
Baron Bradford—
Nec temere nec timide
"Neither rashly nor timidly."
Baron Selsey—
Memor et fidelis
"Mindful and faithful."
Baron Yarborough—
Vincit amor patriae
"The love of my country prevails."
Baron Hood—
Ventis secundis
"Prosperous gales."
Baron Roos—
Je vive en espoir
"I live in hope."
Baron Gwydir—
Animus non officit aequus
"An equal mind is never hurt."
Baron De Dunstanville—
Pro rege et populo
"For king and people."
Baron Harewood—
In solo Deo salus
"Salvation is in God alone."
Baron Rolle—
Nec rege, nec populo, sed utroque
"Neither for king, nor people, but for both."
Baron Carrington—
Tenax et fidelus
"Persevering and faithful."
Baron Bayning—
Stare super vias antiquas
"I pursue the path of my ancestors."
Baron Glastonbury—
Uni aequus virtuti

"Friendly only to virtue."
Baron Bolton—
Aymez loyalte
"Love loyalty."
Baron Northwick—
Par ternis suppar
"The two are of equal antiquity to the three."
Baron Lilford—
Parta tueri
"I will defend that I have won."
Baron Seaforth—
Luceo non uro
"Shine, but not burn."
Baron Eldon—
Sec fine labe decas
"Honor with a stain."
Baron Redesdale—
Aequabiliter et diligenter
"Steady and Diligently."
Baron Hutchinson—
Fortiter gerit cruceum
"He bravely supports the cross."
Baron Ellenborough—
Compositum jus fasque animi
"Law and equity."

Baron Sheffield—
Quem te Deus esse jussit
"Be what God commands you to be."
Baron Barham—
Fortis in arduis
"Brave amidst dangers."
Baron Collingwood—
Farar unus et idem
"Always the same."
Baron Crewe—
Sequor nec inferior
"I follow no inferior."
Baron Beauchamp—
Ex fide fortis
"Strong through faith."
Baron Ponsonby—
Pro rege, lege, grege
"For king, law and people."
Baron Manners—
Pour y parvenir
"In order to accomplish."
Baron Gambier—
Fide, non armis
"Faith, not arms."

18

Crowns, Coronets, and Chapeaus

The crown was developed from the diadem and fillet. The bandeau or fillet was tied around the forehead of primitive man to keep his long hair out of his eyes. In time, priests wishing to distinguish themselves from the fighting men wore a different pattern from these warriors. Eventually the chieftain also chose to be distinguished by a varying pattern.

The diadems or circlets remained simple for a number of centuries but the tops began to close in, or become arched. In the interim, the Byzantine period saw ornate diadems come into being. Edward the Confessor appears to be the first of the Saxon kings to display an arched crown however.

The first Saxon crowns were simple gold circlets heightened at four intervals with plain uprights or projections. Each of these projections usually bore a pearl at the top. The crown of Athelstan is an excellent example of this basic crown. Circa 1035, King Canute, a Dane who ruled in North England, wore a crown heightened by four trefoils.

The arched crown first worn by Edward the Confessor was the type also worn by his successor, King

Left, *Crown of Athelstan;* center, *Crown of Canute;* right, *Crown of Edward the Confessor*

120

appeared as a secondary or smaller symbol between the fleur-de-lis—perhaps a concession to the conquered English. The fleur-de-lis again appeared, but in con-

King Henry IV (1399–1413)

King Henry III (1216–1272)

Harold, and the first three Norman kings (William II, Henry I, and Stephen). This style was then discontinued until its re-adoption by Henry V in 1411. When earlier worn by Stephen, this displayed a series of fleur-de-lis, replacing the trefoil familiar to Saxon crowns. The fleur-de-lis was of course the symbol of the Norman-French.

The Plantagenet dynasty introduced the strawberry leaf to English sovereign crowns. The trefoil later re-

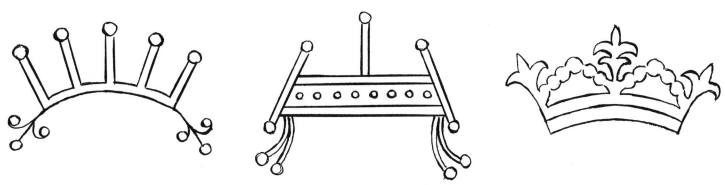

Left, *Crown of William II;* center, *Crown of William I;* right, *Crown of Stephen*

King Henry II (1133–1189)

sort with a new symbol that alternated with it in the same size.

This new device was a cross paty. It was a splayed-limb cross with square ends. This combination of the fleur-de-lis and the cross pattée was originated in the crown of Henry V. Its styling was the basis for the present Royal Crown.

The crown of Henry V, just described, had the fleur-de-lis in pairs with a single cross paty between each of four such pairs. Henry VI's crown reduced the number of fleur-de-lis to four, so that singular alternations of both devices now occurred. Charles I repeated this theme but added two arches to the two *already* a part of the crown. His successor, Charles II, restored the original two-arch conception but depressed them at their intersection.

The crown of Queen Victoria had in it an enrichment of the surfaces rather than any change in styling. Later, in 1880, when she became Empress of India, the arches were again raised at their point of depression, thus effecting the look of an imperial crown. In the 20th century, the Royal Crown returned to the arches depressed below the mound, or orb.

Coronet is a term applied to a crown worn by those members of royalty other than the king and queen. It also applies to crowns worn by all members of the peerage. Those members of the Blood Royal who wear the coronet are the heir apparent, sons and daughters of the sovereign, the sovereign's brothers and sisters, and their sons, and the sovereign's grandchildren.

The coronet of the heir apparent is the same as the Royal Crown, except that it only has one arch. The

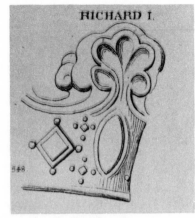

Detail of the King's crown

Detail of the Queen's crown

Edward II   Henry IV

Imperial Crown of Victoria

coronet of the sovereign's other sons and daughters has no arches but contains the same detailing around the circlet. The sovereign's brothers and sisters also wear this coronet. It should be noted that although the surface of the circlet is chased in simulation of containing the same jewels of the Royal Crown, no jewels are actually set there.

The male grandchildren of the sovereign's oldest son wear a coronet that introduces two strawberry leaves in place of two crosses paty. The children of his younger sons and those of his brothers wear a coronet with four strawberry leaves in place of the fleur-de-lis, and with these leaves there are also four crosses paty. The children of the sovereign's daughters wear a circlet with four fleur-de-lis and four strawberry leaves, the crosses paty not appearing.

Crimson caps lined with ermine usually are worn beneath the crown and coronet. The caps worn beneath the archless coronets have a gold tassel on the top. These crimson caps alone once were the headdress of the baron in lieu of a coronet.

The first of the peers to wear coronets until 1444 were the dukes and marquesses. Edward III created the coronet of the duke when he conferred this title on his son. The lower rank of earl appears to go back to Edward II, but the coronet for this rank is said to have first been created by Edward IV. The viscount's coronet was created by James I and the baron's coronet replaced the crimson cap in 1661 during the reign of Charles II.

The various coronets of the early peers had no distinctive pattern to distinguish each rank. When the coronet of the baron was created it carried with it specifics of design that then followed in the higher ranks. These are described as follows:

Duke—A gilt circlet, embossed as jeweled but not actually jeweled. This coronet is heightened with eight abstractly styled gold strawberry leaves. Five are visible in graphic depictions.

Marquess—A gilt circlet, heightened with four strawberry leaves, alternated with four silver balls placed upon small points. Three leaves and two balls are visible in depictions.

Earl—A gilt circlet with eight high rays each topped with a silver ball. Each ray is alternated with a

Left, *St. Edward crown displayed when a queen reigns in England;* right, *Tudor crown used at present time to symbolize a reigning male sovereign*

Ducal coronet   Mural crown   Palisado crown   Naval crown

Eastern crown   Baron's cap   Cap of maintenance   Celestial crown

Crest of Scotland   Crest of England   Crest of Ireland

Triumphal wreath   King of Arms   Civic wreath

Bishop   Bishop

gold strawberry leaf. Five rays are visible in depictions.

Viscount—A gilt circlet with 16 silver balls each touching the next. Nine are visible.

Baron—An unembossed circlet with six large silver balls. Four balls are visible in depictions.

The King of Arms has also been accorded a crown. This is a plain gilt circlet heightened by 16 slim stylized oak leaves alternated in two separate lengths. Across the main area of the circlet is the inscription: *Miserere mei Deus secundum magnan misericordiam tuam.* Nine leaves and the words "Miserere mei Deus" are visible in depictions.

Aside from the crowns and coronets described above, there are found in the crests of arms a variety of crowns and wreaths granted as special honors:

The Naval Crown granted for distinguished naval service. It has since become in addition, an ensign for badges of the Royal Navy. It can also be found as a symbol in civic arms where a town has a nautical background. It is a circlet upon which is surmounted alternately the sterns and sails of an old ship.

The Mural Crown is said to have been granted originally to knights who first sealed the top of a besieged battlement. Accordingly, it is in the shape of a crenellated castle wall with its square-stoned masonry.

The Crown Vallary and Palisado Crowns also represent defensive works. These similar circlets heightened by spear point projections suggest the stakes that confronted a troop of charging cavalry.

The Eastern and Celestial Crowns are also similar; the former granted for distinguished service in the East. The Celestial Crown differs from the Eastern Crown only in the fact that its rays or heightenings each end with a star at the point.

There are also wreaths of honor depicted on occasion—the Wreath of Triumph and the Civic Wreath. The first is composed of laurel sprigs and the latter of oak.

19
Royal Arms

The shield of Richard I gave England its first Royal Arms. His Great Seal was also the first to display them. While it is true that sovereigns before him were accredited with distinctive symbolism, he is the first sovereign to bear devices that were truly heraldic.

Some of the arms that preceded Richard I were literally marshalled into heraldic usage at a later date. Richard II impaled the attributed arms of Edward the Confessor with his own, thus giving them heraldic status. This sovereign also gave such status to the arms of St. Edmund when he granted them to the Dukes of Surrey and Kent as augmentations to their existing arms.

Dwelling momentarily with *pre*-heraldic arms, some familiar motifs or symbols arose from the seven Anglo-Saxon kingdoms (Heptarchy) of 449–828 A.D. These kingdoms displayed the cross, lion rampant, saltire, crown, horse salient, swallow, seax dragon, and paly of eight. Heraldry gave hereditary and systematic use to these devices several hundred years later.

The Saxon and Anglo-Danish kings of the period between the Heptarchy and the Norman Conquest showed a leaning toward the cross flory or moline. This was again supplemented in some situations by a bird symbol, in this case the dove rather than the swallow of the earlier South Saxons. Harold, the last of the pre-Conquest kings, displayed the first royal use of the cross in a powdered field. He also apparently used animal

heads (leopards) for the first time. Again he reminded that all that preceded Richard I was still non-heraldic in nature.

Royal Arms, Westminster Abbey

127

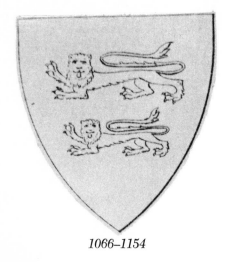

1066–1154

1154–1340

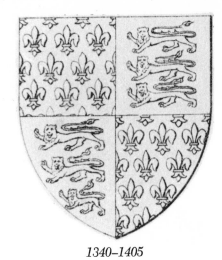

1340–1405

1405–1603

Stuarts

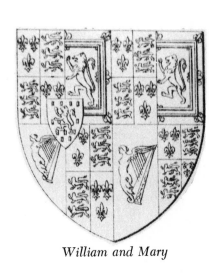

William and Mary

1707–1714

1714–1801

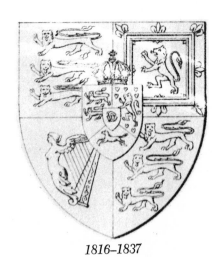

1816–1837

Royal Arms of England

London

Birmingham

Gloucester

Canterbury

Litchfield

Chester

Winchester

Hereford

Southwark

Bangor

Manchester

Oxford

Salisbury

Chichester

Landaff

Durham

Ecclesiastical Heraldry

Tavistock

Colchester

London

Dumbarton

Lancaster

Richmond

Birmingham

Wareham

Stamford

York

Canterbury

Worcester

Monmouth

Newcastle-upon-Tyne

Winchester

Wakefield

Bury

Durham

Gloucester

Leeds

Civic Heraldry

The lion which appears as the first symbol used heraldically by Geoffrey of Anjou, appears to come into the first Royal Arms also by way of Norman initiation. While Geoffrey, Henry I's son-in-law, bore six small lions (lioncels) Henry himself bore just one as a badge. It is interesting that Henry II may have borne two as a badge symbol of being second in this line and that

Great Seal of Richard I (circa 1198). This is the first seal to show the Royal Arms

Richard I, his successor, eventually bore a shield with three.

Richard I was a member of a long-ruling house known as the Plantagenets. From his reign on, a number of ruling dynasties was created, including the Houses of Tudor, Stuart, Hanover, Sexe-Coburg, and Windsor. Each house had separate Royal Arms that existed the length of the reign.

Though the Plantagenets were the first of these ruling houses, the arms that they created remain the core of the present Royal Arms of England. These are the familiar gules, three lions passant or. They are in fact termed *England* in blazoning.

These lions or *England* remained the Royal Arms from about 1198 to 1340 when the introduction of quartering influenced a change. Edward III took advantage of this new form of marshalling to reflect his claim to the French throne. This was done by quartering 1 and 4, the Royal Arms of France Ancient, with England. These bearings remained in effect until 1405.

About this time, the French King had reduced the powdered field of fleur-de-lis (floretty) into a simpler charge of three such flowers. The English King Henry IV, in order to properly maintain England's earlier claim to the French throne, adjusted the quarterings in his own Royal Arms in a like manner. These new quarters were termed France Modern.

It has been found that the quarterings 1 and 4 of France were occasionally placed 2 and 3, supposedly when an English sovereign carried these Royal Arms

KING EDWARD III.

EDWARD PLANTAGENET.
THE BLACK PRINCE

LIONEL PLANTAGENET.
OF ANTWERP.

JOHN PLANTAGENET.
OF GHENT.

EDMUND PLANTAGENET.
OF LANGLEY

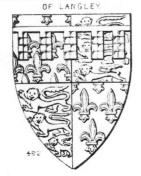

EDMOND, THOMAS & HENRY PLANTAGENET.
OF LANCASTER

Cadency labels of the Plantagenets

on visits into this country. The superiority of England was alleged to be evidenced by its now being shown in the first quarter. In a later version of the Royal Arms, 1707–1801, *France Modern* was regularly quartered 2 while England was quartered 1.

The Order of the Garter, which was created by Ed-

Philip and Mary

ward III in 1344, became a part of the Royal Arms from the time that they were first quartered. This garter, which encircles the shield, bears the inscription *Honi soit qui mal y pense* ("Evil to him who thinks evil").

Seal of Henry VII

The reign of Henry VII marked the House of Tudor's rise to power. This dynasty lasted from 1485 to 1603, ending with the death of Elizabeth I. The Royal Arms of this house quartered France Modern and England with the shield encircled by the Garter. The motto *Dieu et mon Droit,* created by Richard I but not used consistently until re-adopted by Henry VI, became the permanent motto of the Tudors and the houses that followed.

The Royal Arms of Scotland became quartered with those of England to initiate the reign of James VI of Scotland upon the English throne. This same House of Stuart also introduced the arms of Ireland as a quartering in their Royal Arms. The Royal Arms of Scotland are or, a lion rampant within a double tressure flory counter flory gules. The arms of Ireland, based on their badge in the Tudor period are azure, a harp or stringed argent.

To provide for these new quarters, the Royal Arms of England were grand-quartered 1 and 4 while Scotland was quartered 2 and Ireland 3. The Garter continued to encircle the arms.

The Royal Arms disappeared during the Commonwealth (Revolutionary period of Oliver Cromwell), 1649–1660. The Arms of the Commonwealth displayed quarterly 1 and 4 argent, the cross of St. George gules for England; 2 azure, the saltire of St. Andrew argent for Scotland and 3, azure, a harp or stringed argent for Ireland; and on an inescutcheon, sable, a lion rampant argent. The inescutcheon represented Cromwell's personal coat. During this period, the motto *Pax quaeritur bello* replaced *Dieu et mon droit.*

Charles II returned to the throne after the death of Cromwell in 1658 followed by James II in 1685, William (III) and Mary (II) in 1688, and by Queen Anne in 1702. The Stuart Royal Arms returned with Charles II and remained unchanged until William III differenced them with an inescutcheon of his paternal arms of Nassau (azure billety and a lion rampant or).

During his joint reign with Mary II, William III's arms were impaled with the undifferenced Stuart Arms representing Mary. Queen Anne bore the Stuart Arms alone for the first five years of her reign, but then re-marshalled them to mark Scotland's union with England. Thus in 1707 the Royal Arms were: Quarterly 1 and 4 grand quarters, England impaling Scotland; 2, France Modern; 3, Ireland.

George I's accession to the throne marked the reign

Arms of King George

Arms of the House of Hanover

Arms of the House of Nassau

Arms of Queen Charlotte

an escutcheon of Hanover: What is described as an Electoral Bonnet surmounted the escutcheon of the earlier Hanover sovereigns, while the Arms from 1816 to 1837 featured a crown in recognition of Hanover becoming a kingdom. This change in quartering finally brought about the removal of the arms of France. These new Royal Arms remained in effect during the reigns of George IV and William IV.

When Queen Victoria succeeded to the English throne, the ancient Salic Law of the Germanic people

of the Germanic House of Hanover in 1714. The previous Royal Arms were altered to place the arms of Hanover in the fourth quarter. In this fourth quarter there appears: 1, Gules, two lions passant guardant in palce or 2, Or, seme of hearts gules, a lion rampant azure 3, Gules, a horse courant argent; and over all an inescutcheon gules charged with the crown of Charlemagne or. The three impaled coasts represented the Dutchies of Brunswick, Luneburg, and Westphalia respectively.

Although Hanovers ruled until 1837, the Union with Ireland caused the arms again to be re-marshalled in 1801. The Royal Arms at that time became: Quarterly, 1 and 4, England; 2 Scotland; 3 Ireland; and over all

The present Royal Arms

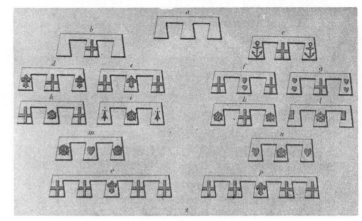

The labels of the Royal Family (circa 1814)

Arms of the Prince of Wales (circa 1814)

Obverse   The Great Seal of Queen Elizabeth II   Reverse

Great Seals of English rulers (top left, King John; top right, Henry IV; lower left, Edward V; lower right, Henry VIII)

Great Seal of Edward IV (1461–1471). Note improved detailing on both obverse and reverse sides

prevented her from also becoming Queen of Hanover. It was therefore necessary to remove the Hanover escutcheon from the new Royal Arms. Thus the Royal Arms became: Quarterly 1 and 4, England; 2, Scotland; 3, Ireland; the shield encircled with the Garter. These arms have remained unchanged to the present time.

The House of Saxe-Coburg was formed with the issue of children from the marriage of Queen Victoria and the Prince Consort, Albert. Edward VII became king upon the death of Queen Victoria in 1901. His son, George V, ruled England from 1910 to 1936.

In 1917 during the reign of George V and owing to the Anglo-German hostilities of World War I, Saxe-Coburg and Gotha was dissolved as the name of the ruling family and the name Windsor replaced it. The death of George V in 1936 brought Edward VIII to the throne. His abdication in the same year made way for his brother, the Duke of York, to reign next as George VI. In 1952, his daughter became Queen Elizabeth II, the present ruler of England.

Great Seals of English sovereigns (top, King James I; center, King George I; bottom, Queen Victoria)

20

Ecclesiastical Heraldry

Church heraldry is presently found in the arms of the various bishoprics or sees throughout England. Many of the symbols representing these church jurisdictions come from the personal seals of the original bishops. Such seals, it has already been stated, existed before heraldic arms. Pre-Reformation arms of many religious houses bore other ecclesiastic symbols, but the suppression of monasteries at that time caused such symbols to vanish.

Arms of Westminster Abbey

The inanimate symbols commonly seen in ecclesiastical heraldry are the crosier, key, palium, sword, mitre, crown, saltire, and cross. The figures of Divine beings are also seen occasionally in church arms. The arms of the Chichester display the seated figure of the Almighty with His hand raised in benediction. The See of Salis-

bury depicts the Virgin Mary with the Infant Christ in arm.

The crosier, or pastoral staff, of the bishop and that of the abbot are distinguished from one another in heraldry. The abbot's crosier has a crook whose sharp curve remains fully turned into the staff. The bishop's crosier, however, takes an outward turn near the end of this same curve. This difference in the latter's staff is presented to show his external or wider jurisdiction over that of the abbot.

The pallium is displayed only in the Sees of the Archbishops. This symbol differences his jurisdiction above that of the bishop. Both arms are nonetheless surmounted by a mitre. The mitre of an abbot does not have the pendant labels or enfulae seen in the arms of these higher church officers. A crest never appears where these caps surmount the shield nor do supporters or mottoes.

The personal arms of archbishops and administrative bishops may be impaled on the sinister side of the shield alongside those of their sees. Those without jurisdictions display their personal arms alone. A rare situation occurs in the arms of the Bishop of Durham. Since he formerly held the title of Count Palatine, his mitre rises out of a ducal coronet. Other bishops' mitre depictions, apparently influenced by this singular example, are incorrectly shown in the same manner.

The mitre of the Bishop of Durham bears another

distinction from that of the common bishop. His mitre above the shield shows a sword and a crosier placed behind it in saltire, whereas the other bishops show two crosiers placed in saltire behind the mitre.

The Roman Catholic heraldry varies mainly from the Episcopal in the matter of the cap and accessories that this religious branch surmounts above its arms. The Pope's arms show his tiara or triple-crown with the keys of St. Peter placed in saltire behind the shield. Cardinal's arms display a red, wide-brimmed cap with a pyramid of 15 connected red tassels pendant from each side of it. The hat is of such size and width that the tassels hang just clear of each side of the shield.

The hat surmounting the Patriarch's arms is of the same form and carries the same number of tassels. Both the hat and the tassels, however, are green as compared to the red of the Cardinal's. Archbishops' arms also show a green hat but fewer green tassels (ten on each side). Bishops' arms continue the display of the green hat but the number of green tassels is further reduced to six on each side.

Archabbots' arms also are distinguished by the same green hat and numbered tassels. Abbots' hats are black with three tassels per side. Local superiors (Prior, Guardian, and Rector) are known also by their black hat with only two tassels on each side.

Examples of ecclesiastical heraldry: Pope (top left) Bishop (top right), and Cardinal (bottom)

21

Civic and Corporate Heraldry

Civic heraldry began in the 14th century, at a time when several cities and towns adopted identifying arms that they placed within their official seals. As was done with personal arms, the heralds duly recorded these civic arms. This practice of merely recording but not authorizing civic arms continued through the next century.

In the 16th century however, such devices could only be borne if granted by the Kings of Arms upon official petition. As it became the jurisdiction of these heraldic officers to issue such grants, county councils and urban and rural district councils also applied for identifying arms.

Most of these early arms had some local symbolism or else contained the personal cognizance of a sovereign or feudal lord whose followers settled in the town identified by the arms in question. Some landmark of the area such as a castle or port feature could provide the basis for a shield of arms.

There were just a handful of towns involved in these early civic arms, so that most of the official heraldry existing presently is of modern creation. Although new arms are more complex in design and the symbolism is more far-reaching, the attempt is usually made to retain the character of the early bearings. Present-day civic heraldry has more to draw upon than the earliest arms. History and tradition have accrued in these towns since then.

The Arms of London is the classic example of early civic arms. Its chief charge is the cross of St. George, Patron Saint of England, with a secondary charge, the

Seal of Winchelsea City

sword of St. Paul in canton. These bearings have been in use since about 1450. The crest that came into being in the 1500s contains a wreath, a cross, and a dragon's wing. For supporters, the arms display two dragons charged with a cross on the underside of the wings. These supporters, added in the 1600s, were the last component of the achievement.

The Westminster arms granted in 1601 may have

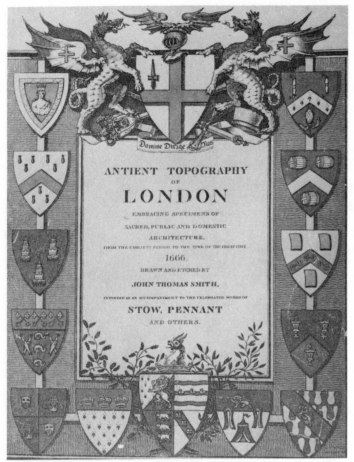

Title page showing Civic Arms of London (circa 1820)

been the first to be issued through the King of Arms. These arms are as follows: azure, a porticulles or, on a chief gold, a pale bearing the arms of Edward the Confessor between two Tudor Roses. The Arms of England, St. Thomas Becket, and the Earls of Gloucester appear in other early civic shields.

Arms of Westminster City

Arms of craft guilds, from an early 19-century print

Many towns and cities grow out of industrial communities. It is therefore common to find some symbol of the industry represented in the civic shield. These may be the product manufactured or the tool of the craft involved. Agricultural symbols such as garbs of wheat are often found. The more unusual arms are those depicting a locomotive and an airplane.

Modern corporate arms, since they too deal with industry, are closely allied with those civic arms just described. Guild arms also display the same type tools of their craft found in the arms of certain industry-oriented civic shields. Some examples are blazoned below of the corporate arms, merchant companies, and guilds:

Bank of Scotland—arms granted 1701. Azure, a saltire argent between four bezants.

Central London Railway—arms granted 1898. Argent on a cross gules, voided of the field, between two wings in chief sable and as many daggers erect in the base of the second, in the fess point a morion winged of the third, on a chief also of the second, a pale of the first, thereon eight arrows, saltire-wise, banded also of the third, between, on the dexter side three bendlets enhanced, and on the sinister, a fleur-de-lis or Crest: a representation of a locomotive proper, between two wings or. MOTTO: "Foward."

Some corporations are allowed the use of supporters. The two examples of corporate arms given here have either not applied for or have not been granted these accessories.

Fishmongers' Company of London—arms granted 1536. Azure, three dolphins naiant in pale argent finned or, between two pairs of lucies in saltire proper, over the nose of each lucy a ducal coronet gold; on a chief gules three pairs of keys in saltire wards outward or. CREST: two cubit arms erect, holding in the hands proper a regal crown of the last.

Drapers' Company of London—arms granted. Azure, three clouds proper, radiated in base or, each surmounted with triple crown or, capes gules. CREST: a mount vert, thereon a ram couchant or, attired sable.

Carpenters' Company of London—arms granted by Edward II. Argent, a chevron engrailed between three pairs of compasses extended sable.

Masons' Company of London—arms granted by Edward VI. Sable, on a chevron engrailed between three quadrilateral castles argent, a pair of compasses extended of the field. CREST: a castle as in the arms.

Worshipful Company of Skinners

Worshipful Company of Curriers

Colleges, universities, public schools, and institutions round out the remaining groups who bear arms. Of the colleges, Oxford and Cambridge, the perennial rivals, stand out among the schools of higher learning.

Oxford University—arms granted c. 1450. Azure, be-

Arms of Oxford University

tween three open crowns or an open book proper, leathered gules, garnished and having on the dexter side seven seals gold, and inscribed with the words "Dominus Illuminato Mea."

Cambridge University—arms granted 1573. Gules, on

Arms of Cambridge University

a cross ermine between four lions passant guardant or, a closed book of the first; edged, clasped, and garnished gold.

Eaton College—arms granted 1449. Sable, three lilies slipped and leafed argent; on a chief per pale azure

Arms of Westminster Deanery

and gules a fleur-de-lis and a lion passant guardant or.

Tonbridge School—founded 1553, arms granted 1923. The quartered arms of the founder, Sir Andrew Judd, viz.: Quarterly 1 and 4, a bar raguly between three boars' heads couped close argent, and quarterly 2 and 3 azure, three lions rampant or, all quarters indivisibly joined by a fillet cross or.

The College of Arms—founded 1484. Argent, a cross of St. George between four doves, their dexter wings elevated and inverted, azure. CREST: Form of crest-coronet or, a dove rising azure. SUPPORTERS: Two lions rampant guardant argent, ducally gorged or.

Lyon Office of Arms—Scotland. Argent, a lion sejant affronté gules holding in his dexter paw a thistle slipped vert, and in the sinister an escutcheon gules; on a chief azure, the cross of St. Andrew.

The Corporation of Lloyds—arms granted 1926. The shield divided fesswise displays in the chief half the

Graham-Paige motors

arms of the City of London and in the base half azure, a fouled anchor cabled or. CREST: A ship representing H.M.S. La Lutine, wrecked 1799, whose bell is rung before bulletins at Lloyds'.

The British Broadcasting Corporation—arms granted 1927. Azure, in an orle of seven estoils argent, a representation of the globe. CREST: On a helm argent with a mantling azure and or, a statant lion or, holding in its sinister paw a thunderbolt proper. SUPPORTERS: Two eagles proper, each gorged with a collar azure from which is pendant a bugle or horn.

Arms of British Broadcasting Corporation

22

Flags

Flags existed well before the development of heraldry, the earliest ones being of modest proportions. By the time that heraldry was becoming systematized, some flags were so large that they were mounted on wagons in order to be displayed and transported. The small flags that first existed bore the same type of simple forms as the shield ordinaries. Sometimes the flags instead displayed cut-out animal figures. These flags

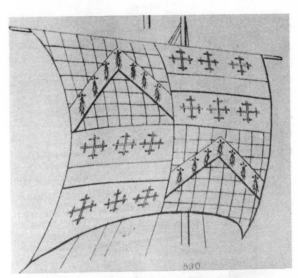

Nautical pennon of the Earl of Warwick

were generally tapered lengthwise and ended in three points. Later they were modified into two-pointed (swallow tail) flags as well as into single-pointed ones, which were called *pennons*. It is from this term that the word "pennant" was derived. A single-pointed pennon whose bottom side was straight rather than tapered was called a *pavon*. Such flags were carried by the knight bachelor and displayed his personal badge or shield device.

The wartime knight was expected to serve his king

143

for a period of not less than 40 days from the time that he entered hostile ground. His esquire, aspiring to knighthood, would carry a smaller pennon signifying his lower status. His flag was therefore called a *pennoncel* (small pennon) or *pensil*. These small flags did not follow any set dimensions, although the average pennon clearly outsized the like pennoncel.

When the knight bachelor was honored for bravery, a ceremony would be conducted on the field of battle.

Banner of the Earl of Lincoln

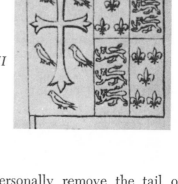

Banner of Richard II

Squire with pennoncel

Here the king would personally remove the tail or tails from the knight's pennon, converting it into a rectangular banner or, technically, a *banneret* (small banner). The knight bachelor thus became a knight banneret. If the knight accepted this honor he would be expected to now provide and support 50 or more men-at-arms to hold his title. It was therefore not uncommon for some poorer knight bachelors to respectfully decline this higher grade of knighthood.

The banner, formed by the removal of the tails was generally oblong; twice as high as wide. Square banners, however, were sometimes carried by knight bannerets as well. There is no known reason for this variance. Banners were also carried by members of the nobility and royalty. Here, too, the basis for this action has not been established. It might be conjectured that the banner was first borne by the peers and sovereigns and the privilege was extended to the knight banneret as a significant honor for his gallantry.

The banners of the nobles and kings often contained

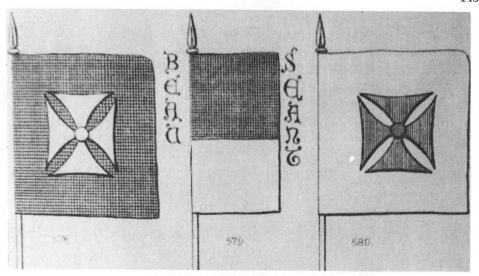

Knights Templar banner

BANNER of SIR ROBERT CURSON.

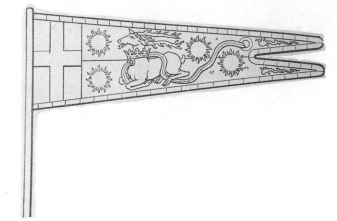

Three examples of Swallow-tail pennons.

BANNER of LORD DACRE.

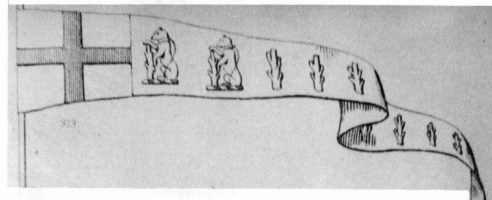

Beauchamp standard

Royal banner of England

Standards of Edward III
D'Aubernon   *From Bayeaux Tapestry*

symbols that were different from those found on their shields. The first banner borne by a sovereign of which there is a description is that of Edward I. His flag displayed gules, three leopards courant, or. This flag was observed at the siege of Caerverlock in the year 1300.

The reign of Edward III saw the introduction of another flag, which was called the *standard*. It was a return to the swallow-tail and single-pointed style. These flags were distinguished from the earlier knightly pennon by their immense width. The size of these standards was proportionate to the rank of the owner. It has been suggested that the sizes varied thusly:

An emperor's	— 11	yards.
A king's *great standard* (not borne in battle)	— 11	yards.
A king's *ordinary standard*	— 9	yards.
A prince's or duke's	— 7	yards.
A marquess's	— 6½	yards.
An earl's	— 6	yards.
A viscount or baron's	— 5	yards.
A knight banneret's	— 4½	yards.
A baronet's	— 4	yards.

The great standard was confined in its use to the pageantry associated with tournaments. The royal standard, in particular, would certainly be too unwieldy and impractical to carry into battle. Standards were usually divided lengthwise into two separate tinctures. These two tinctures could also be found continuously alternating in the piping or edging around the flag. Because of the standard's large area, the badge device was often used repeatedly to form a scattered field.

The cross of St. George found in early arms was the symbol of the Patron Saint of England. The cross of St. Andrew, the Patron Saint of Scotland, was combined with the former cross to form the Union flag in 1606 when these two countries were united. In 1801, when Ireland joined the Union, its cross of St. Patrick was added to form the present Union Flag of England.

The Union Flag appears in canton upon the flags of the Army, Royal Navy, Royal Air Force, and Royal Marines.

Cross of St. George

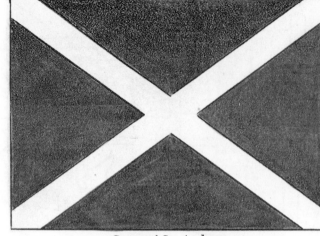

Cross of St. Andrew

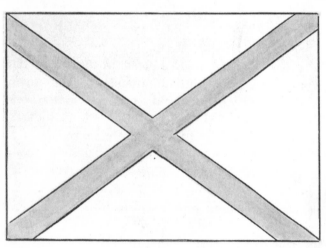

Cross of St. Patrick

First Union flag, 1606–1801

Present Union flag

Origin of "Union Jack"

THE QUEEN'S COLOUR

THE REGIMENTAL COLOUR

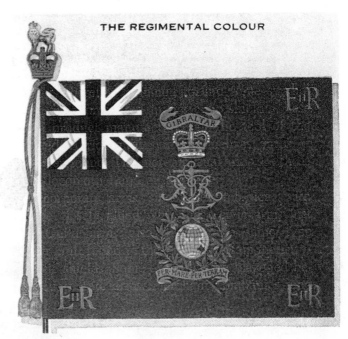

Colours of the Royal Marines

The Queen's Colour
for the Royal Air Force in the United Kingdom

College of Arms
September, 1963

J. D. Heaton-Armstrong

Clarenceux King of Arms
I. R.A.F.B.

23

Orders of Knighthood

Orders of knighthood have a distinct place in heraldry since they are represented symbolically in the arms of member-knights. In the Middle Ages, knighthood was earned by military service or other service to the king or country. Some became knights by holding land under feudal lords with the understanding that they were pledged to perform military duty if required.

It was expected that knights, in addition to their military duties, would take part in chivalrous exercises (tournaments). Those knights not inclined to honor such obligations could be excused upon payment of a fine. As a result, other knights wishing to distinguish themselves from their less tournament-minded comrades formed separate orders of chivalry.

Although some orders of knighthood were founded on this principle of military participation and chivalry, they were preceded by two religious orders established during the Crusades—the Knights of St. John of Jerusalem (Hospitallers) and the Knights of the Temple (Knight Templars or Templars).

The Hospitallers's original function was to care for the sick and to assist pilgrims in the Holy Land. This order was formed in 1092 at which time it wore a black habit with an eight-pointed silver cross. In the latter half of the 13th century, it took on a military aspect and its attire during military service was a red surcoat charged with a plain white cross.

Knight Templars

150

The Templars came into existence about 20 years after the Hospitallers. They served in a similar manner as their predecessors. Their surcoat colors were reversed from the Hospitallers, being white with an eight-point red cross on the shoulder. The Templar banner parted fesswise sable and argent bore the inscription "Beau Seant," their battle cry.

The Order of St. Anthony, next established in England in the 14th century, was symbolized by the Tau Cross. The House of Lancaster, while not a knightly order, developed a neck chain or collar made up of S's that served to mark their adherents. It was inspired by the badge of Henry IV who also featured S's. While no proof was found of its meaning, the S symbol is believed to be derived from the word "Sovereygne," Henry's motto.

This same collar was modified by Henry VII when he added a porticullis for a pendant and then used this same symbol for alternate links between the S's. Henry VIII gave the collar the significance of a knightly order when he restricted it to this rank. Presently, it is worn in a somewhat modified form by the Heralds, the Lord Mayor of London, and the Lord Chief Justice.

The House of York in rivalry to the Lancastrians, also adopted a collar. This was composed of suns alternating with white roses and the pendant was a white lion. Another version of this collar has the roses placed en soleil and a white boar substituted for the lion.

In commemoration of a tournament he sponsored yearly, Edward III established the Order of the Garter in 1348, which is considered the highest order of chivalry in England. Its symbol is the dark blue buckled garter inscribed with the motto *Honi soit qui mal y pense* ("Evil to him who thinks evil"). The dark blue garter, originally light blue until the reign of George I, encircles the arms of the members of this order.

The order's practice of encircling the arms became general in the reign of Henry VII and, as a result, other orders followed this custom with their devices. The Order of the Garter also displays a gold collar of 26 Garters, each encircling an enameled red rose. Its badge pendant is an equestrian figure of St. George slaying the dragon. The badge ribbon is blue.

The original Order of the Bath was said to have been created by Henry IV in 1399, in commemoration of his accession to the throne. After its later dissolution, it was revived in 1725 by George I. Its name is derived from the symbolic act of bathing performed by all aspirants to knighthood. This order, as do other orders, now have Military and Civil Divisions. In each group are the Knights Grand Cross, Knights Commanders, and Companions. These divisions were added in 1815.

The arms device of this order is a red circlet edged with gold. Its motto in gold letters is *Tria juncta in uno*.

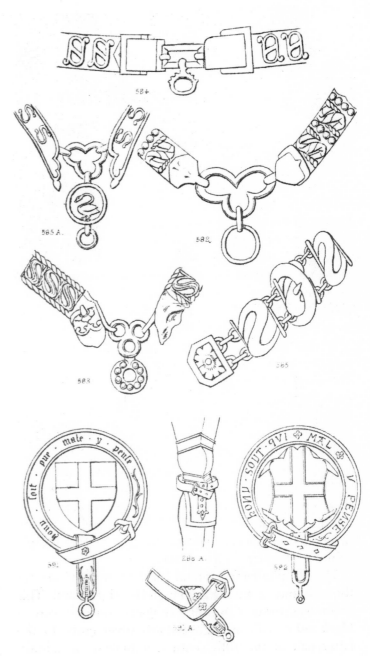

Lancastrian collars of SS and insignia of the garter

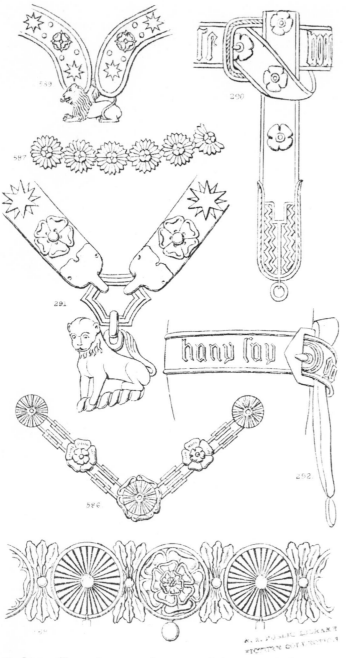

Yorkist collars of suns and roses and insignia of the garter

Star, badge, and collar of the most noble Order of the Garter

The circlet of the Military Division is enclosed by two laurel branches, and a blue scroll accompanying the circlet bears the words *Ich Dien*. The collar is composed of nine Imperial Crowns, each crown with four arches. These crowns are alternated with a connected series of a single rose, thistle, and shamrock, all issuing from a gold sceptre. White knots connect these flowers with the crowns. The badge ribbon is crimson.

The badge of the Military Division is an eight-point white enameled cross with small gold lions between the limbs. The laurel wreath, red circlet, and motto found in the arms form the center device of this cross. The

Civil Division features the same center device without the cross. In this device, however, the circlet itself is gold rather than red.

The Most Ancient and Most Noble Order of the Thistle was created by James II in 1687. The circlet is green edged with gold and the motto, *Nemo me impune lacessit,* is inscribed in gold letters. The gold collar has 16 sprigs of thistle and rue appearing alternately in proper colors. The badge of this order depicts St. Andrew attired in green and purple displaying his symbol of a white saltire before him.

The Most Illustrious Order of St. Patrick was created by George III in 1783. This Order presently is extremely small in membership (6) partially due to the fact that no Knights have been added since 1922, except for those members in the Royal Family. The circlet of the Order is sky-blue edged with gold and inscribed in

Star, collar, and badge of a Knight Grand Cross (civil division), Order of the Bath

Method of wearing the garter of that order of knighthood

gold letters is *Quis Separabit.* The gold collar has a crowned harp as the center piece, while the rest of the collar alternates linked harps and roses, the linking device being four looped knots. The badge beneath the crowned harp displays on a white field the red saltire of St. Patrick surmounted by a green shamrock in turn charged with three gold crowns. The entire design is encircled by a gold border studded with green shamrocks. The badge is worn on a sky blue ribbon.

The Most Distinguished Order of St. Michael and St. George was created in 1818 to confer honor upon Maltese and Ionian natives. It now includes among its recipients members of the Diplomatic and Colonial services. It also has been lately conferred upon members of the military involved in foreign affairs. It has three classes: Knights Grand Cross, Knights Commanders, and Companions.

The circlet is blue edged with gold and inscribed *Auspicium Merlioris Aevi,* in gold letters. The collar

Knights Grand Cross Star

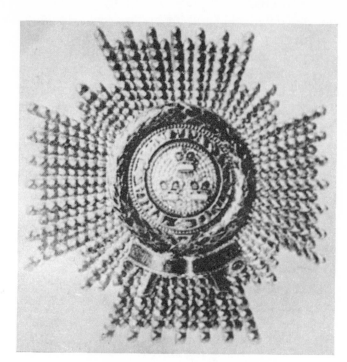

Knights Commander Star

Badge, Military Division

Companions Star

*Insignia of all classes, **Most Honorable** Order of the Bath*

Star, collar, and badge of the Order of Saint Patrick

designed to resemble a ribbon knotted at the bottom. It bears the inscription in diamond letters: "Heaven's Light our guide." The collar is composed of cojoined red and white roses alternating with lotus-flowers. Between these two devices are crossed and tied palm branches. All are enameled proper and connected by a double gold chain. The center piece is the Imperial Crown from which depends the badge.

The badge is a five-pointed star set with diamonds. Below the star is an oval medallion containing an onyx relief profile of Queen Victoria. The motto encircles this in diamond letters on a blue border. The badge of the two lower Divisions is of chipped silver instead of diamonds. Its ribbon is light blue edged with white.

The Most Eminent Order of the Indian Empire was founded in 1877. It has three classes: Knights Grand Commanders, Knights Commanders, and Companions. The circlet is Imperial purple edged with gold, bearing in gold letters the motto *Imperatricis Auspiciis.*

consists of gold crowned lions alternated with white enameled Maltese crosses that are linked by gold chains alternately bearing the letters SM and SG. The center piece displays two winged lions counter passant guardant ensigned by the crown. Each lion has a halo above its head and holds a book and seven arrows.

The badge is a 14-point cross of white enamel edged in gold and ensigned with the Imperial Crown. The center contains the circlet and motto, and within the circlet are the two figures of St. Michael and St. George. St. Michael is seen trampling upon Satan while St. George is found slaying the dragon. The ribbon of the badge is Saxon-blue and scarlet.

The Most Exalted Order of the Star of India was founded by Queen Victoria in 1861. It has three classes: Knights Grand Commanders, Knights Commanders, and Companions. The pale blue enameled circlet is

Star, collar, and badge of the Order of St. Michael and St. George

Imperial Order of the Crown of India

Star, collar, and badge of the Order of the Star of India

The collar has for a center piece, an Imperial Crown flanked by two elephants. The gold collar itself has alternate Indian roses, peacocks, and lotuses linked by double chains. There is no enameling on this collar. The badge is a stylized or heraldic rose enameled in scarlet with green sepals. The center of the rose contains the same profile of Queen Victoria as described above, except in gold. The ribbon is purple-blue.

The Royal Victorian Order instituted by the Queen in 1896 has five classes: Knights Grand Cross and Dames Grand Cross, Knights Commanders and Dames Commanders, Commanders, and Members of the Fourth and Fifth Classes.

The circlet is blue, is edged in gold, and bears in gold letters the word "Victoria." The collar is gold with alternate octagonal and oblong pieces. The oc-

tagonal pieces are blue with gold rose inserts jeweled with a carbuncle. The oblong pieces each contain a portion of the inscription, Victoria-Britt. Reg.-Def. Fid.-Ind. Imp.

In the center of the collar is a decorative gold frame containing an octagonal piece in blue enamel edged in red and charged with a white saltire. The saltire bears a gold medallion of Queen Victoria upon it. The badge consists of a white enameled cross of eight points bearing the circlet described earlier and ensigned with the Imperial Crown. The cypher VRI appears in gold on crimson within the circlet.

The cross of the Fifth Class badge substitutes frosted silver for white enamel. The ribbon is dark blue edged on each side with narrow stripes of red, white, and red.

The Royal Order of Victoria and Albert

The Most Excellent Order of the British Empire was founded in 1917 and soon after was separated into Military and Civil Divisions. This Order has five classes: Knights Grand Cross and Dames Grand Cross, Knights Commanders and Dames Commanders, Commanders, Officers, and Members. The circlet is scarlet, is edged in gold, and the gold letters bear the motto "For God and the Empire." The collar is of silver-gilt and consists of alternate medallions of the Royal Arms and the Cypher GRI connected by interlacing knots. Between each knot is the Imperial Crown, which is placed between two heraldic sea-lions, counter-rampant reguardant, each grasping a trident.

The badge, also of silver-gilt, consists of a cross patonce of pearl grey enamel, ensigned with the Crown and charged with the circlet described above. Within the circlet are the crowned figures of King George V and Queen Mary. The badge of Officers does not have the pearl grey enamel of the higher classes.

The order of Baronets, while hereditary, ranks below the peerage. This rank was created in 1611 by James I to honor those who helped to colonize Ulster. This honor appears as an augmentation to the arms of the Baronets of England and Ireland. Its form is, an escutcheon argent, a sinister hand erect, couped at the wrist and appaumé gules.

In 1625 Baronets of Scotland were created, relative to the colonization of Nova Scotia. These Baronets augmented their arms with either an inescutcheon or canton bearing the Arms of Nova Scotia: Argent, on a saltire azure an escutcheon of the Royal Arms of Scotland.

The later Union of England and Scotland dictated that new creations of baronets be Baronets of the United Kingdom. The augmentation for this rank is the same as the Baronet of Ulster or Ireland.

In addition to this Order and the previously described Orders of Knighthood, there are several other Orders and insignias of honor that carry no rank or precedence:

Knights Bachelor
The Order of Merit, 1902
The Royal Victorian Chain, 1902
The Order of the Companions of Honour, 1917
The Distinguished Service Order, 1886
The Imperial Service Order, 1902
The Order of St. John of Jerusalem

There are also medals of great honor—such as the Victoria Cross, the Albert Medal, and the George Cross —that may appear with a ribbon below the shield in the proper order of importance, the dexter side being the side of precedence.

Certain instances exist where officials are granted insignias of office other than, or in addition to, an official coat of arms. The Earl Marshall, King of Arms, and the Heralds are three pertinent examples. The Earl Marshall displays two gold batons tipped in black placed in saltire behind his shield. The Kings of Arms, in addition to their regular arms and crowns, display a collar of S's around the shield. Their badge of office is placed below the shield. The Heralds also display the collar of S's relating to their office. Others who possess insignias of office are:

The Hereditary Lord High Steward of Ireland (The Earl of Shrewsbury): a white wand in pale behind the shield.
The Hereditary Keeper of Stirling Castle (The Earl of Mar and Kellie): a key and baton in saltire behind the shield.
The Lord Chief Justice of England and Sergeants at Arms: a collar of S's encircling the shield.

As mentioned in the chapter on Marshalling, insignias of Knighthood and other decorations possessed by either men or women are not to be borne with the arms of their spouses. Exceptions are where the order is hereditary.

Two shields must be used where either mate possesses personal, non-hereditary honors. In the case of the married man his office or honors are impaled with his paternal coat alone. This shield is placed to the dexter while his impaled marital arms are placed to the sinister. Where the husband's circlet of an order of knighthood is displayed, a conventional type wreath may be used with the wife's arms for balance.

A woman possessing the right to display a circlet of a knighthood must do so by encircling the escutcheon within her husband's arms. In addition to this, she must place his paternal coat to the dexter side of their marital arms. It will then become clear that the escutcheon is hers and not his.

Some badges or decorations are only bestowed upon men, so when they are displayed beneath the marital arms, it is still evident which mate possesses them. If, however, such honors are open to both sexes, the procedure involving two shields must again be employed.

24

College of Arms

It should be noted that the herald, although associated with other duties, saw his initial service in calling the tournaments. His later function as a royal messenger was a natural outgrowth of his tournament service. His role in traveling to foreign courts to proclaim a coming tournament inevitably led to his also being entrusted with messages of state. The knowledge that he possessed in regard to armorial bearings decreed that his name be given to the science built upon such devices. How his own title originated, however, is still a matter of conjecture.

Some writers credit the origin of the word "herald" to a combination of two Anglo-Saxon words, *here* (an army), and *wald* (strength or sway). This word combination is perhaps a reference to the herald's empowerment to carry a message of war or peace. A term of German origin has also been considered as a basis for the word *herald; herold*, meaning "caller of champions." The latter term, in the face of certain facts, seems the more likely. It has been established that the tournament was the herald's first area of service. The German word *herold* applies to this duty. It has also been documented that the Germans first derived a version of these war games in the 10th century. It therefore seems conceivable that their word would be coined before any others.

The expansion of English tournament participation and the scientific and expanded use of armorial bearings eventually led to the herald's preoccupation with these matters above all others. The first heralds were independent personages on temporary hire only when an occasion warranted their services and by whomever would employ them. Their effectiveness soon encouraged noblemen to put them on permanent retainer.

When heralds acquired this status it was not unusual for them to be given the family names of the nobles who retained them. In some cases names were provided from the noble's castle or badge symbol. One famous castle name drawn upon for this purpose was Windsor. A final close identification of the herald with his employer was the herald's authorized assumption of the latter's armorial devices.

The granting of rights to the heralds to use the arms of their masters was not considered objectionable. In other cases, however, a number of arms was assumed or copied without proper authority. This brought about a troublesome period in the history of English heraldry.

In 1286 the German nobles, in view of the same ignoble practices, adopted a policy of forbidding a man to use arms already possessed by another. Sometime before 1348, the English also had an inferred ruling of this type in their court of law. The false assumption of arms was of course resented by the nobility who felt that they alone had the right to bear such arms.

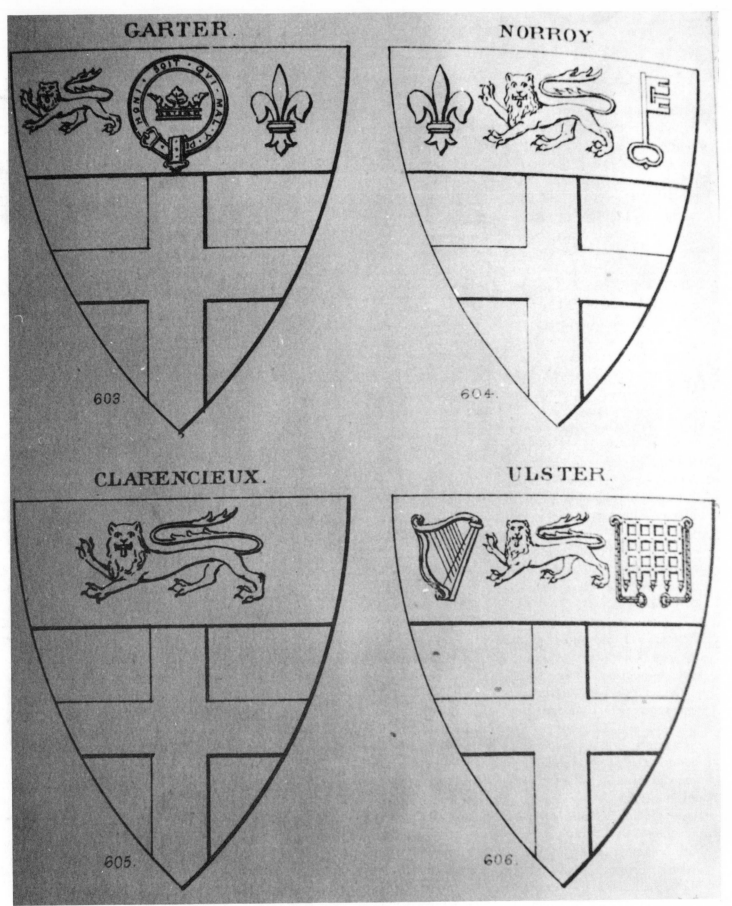

Arms of the Kings of Arms

At one point, in an attempt to thwart the use of false achievements, some major tournaments required that participants display quartered arms (arms that represented nobility on both sides of the family).

The decline of the feudal period brought an end to the herald's service in the feudal lord's behalf. Their permanent service to the king continued, however. In the exclusive employ of the king, the herald gained further stature; so much so, that aspirants to this office would now require training. These apprentices, hoping one day to earn the grade of herald, were termed "pursuivants of arms" (pursuers of armorial knowledge). The pursuivants were under the administration of the senior herald, who accordingly was designated King of Heralds or King of Arms.

Two Kings of Arms in the course of time jointly held authority in England, but their jurisdiction prevailed in different and separate provinces. The Trent River was considered the geographic boundary line between their two sectors of authority. In the northern half of England, the Narroy King of Arms held office and in the southern half below the Trent, the Clarenceaux King of Arms officiated similarly.

The year 1417 proved an eventful one heraldically. It was at this time that Henry V declared the long-inferred ruling against wrongly assumed arms to be a positive one. He stated that from that date forward no arms shall be taken unless they are of the bearer's ancestry or granted to him by someone of unquestioned authority. In the same year Henry V created the Garter Principle King of Arms to enforce this edict. While this office concentrated on administering the Order of the Garter, it also included supervisory authority over the two other Kings of Arms. The following year the sovereign notified sheriffs in various counties that they were to aid in the enforcement of his 1417 proclamation. He made one exception known at this time: Those who fought at Agincourt would not be denied the arms they presently held.

Motivated by the fraudulent use of arms, in 1413 the Kings of Arms began an extensive but voluntary search into the rights of many of the subjects to bear arms. In the next century, their oath of office charged them with the obligation of doing so. These inspections that carried the heralds to all parts of the kingdom were called *visitations*.

If the King of Arms were to uncover a misuse of arms, he was empowered to remove or deface these arms. He was also to denounce the guilty party or parties by proclamation. If, on the other hand, a claim to arms proved legitimate, he would properly record the fact for all time. The visitations of the heralds were conducted at intervals of about 30 years during the 15th and 16th centuries. The last visitation occurred in 1686.

Prior to the 1417 edict of Henry V, a Court of Chivalry was already in existence to deal with disputes over the right to armorial achievements. Presiding jointly at this court were the Constable and the Marshal. Frequently, a herald's authoritative testimony had much to do with the outcome of the case.

The Marshal soon became the King's representative in all matters of heraldry and the three Kings of Arms were answerable to him. His title was then changed in 1386 from Marshal to Earl Marshal. The Duke of Norfolk was the noble selected for this office, and it is a

Duke of Norfolk. Portrait shows batons of office seen in his coat of arms.

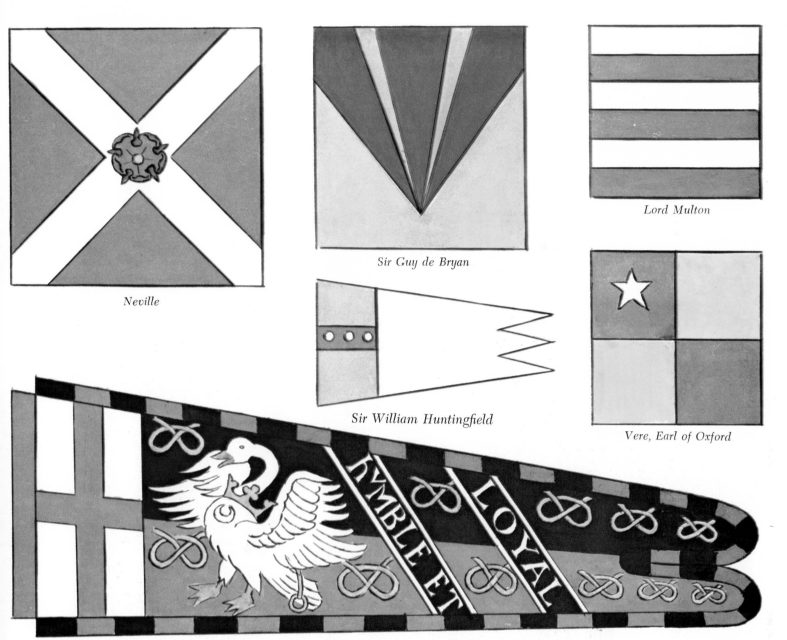

Neville

Sir Guy de Bryan

Lord Multon

Sir William Huntingfield

Vere, Earl of Oxford

Standard of Sir Henry de Stafford

Ralph de Monthermer

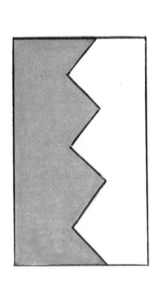

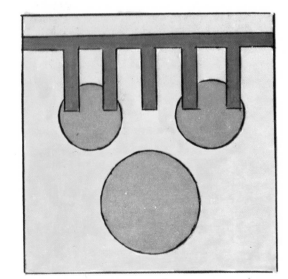

Courtenay, Earl of Devon

Standards, Banners & Pennons

Proclaiming the Coronation. The Somerset Herald *proclaims the Coronation of George V on July 22, 1910, at the Royal Exchange*

hereditary office that has been handed down since its creation.

In 1484 the three grades of heralds were incorporated by Charter though they continued to remain in the Royal Household. Under the sanction of Richard III, the heralds now became the College of Arms. In 1554 a former townhouse of the Earl of Derby was assigned to the College as a headquarters and a repository for their valuable armorial documents. This first building burned down with the Great Fire of London in 1666 but it was replaced with another on the same site. The records contained in the original building were luckily saved.

Although housed and incorporated together, some confusion existed between heralds as to which King of Arms held final authority for the creation and granting of arms. It was not until 1673 that, after much debate, a lasting decision was reached. It was agreed King of Arms who had the particular territorial jurisdiction over the arms involved would, in consort with the Garter Principle King of Arms, decide that issue. In other words, the North or South location of the applicant would itself determine which King of Arms was properly empowered to make a joint decision with the Garter Principle.

The provision was included, however, that the application for grant of arms must be preceded by a warrant from the Earl Marshal. These grants of arms, once given, were termed *patents* in the same manner that inventions are recorded and protected in the United States. A facsimile of the arms plus a blazoning are included in the form deposited with the College. With the establishment of this system, the total sum of records from both Kings of Arms were now kept as one. The Garter Principle King had also been enacting grants of arms prior to the ruling and his records were of course joined with the others. It should be of interest to learn, in again mentioning the Garter King of Arms, that the first known record of a grant of arms by his office occurred in 1439. It was issued to the Draper's Company of London by Sir William Bruges, the first Principle King of Arms.

The documents contained within the College often make mention of specific heralds or King of Arms performing visitations. In 1530, for instance, Henry VIII commissioned Thomas Benolt, Clarenceaux King of Arms, to establish commissions made up of sheriffs and local authorities to examine the various arms claims of their townspeople. Between this date and 1686 previously mentioned as that date of the last visitation, 23 visitation commissions were created. Of this number, the Clarenceaux King of Arms supervised 13 and the Norroy King of Arms, seven.

The services of the heralds and pursuivants were greatly needed during the above visitations. They would be *deputized* to act in the name of the King of Arms to cover the territory under each chief herald's control.

One of the gigantic products of the herald's early searching is a collection of visitation records that fill over a hundred large volumes. Although some few copies have been granted to other libraries, it remains the largest genealogical survey in the world. The searching into the ancestry of various arms applicants or claimants made many heralds astute genealogists and it is well understandable that they have continuously authored many fine heraldic works. Those who follow this science are deeply indebted to them for their knowledge and effort.

Northern Ireland, Scotland, and the Irish Republic keep their separate records. The visitations that occurred in Ireland during the Middle Ages were infrequent and covered only a fraction of the country. As a result, the Ulster King of Arms, the heraldic officer of Northern Ireland, had to use a different criterion for judging the legitimacy of claims to arms.

If an Irish family can show that it has used the same arms continuously for three generations or 100 years, their claim to them is recognized. The Irish Republic uses this same principle in the granting of their arms. This rule was once also practiced in England but later abandoned.

The equivalent of the King of Arms in the Republic of Ireland has the title, Chief Herald of Ireland. He has also lately assumed the duties once undertaken by the Ulster King of Arms, who had been the Chief Herald there and in Northern Ireland. In the latter country, the Ulster King has also had his duties undertaken by another heraldic officer. In this case it is the Norroy King of Arms.

The Scottish King of Arms is titled Lord Lyon King of Arms and holds office in Edinburgh. In this country the laws of cadency vary somewhat with England. Only the oldest son inherits the arms of his father.

Younger sons at the time of their fathers' death, must add marks of cadency approved by the Lord Lyon before such arms are officially entered in the Public Register of Arms and Bearings. If one of the younger sons subsequently dies, the differenced arms of the other sons must be *re-differenced* so that the deceased younger son's male heir may alone properly inherit the *initially* differenced arms.

When King Henry V issued his edict against false assumption of arms, it marked the point henceforth where arms could only be acquired through heraldic laws of inheritance or by duly constituted authority. The proof justifying present-day claim must appear in the records of the visitations, confirmed by the then King of Arms.

The present College of Arms includes six Heralds and four Pursuivants. The last heraldic office was created during the time of Henry VIII. Below are listed the names of the heralds established by royal decree and the sovereign who created the office:

Windsor Herald	— Edward III
Lancaster Herald	— Edward III
York Herald	— Edward III
Chester Herald	— Edward III
Richmond Herald	— Edward IV
Somerset Herald	— Henry VIII

The four Pursuivants' names now follow, along with the derivation of each:

Rouge-Croix — derived from the red cross of St. George, patron saint of England.

Blue Mantle — in honor of the French coat of Edward III.
Rouge-Dragon — in honor of one of the (shield) supporters of Henry VII and the badge of Wales.
Portcullis — instituted by Henry VII from his badge of cognizance.

In the matter of herald's names, it should be immediately apparent that they are derived from names granted by early feudal lords as outlined in the beginning of this chapter.

In Scotland, the Lord Lyon is assisted by three Heralds. These are:

Marchmont Herald
Rothesay Herald
Albany Herald

In addition there are three Pursuivants:

Dingwall
Unicorn
Carrick

The bearing of arms in Great Britain is not compulsory for those having the right to do so. Those whose arms patents already are in effect pay Inland Revenue, a heraldic tax each year for the continued privilege of displaying their achievements. On the basis of total early taxes received, a goodly number of armigerous families, corporations, institutions, etc., do avail themselves of this option. The tracing of family arms or the recording of same is naturally the province of one of the four Kings of Arms or their offices.

25

Original Source Material

Much of what is known today about English heraldry was garnered from three sources of information: the still-existent personal seals of early arms bearers, the monuments of such persons, and the records of their arms in the keeping of the Herald's College.

Manuscripts, which provided a good portion of the data, dealt with arms in various ways. Some merely blazoned (described) the shield devices, others were detailed in abbreviated drawings *tricking* previously explained in the text, and a third group was displayed in color and possibly blazoned as well.

One form of painted arms appeared in vellum skin rolls. One well-known roll was 5'3" long and 6¼" wide and was composed of three skins sewn together on which the shields were aligned in short horizontal rows. Some rolls were later cut into small sections and bound into books. As a consequence, the term *Rolls of Arms* came to mean such arms now in book form as well as those still in rolls. For purposes of cataloguing, all arms in series form are now so classified.

Some manuscripts were the works of monks or churchmen such as Matthew Paris and Father Menestrier. Works of this nature were called Illustrative Rolls, one of four classifications given to records of arms.

Some of these illustrative manuscripts were not heraldic but were historical texts or chronicles as they were called. This fact notwithstanding, many shield devices were decoratively emblazoned in the margins alongside the text.

A second category under which rolls are classified is the *Occasional Roll,* which commemorates a great battle or important tournament. Unfortunately, a few of these rolls are merely blazoned, but heralds were able to translate and re-create them as necessary. Examples of these commemorative rolls are:

Battle of Falkirk 1298
Siege of Caerlaverock 1300
Tournament of Dunstable 1308
Battle of Boroughbridge 1322

General Rolls (the third category) usually begin with arms of European rulers and move down in rank to knights and esquires in no particular order. Some rolls only depict the arms of sovereigns.

Local Rolls are few, but are of no less importance. One such roll called the Parliamentary Roll (circa 1310) contains 1110 coats of arms arranged according to county. A later one circa 1370 holds more than 1800 shields and crests encompassing most of Europe in scope. The roll is arranged by Kingdoms and lordships. The English section contains 78 coats of arms.

No early roll of Scottish Arms has been found except for those arms included in the last mentioned roll. This latter roll, incidentally, is the oldest roll that can be attributed to a specific herald. It has thus been established that four categories exist: the Illustrative Rolls, Occasional Rolls, General Rolls, and Local Rolls.

The earliest known roll of arms is one compiled during the reign of Henry III. This is known as the Glover

Early seals of knights and nobles (upper left, House of York; upper center, House of Lancaster; upper right, House of York; center, Simon de Monfort; lower left, Robert de Vere, Earl of Oxford, 1263–1296; lower right, William Montagute, Earl of Salisbury, 1337–1343)

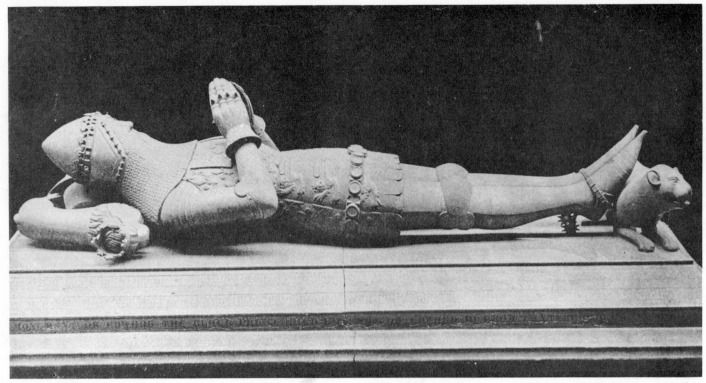

Effigy of the Black Prince on his tomb in Canterbury Cathedral. Effigies such as this provide one of the three sources of authoritative information on medieval heraldry and armor

Painted glass, 1585, from Gilling Castle, Yorkshire

Examples of stained-glass windows depicting coats of arms (upper left, circa 1579; upper right, Shield of Edward VI when he was Prince of Wales, circa 1517; lower left, Arms of the Black Prince showing the first three-point label argent, circa 1360; lower right, Quartered arms of Sir Edward Norris and wife, circa 1510)

Westminster Abbey where many original traces of heraldry can be found. Stall plates or monuments, as seen on page 169, are examples.

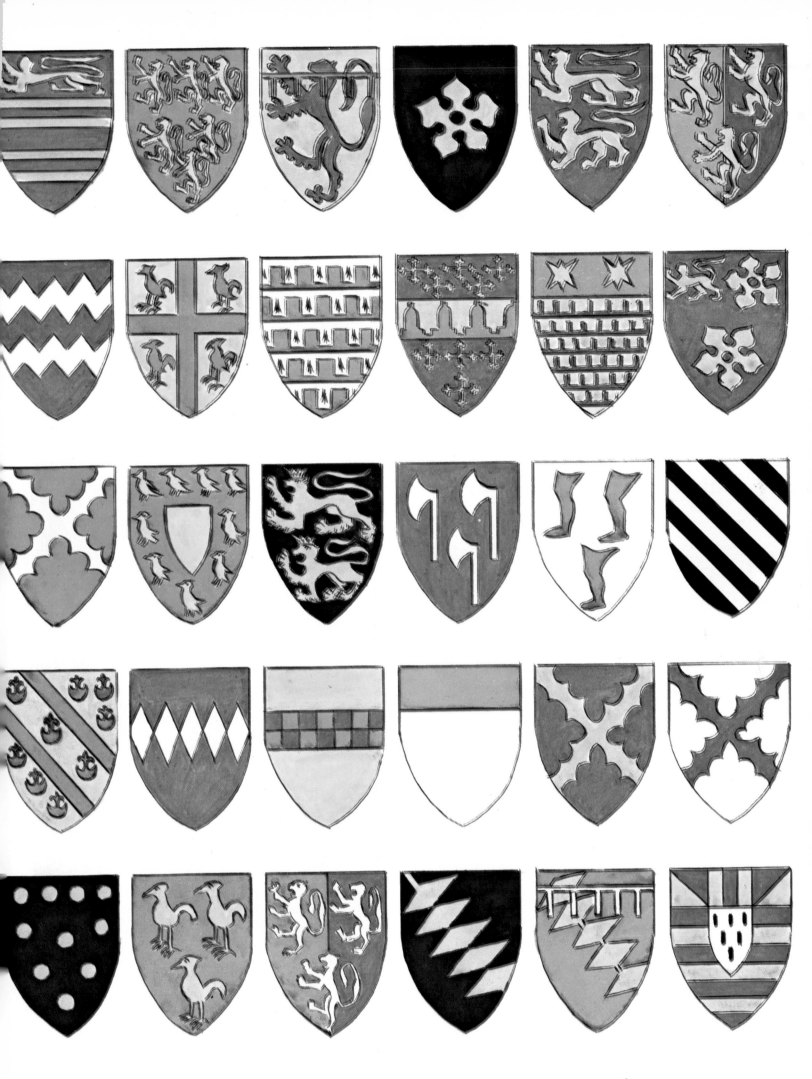

SHIELDS FROM AN EXISTING ROLL OF ARMS
Early Fourteenth Century

SHIELDS FROM AN EXISTING ROLL OF ARMS :::
Middle Fourteenth Century

Stall plate, Lord Bourchier, K.G., 1421

William de Valence, Earl of Pembroke, 1296

Sir Simon de Felbrigge

Sir John D'Abernon

Roll and depicts the arms of the feudal lords and knights of that time. It is the work of Robert Glover, Somerset Herald, who in 1586 emblazoned 218 coats from an earlier transcript.

Sir Anthony Richard Wagner, Garter Principal King of Arms, has compiled an authoritative list of the above rolls, detailing their contents and locations. These are enumerated in his "Catalogue of English Medieval Rolls of Arms," 1950. His work also includes other sources such as will be described in a later chapter.

Blazoned roll of arms (Camden roll) from Some Feudal Coats of Arms *by Joseph Foster, 1902*

26

Abatements—Fact or Fancy?

The presently accepted heraldic meaning of the word abatement means "a difference for illegitimacy." Writers of the 16th and 17th century gave a different interpretation to the word, which has since been rejected by modern heraldists. The early writers considered abatements to be stains or marks of dishonor placed as punishment upon the shield. Not only did these writers advance this conflicting definition, but they also submitted nine different marks to illustrate its supposed meaning.

These supposed marks were single tinctured figures that were overlayed or intruded upon the arms of the wrongdoer. Each figure was tinctured either tenne or sanguine (livery colors), had a distinctive shape, and was assigned a particular position so as to indicate the specific nature of the offense.

Gerald Legh, in his *Accidens of Armorie,* 1562, was among the first English writers to mention these "abatements." A much respected Officer of Arms and writer, John Guillim, writes of these marks in his *Display of Heraldry,* 1610, and abatements are again defined in Favine's *Theatre of Honour and Knighthood,* 1619. Another Frenchman, De la Colombiere, also deals with this subject in one of his books, *La Science Heroique* (English translation), 1648. Selden, in his *Titles of Honour,* 1673, places the same meaning on the word abatement, as his predecessors.

The marks are described below with the offense related to each:

1. A delph tenne—for revoking a challenge.
2. An escutcheon reversed sanguine—for deflowering a maid or widow.
3. The entire coat reversed—for treason.
4. A point dexter tenne—for boasting of marshal acts.
5. A point in point sanguine—for cowardice.
6. A point Campion tenne—for killing a prisoner.
7. A gore sinister tenne—for fleeing from his colors.
8. Two gussets sanguine—for adultery.
9. A plain point sanguine—for lying to the sovereign or general. Drunkenness is alternately mentioned as the basis for this mark.

Two distinguished barristers at law, C. and A. Lynch-Robinson, in their book *Intelligible Heraldry,* 1949, place belief in the former existence of these marks. They submit, as they would a point of law, that if there are proven marks of honor (augmentations), there must surely be marks of dishonor to balance them. This position taken in modern times is unusual since post-Medieval writers as early as M. A. Porny in 1795 have taken a negative view on the existence of marks of dishonor.

The full truth on "abatements" may never be established as early writings have been shown to be clouded with mis-information and theories based on the morals and thinking of the day.

Much authoritative criticism has been registered against many of the early heraldic writers for their fanciful interpretations of symbols and other matters, so their writings on this subject must also be judged in the same light. Aside from this fact, no dishonorable marks of this type appear in any existing or recorded arms.

In opposition to the writings that propose such marks existed are contemporary accounts describing the wrongdoer's shield being dragged through a dung pile or being torn apart rather than being marked as earlier suggested. This would indicate, at least, that *some* punitive action *was* taken affecting the shield. Doubt has been expressed by armorists that any family's arms would be expected to permanently (or even for a long period of time) display such marks of dishonor even had they actually existed.

This being the case, their traces would be extremely hard to unearth. It might also be possible—but not probable—that these marks may have been proposed but never acted upon. Some heraldic writers were also officers at arms either in France or England, so that one of them may have suggested the use of such marks, introducing them prematurely in a treatise on heraldry. Later writers may have later presumed them to be in effect. This is all theorizing, however, and no positive credence should be placed upon it.

The early position taken on abatements serves some constructive purpose in the final analysis. In listing the misdemeanors and crimes of which these supposed marks were indicative, we indirectly learn of the high standards of virtue that were set for the man-at-arms in those days.

The supposed marks of abatement can be found on page 177. They are seen in the playing cards printed in 1675 by Richard Blome.

27

Heraldic Playing Cards

Playing cards made their appearance in Europe during the latter part of the 14th century. While their introduction to all countries was almost simultaneous, it is believed that Italy was the first country to receive them from the Orient, and there is definite logic to support this theory.

Venice was the first European stop for ships returning from the East. It had already been established that the Chinese had invented cards. Therefore, in all likelihood, sailors and merchants disembarking at this port would have occasion to display them here prior to other European cities.

The first Chinese cards used symbols adopted from those found on their paper money, such symbols denoting different values. European nations created new symbols for decks of their own design. The French in the early 15th century developed the suit symbols that are presently used. These suit designs were attributed to a famous knight, Etienne Vignoles, also called Lahire. These cards were called by their French names as follows:

Coeurs	(hearts)
Carreaux	(diamonds)
Trefles	(clubs)
Piques	(spades)

About 1440 kings appeared on *court cards* in the form of French heroes, namely Lancelot, Roland,

Arms of Four Fraternities of French playing Card Makers (upper left, Card Makers of Paris; upper right, Card Makers of Rouen; lower left, Card Makers of Lyons; lower right, Card Makers of Le Mans)

French Playing Cards (left, Prince of Carreaux; right King of Clubs), from Heraldic Playing Cards *of C. Oronce Fine de Brianville, 1655–1665. (Courtesy the John Omwake Playing Card Collection on permanent loan to the Cincinnati Art Museum from the United States Playing Card Company)*

Valery, and Hogier. Later in the century, Caesar, Charlemagne, Alexander, and David replaced the earlier figures as kings and the former group became knaves in the deck.

Queens, which were also a part of these early French decks, were supposed to represent Joan of Arc, Judith of Bavaria, the biblical Rachel, and Marie Anjou. The way that these and the other court cards were generally assigned to suits is as follows:

KING	Spade	— David
	Heart	— Charlemagne
	Diamond	— Julius Caesar
	Club	— Alexander the Great
QUEEN	Spade	— Joan of Arc
	Heart	— Judith of Bavaria

	Diamond	— Rachel
	Club	— Marie Anjou
JACK	Spade	— Hogier the Dane
	Heart	— Lahire
	Diamond	— Roland or Hector
	Club	— Lancelot

In 1655, one of the earliest decks of heraldic playing cards was created. With heraldry a science, it had become a practice to teach it mainly to the youth of the privileged class inasmuch as it involved them. In this form, heraldic cards essentially served the same purpose as the flash cards do for youngsters today. Additionally, the color and symbolism of heraldic devices fitted into the styling already well established in playing cards.

The creator of this early heraldic deck was a Frenchman named C. Oronee Fine de Brianville. Each suit of these cards represented the arms of a separate European country not including England. De Brianville's original deck was repeated in a second series in 1659 and a third in 1665. These decks were reproduced in Italy in 1667, 1681, and 1715.

In 1692, a French priest named Father Menestrier

French Playing Cards, 1692. Four of Fleurdelys and the Roy des Fleurdelys, from Jeu de Cartes du Blason *by Pere F. C. Menestrier, 1692. (Courtesy the John Omwake Playing Card Collection on permanent loan to the Cincinnati Art Museum from the United States Playing Card Company)*

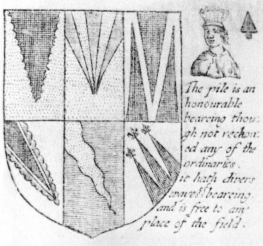

The pile is an honourable bearing though not reckoned any of the ordinaryes. ...e hath divers ...oues bearing, and is free to any place of the field.

(1) O. a pile engrailed S. (2) O. 3 piles B. (3) A. 3 piles one issuing out of the cheife between 2 others reversed S. (4) A. a pile in bend issuing out of ye dexter corner S. cottised engrailed G. (5) B. a pile waved issuing out of ye dexter corner bendwayes O. (6) A. a tripple pile flory on ye topps issuing out of ye sinister base in bend S.

The saltier was made ye hight of a man and was driven full of Pinns, and served to scale ye walls of a Citty.

(1) A. a saltier G. (2) B. a saltier quarterly quartered O. & A. (3) G. a saltier O. surmounted of anether S. (4) ¼ pale A. & B. a saltier counterchanged.

This ordinary as ye rest is born engrailed wavy or the like er between, or charged with a charge as ye ordinaryes are.

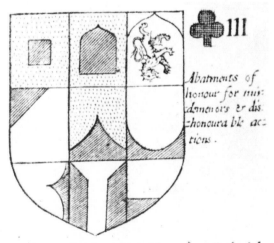

Abatements of honour for misdemenors & dishonourable actions.

(1) A. a delph tenne due to him yt revolketh a challenge. (2) O. an Escocheon reversed sanguine, due for deflowering a maid or widdow. (3) ye whole (Ceate reversed viz. a lyon rampant) due to a traitor. (4) A. a poynt dexter tanne, due for too much bosting of his marshall acts. (5) a poynt in poynt sanguine due to a coward. (6) O. a poynt Campion tenne, due to him yt billeth his prisoner. (7) A. a gore sinister tenne, due for flying from his colours. (8) A. 2 gussets sanguine, due for adultry. (9) O. a plaine poynt sanguine, due for telling lyes to his soueraigne, or Generall.

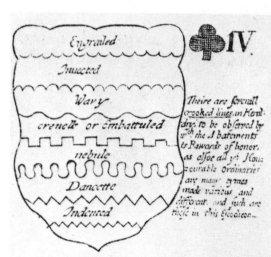

Engrailed
Invected
Wavy
crenelle or embattuled
nebule
Dancette
Indented

Theire are severall crooked lines in Heraldry, to be observed by wch the Abatements & Rewards of honor, as allso all ye Honourable Ordinaryes are many tymes made various and different, and such are those in this Escocheon.

And note yt when any of ye sd charges are drawn with any of ye sd lines, then they are to be blazoned a Cross, a cheif, Bend, saltier &c. engrailed, Invected, wavy or the like.

English Playing Cards, 1888. Facsimiles of a heraldic series by Richard Blome, printed in 1675. They were issued by the Worshipful Company of Playing Card Makers, London, in 1888, and given at first to the ladies at the annual banquet of that year. (Courtesy the John Omwake Playing Card Collection on permanent loan to the Cincinnati Art Museum from the United States Playing Card Company)

English Playing Cards, 1686. King of Clubs from the Arms of the English Peers in 1684. (Courtesy the John Omwake Playing Card Collection on permanent loan to the Cincinnati Art Museum from the United States Playing Card Company)

created another heraldic deck. He also did a treatise on heraldry that has been cited by later writers in this field. A French printer named Daumont produced still another deck in 1698.

The earlier Deck created by Lahire was made expressly for *piquet*, a game of knights and chivalry. The card we call *jack* originally was *knave* and meant son. The Spaniards called him *rogue* or *jack a napes*, from whence it was shortened to jack.

The English also created some heraldic decks in the 17th century. The deck by Richard Blome in 1675 used the heart suit to denote ten persons of rank from king to squire. The three other suits outlined the various charges of heraldry. Another deck titled "The Arms of the English Peers" followed in 1684. A decade later, a Scottish goldsmith produced a deck with a lengthy title, "The Blazoning of the Ensignes Armorial of the Kingdoms of Scotland, France and Ireland and of the coats of arms of the Nobility of Scotland." This is the only known deck of Scotch origin.

The dress and figure of Henry VIII is that which is presently seen in modern playing cards. The Queens are symbolic of Elizabeth of York. The flower carried by the Queen is the Tudor rose symbolizing her marriage to Henry of Lancaster, ending the War of Roses.

28

The Tournament

Heraldry received the greatest momentum—if not its spark of life—from the tournaments of the Middle Ages. Ironically, the exact origin of these events has never been fully established. The Germans in the tenth century were known to have some similar form of contest, but it has been found that rules for the tournament as we know it were first devised in the year 1066. The proponent of these rules is said to be a Frenchman, Geoffroi de Preulli of Anjou. He is not to be confused with the Geoffrey of Anjou, who in a later century is cited in the origin of heraldry.

The first manuscript record of tournaments conducted under such rules comes to us in the 11th century. These martial exercises, as the tournaments were sometimes called, were designed both as preparatory training for war and as a means of displaying individual skill and prowess with weapons. The fact that tournament rules were founded in the year of the Norman invasion of England may be significant.

The derivation of the word *tournament*, like the origin of the event itself, is an unsettled point. An author writing close to the period of the tournament says that the word comes from *par tour*, which in French means "by turns." This is the manner in which the French horseman, with outstretched lance, charged the quintain, an upright post with or without a suspended shield serving as a target.

The obvious purpose of these targets was to improve aim, and they later became more varied or complex. Another form of these lance targets was a dummy on a post equipped with a wooden sword. If a designated space between his eyes was not hit properly, the dummy would pivot around on contact and slap the horseman sharply with the sword. Sandbags were also rigged with a pivot system to pound the thruster of a misdirected lance.

A later form of the quintain was again a post, but with a metal bar affixed to it at right-angles. From this bar a ring held in spring tension was the target of the horseman. This exercise was aptly called *running at the ring*. The intent of the horseman in this case was to strike the ring and transfer it to his lance point. This exercise, like the other, was without particular risk of injury and so was popular as a general sport for a long period. It also could be practiced with weapons other than the lance.

This practice was in preparation for the joust, which, in addition to demanding accurate lance aim, called for steadiness in the saddle and quick disposal of the splintered lance stump after body contact. The term *joust* has been wrongly applied to mean the same thing as tournament. A tournament was a contest of *group* participation or *en masse*, with troop against troop on horseback. The joust was *individual* combat, mainly with lance and always within an enclosure called *the lists*. The sword, in contrast to the jousting lance, was

Jousts at Ingleleuerch, from "Froissart's Chronicales,"
British Museum

the tournament's main weapon, but not necessarily its only weapon. Tournaments could and did include jousts but either event could be run independently.

The early tournaments were like a simplified version of modern army maneuvers, but unlike the latter war games tournaments were also intended to entertain an audience of assembled townspeople. Participants were usually divided into two forces of mounted troops who carried out a pre-arranged series of strategies. Their weapons were generally rebated swords (unpointed and dull edged) and no injuries were intended. In the heat of a mock skirmish, however, spirits were high and often the strategy and the rules were forgotten. It was not long before the *melee*, as it was called, was completely out of control.

Numerous fatalities were not uncommon as a result, and in Germany, for instance, in the year 1240, 60 deaths occurred during one such tournament. In addition, many of the jousts between individual contestants became angry or rough events ending in death or crippling injuries. It was understandable in the light of these influences that some English sovereigns banned the tournament from being conducted within the kingdom. Such bans occurred four times in the 13th century, in 1220, 1234, 1255, and 1299. The Pope also threatened participants with excommunication. This did not deter the more adventurous knights and nobles from traveling to France where tournaments were still allowed.

Richard I (the Lion Hearted), himself an adventurer, revived the tournaments in England and later Edward III did much to encourage and enhance them. The latter sovereign held an event in 1344 on an invitational basis, in which 40 of the best competitors from six nations vied for prizes. A special feast was arranged as a part of the affair and this, with the tournament itself, became a yearly ritual from that year forward.

The meeting arranged by Edward the III to select specific jousting opponents or teams became known as a "round table." In time, about 1352, he actually did construct a round wooden table of huge proportions, which he housed within a circular building measuring 200 feet in diameter. This was apparently done in emulation of the fabled King Arthur, who thus avoided showing partiality or precedence in his seating arrangements. The feast with its dance and the jeweled prizes of the tournament were a great inducement toward wide participation. In some tournaments sponsored by royalty or nobility, even the necessary armor and weapons were provided.

The lists or spectator stands usually had no more than four to six rows of simple benches that rose to about six feet from the ground at the highest tier. There were, however, special higher galleries for the ladies and distinguished guests. These galleries were vividly decorated with bunting and the shields of the tournament leaders. The number of benches set up for any given tournament depended, as a rule, upon the number of contestants participating.

The first authorized lists for tournaments were all in the south of England and were five in number. The earliest lists were open at both ends except for a simple barrier. Later these lists became enclosed quadrangles with high double barriers at the ends to keep the horses from leaping over at the end of a gallop. The choice of location of future lists often depended on whether a town had a banquet hall large enough for the feast held in conjunction with the tournament. A typical size tournament field ran 270 feet wide by 350 feet long, or one-quarter longer than wide.

Prior to the tournament, the squires (attendants) of the competitors would both guard and display their master's crest, shield, or other identifying personal devices. Since an unhorsed knight could be trampled by other hoofs, these attendants would be ready to spring from between the barriers to drag their master off to safety. There was also a danger of injury from the impact of the fall itself. This was minimized by a thick covering of sand and leather remnants from tanning.

At the start of an event, trumpets sounded and heralds announced the entry of each contestant. Musical flourishes could be heard at each dramatic moment of the joust—especially at the moment of victory. The winner of personal combats usually was awarded the armor and the horse of the loser. If the loser was still alive, he could pay a ransom for the retaining of this equipment.

Chivalry was evident in these contests since the competitors displayed tokens of favor from the ladies on their lances or crests. The women were also honored with the privilege of awarding the prizes to the victors. The custom of affixing a ladies ribbon, garment strip, or kerchief to the helmet crest led eventually to the development of two more heraldic devices—the torse and mantling. These became regular crest accessories.

Chivalrous acts were not solely extended to the fairer sex. The rules of the tournament specified that courtesies be granted to one's opponent, especially if that opponent be fallen or disarmed. Rules varied at the discretion of the marshal or sponsor but they generally added up to the following:

1.) No lances shall be pointed (except by agreement of opponents).
2.) No blows shall be aimed below the waist.
3.) No blows shall be struck at a man's back or while he is disarmed.
4.) Striking a horse or saddle is banned.
5.) No contestant shall be allowed to lay hands on his opponent or his opponent's weapon.
6.) No contestant shall strike the tilt (barrier) with lance.

Violations of these rules were treated in three different ways. The most serious offenses called for imprisonment and forfeiture of horse and armor. Intermediate violations meant disqualification, and lesser infringements meant loss of points in the scoring system.

The scoring system was generally arranged to award

Banquet hall at Knole, a room typical of those halls used for tournament "round tables" and feasts

points or *strokes* in grades of one, two, or three points as shown below:

 a.) Breaking a lance fairly on the body above the waist—1 point.

 b.) Breaking a lance on the shoulder or helmet—2 points.

 c.) Unhorsing the opponent—3 points.

The points scored during a joust were kept on tablets called *checques*. Responsibility for keeping these points correctly marked on these boards rested with the King of Arms or his assistant (Pursuivant of Arms). A typical list of scores showed each participant's name and personal armorial bearings followed by a rectangular form called a parallelogram. This device had a horizontal line running through its center that was continued a full length past it to the right side.

On this center line's extension, the number of short vertical strokes placed upon it indicated the total number of courses in which the contestant had participated. The part of the center line *within* the rectangle had a stroke or point for each lance well broken. The upper line of the box-like form recorded *attaints*, or fairly struck blows to the opponent's head or body. The strokes of the lower line indicated lances ill-broken (those lances that splintered less than a foot from the point, or coronal).

Prizes were also awarded for the best single performance or single blow with each of the various weapons used in a tournament or joust.

Under certain conditions pointed lances or weapons were allowed in jousts upon mutual agreement of the opponents. This occurred generally in meetings be-

Richard, Erle of Beauchamp, justying at Gynes; he cast to the grounde at his spere poynt behynde the horse taile, the Knyght called the Chevaler Ruge c. 1410.
Cotton Ms. Julius E. iv. British Museum.

tween French and English knights where known hostility between the countries existed. In some cases the joust was undertaken by both sides with the knowledge that it would be to the death. Such contests were called *jousts of war* or *joutes à outrance* in contrast to the usual *joust of peace* or *joust of courtesy.*

The death struggles could only be stopped short of fulfillment by the umpire officially casting his baton to the ground. This usually was the case where both sides were able to deal smart but not critical blows or where one opponent was lying helpless. Another struggle less inclined to be interrupted was called *judicial combat,* where an accused man's guilt or innocence was adjudged by his success in a jousting duel. This often directly pitted the accuser against the accused.

The lances used in jousts were about 12½ feet long, or two feet longer than the quintain lance, which incidently weighed seven pounds. The first jousting lances (13th century) were plainly blunted, but later ones (14th century) were fitted with a coronal, a lance head resembling a crown with three flattened points. Additionally, the lances were made of light woods that were prone to splinter with the exertion of moderate force. These two factors reduced injury to a good degree.

As time went by, the rules for jousting became stricter. The 15th-century tournaments required an oath of chivalry from its participants prior to the event. An extra safeguard employed was the *tilt* or wooden fence between the jousters along their line of gallop. This was an improvement on an earlier tilt, which was merely a rope divider with a cloth draped over it along its length. The purpose of the wooden tilt was to prevent the frequent collision of horses.

Armor was becoming more protective as well. A metal shoulder piece called the pauldron came into use about 1430. The top edge flanged out and upward to protect the neck to some degree. The left elbow pieces, or coudieres, became larger and all arm defenses generally improved.

In the 16th-century armor used for jousting became specialized. The upper side of the body, which was more vulnerable to the lance, received extra attention. The breastplate became rounder with the front curved slightly downward to favor the stomach area. A shoulder plate called the *grande garde* now fitted over the pauldron to further protect the left shoulder during jousts. In a certain joust called the Italian or Free

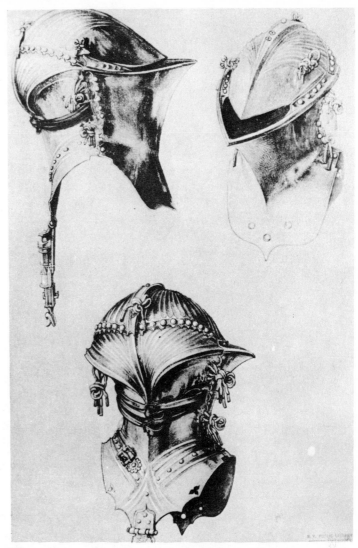

Three views of tournament helmet designed by Hans Holbein (circa 1530)

Course, a concave shield was fixed to the left shoulder. This was the *manteau d' armes.*

To protect the elbow from lance thrusts, a metal piece called the *polder miton* was attached to the vambrance or forearm guard. A neck piece something like the mentonniere protected the neck and lower face. This was called the *volante piece.* Special lance rests called *queues* were attached to the breastplate to absorb the weight. All types of refinements were of course made, but the above changes are the main ones concerned with jousting.

The pageantry of the tournament reached its most colorful heights during the reign of Henry VIII. Fanciful ceremonies and bright attire marked these West-

Tournament armor, early 16th century. From the Royal
Armory at Madrid, founded by King Charles V

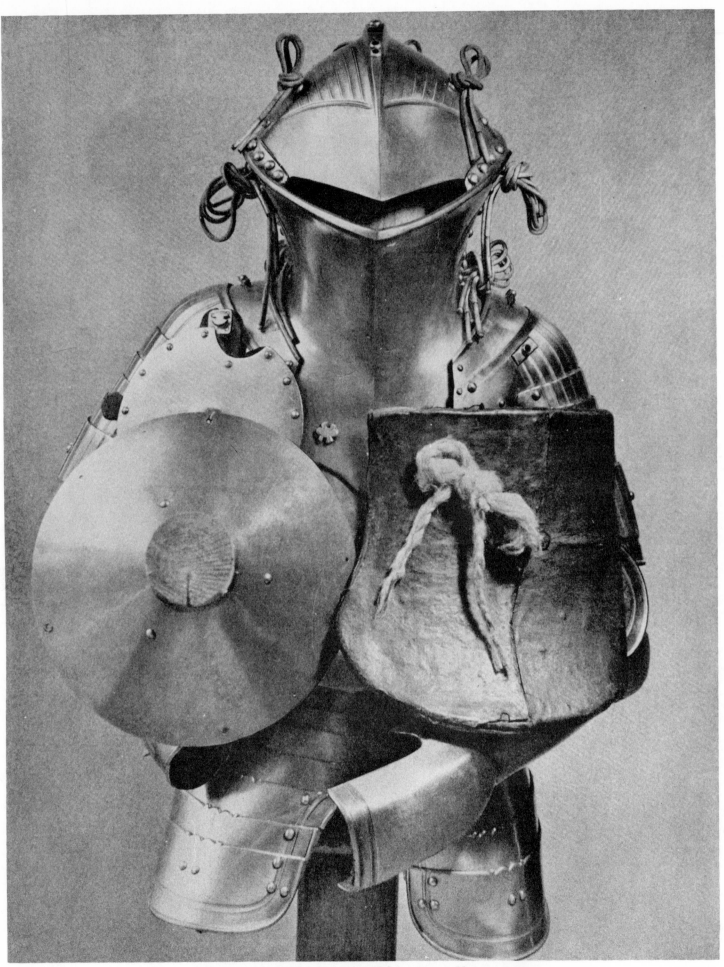

German tournament armor, 16th century. Note manteau
d'armes and helmet lacing. The lacing is depicted in the
collar of the Order of the Garter and is the basis for the
aiguillette, a later military figure

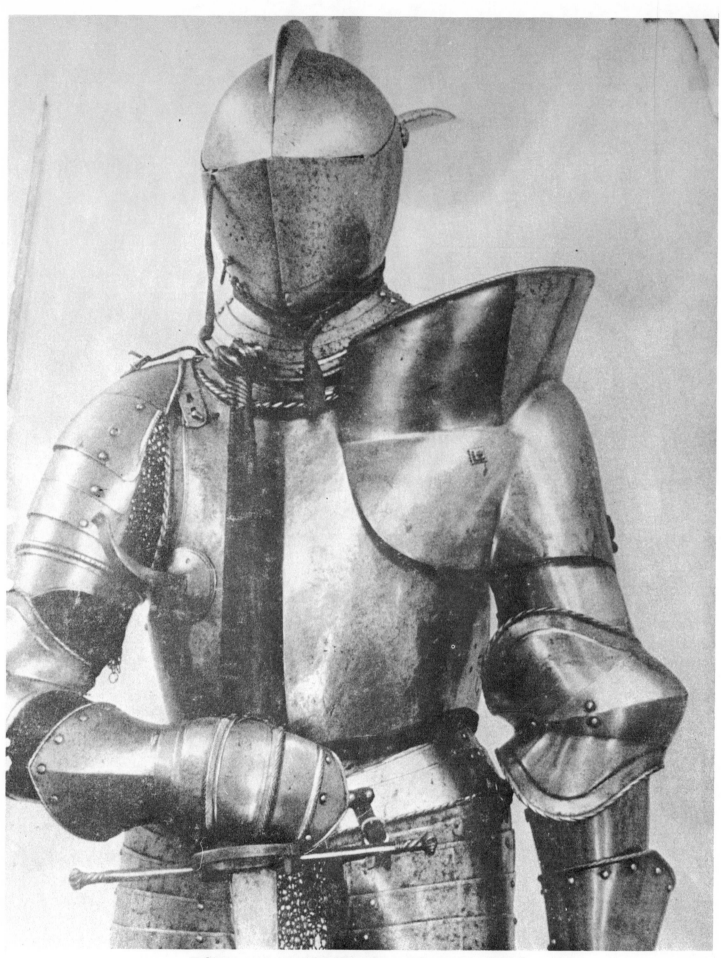

Italian armor, circa 1500. Note the grand guard on the left shoulder as well as the enlarged coudière. The two-handed sword has a hilt of considerable length

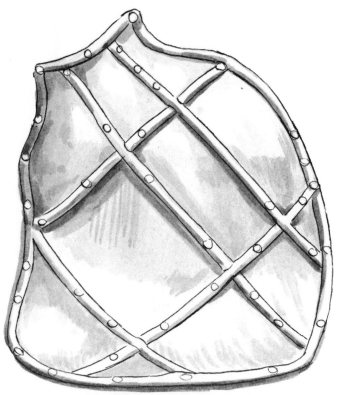

Manteau d'armes (circa 1580)

Sixteenth-century armor displaying Grand Guard

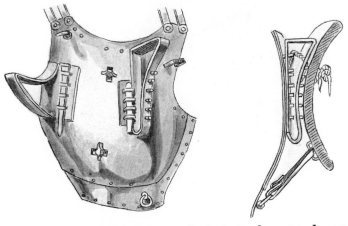

Manteau d' armes, showing method of attachment to breast-plate

German armor for man and horse, 1533

Detailing of horse armor, bridle and saddle

minster jousts of the early 16th century. The horses' trappings were no less resplendent than the gold and silver robes of the contestants themselves. The armor proper had reached its highest stage of development with gold filigree often etched into black and silver plating.

Horse armor originated in the 12th century in the same boiled leather form employed in human body defenses. The horse's head plate was called the *chamfron;* the laminated neck piece, the *crinet;* and the body skirt was referred to as the *peytral.* By the late 15th century complete steel armor was developed for the horse. These horse defenses or *bards* were normally covered by a cloth blanket termed a *trapper.* The trapper served as another vehicle upon which the knight could display his arms or achievements. Horses were often blindfolded and their ears plugged to prevent rearing at the moment of impact in a joust.

The special craftsmanship of an armor suit made a good many as relatively costly to own *then* as a luxury automobile is to own at the present time. Under those circumstances, the quick stripping away of the armor from a fallen knight by the victor is somewhat understandable for that time. However protective the armor became, its weight increased proportionately. A jouster could be carrying 80 or 90 pounds of metal. As a result, his horse with his own armor plus his master could be burdened with as much as 340 pounds.

It is small wonder then that the dramatic gallops of the past settled down to mild trots under this load. This and the development of the musket eventually brought the tournament period to its close.

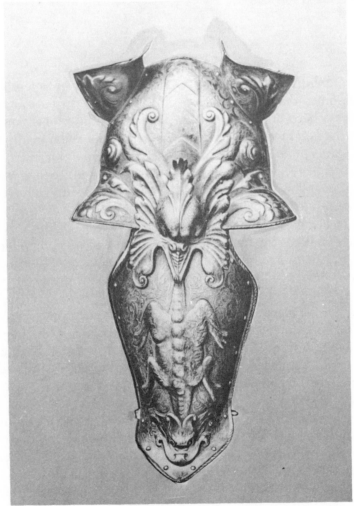

Horse's head armor, 16th century. This armor piece is called a chamfron

29

Armor and Coats of Arms

With the development of heraldry, the display of personal devices spread to areas other than the surfaces of shields. One of the places where arms could be found was on the tunic that the knight wore over his armor. This type of outer garment worn with the earliest of heraldic devices was called the *surcoat.*

The surcoat was a long, loose-flowing, sleeveless tunic. It was usually white or self-colored with a slit down the front and perhaps down the rear to facilitate horseback riding and general mobility. This tunic, like other types that would follow it, had a three-fold value: it prevented the heat from the sun's rays building up on the armor and thus making it unbearably hot for the wearer; it afforded protection against the effect of rain upon the armor itself; and most important, it was eventually used as a symbol of identification, what with the shield or personal device soon to be affixed upon it. This, in fact became the first "coat of arms."

King John, brother of Richard the Lion Hearted, was considered the first sovereign to wear this surcoat, while Richard was believed to be the first king to bear arms upon it. King John's personal seal depicts him in this tunic. In a like manner, other early 13th-century seals of the royalty of France and Scotland show them similarly attired.

The appearance of the surcoat coincided with a period of change in defensive armor. As a consequence this period was generally referred to as "the Surcoat Period" in armor. This time span (1180–1250) was also known as the chain mail period. Interlinked chain mail was substituted for the *jezeraint,* mascled and scale armor of the preceding Norman period.

Also new to body defense was the *pot-helm,* a closely fitting iron head-covering with no openings except eye slits (occularia). This innovation, as suggested in Chapter 1, had as much or more to do with the origin of heraldry than any other factor, since it alone created a need for a new means of personal identity in battle or tournament.

The pot-helm, in some cases looking much like an inverted metal cooking utensil, was either flat or nearly flat on top. It did not quite reach the shoulders, being supported by the head itself. Since the helmet top necessarily touched the head, an iron skull cap (*pot-de-fer*) was worn beneath it. This pot-de-fer was usually placed under the chain-mail hood (*coif-de-mailles*) worn at this time.

The first pot-helms, as earlier stated, had no holes except for eye slits. Whatever little air the wearer was able to get came from these holes. Later gratings or rows of holes (*ventaille*) were created below the occularia for breathing purposes. During this same period,

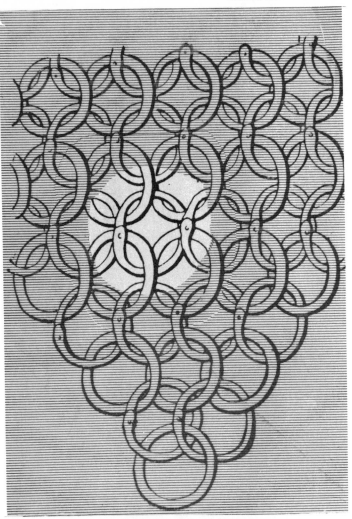

Chain mail detail. Highlighted circular area shows one link interlinked with four others around it

ticated crest of all is credited to Richard I (The Lion Hearted), who displayed a helmet with a fan or winged-shaped metal ornament atop his helmet plus an embossed lion on the crown.

The last important defensive change was the styling of the shield. The *heater shape* described in Chapter 2 gradually came into wide and prolonged usage during the Surcoat Period. The first devices upon it, however, were non-heraldic in nature for a time. As a last thought on this period, it should be understood that most of its innovations slightly *preceded* their application to heraldic usage.

In the next armor period (1250–1325) the surcoat remained in style but armor continued to change. Banded mail supplemented, then succeeded, chain

the crest was introduced to armor and to heraldry. This was an ornamentation fastened to the top of the helmet. Because of its hard leather or metal construction, it was also considered to be protective mainly against a sword cut and somewhat helpful against the mace or pole-ax. It was *doubtful* that in its initial use the crest was meant to bear a heraldic device, but the idea of using it for just such purpose was readily adopted.

The names of three men are identified with the first appearance of the crest. The first is Geoffrey, Count of Anjou, the noble also associated with the first example of the true heraldic device. His monument effigy shows him attired in cap whereon one of his lion symbols is affixed. Philip d'Alsace, Count of Flanders (circa 1181), shows a similar device on his helmet. The most authen-

Chain mail hauberk. Hauberks were also constructed of banded mail

mail. Metal shoulder guards called *ailettes* were added to body defense. The conical helm borne on the shoulders succeeded the pot-helm and with it the helmet crest was further developed. The use of plate armor with mail now began.

Banded mail herewith reverted to the old use of

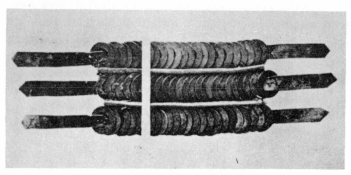

Banded mail reconstructed

narrow hard leather strips as a means of engaging holed metal discs into rows of armor. It was said to have more flexibility than chain mail and yet was more resistant to arrows from the long bow and sword cuts. This body protection remained in use for a hundred years.

Another evil of chain mail was the friction or pull that it placed upon the knees or elbows. Metal plates now covering these body joints allowed the mail to be terminated before reaching these areas. These knee devices, called *genouillieres,* were then joined to the mail at the upper and lower points of termination.

The ailettes or shoulder guards apparently inspired the epaulettes of modern times since the idea of displaying symbolism on a shoulder device is evidenced in both cases. These devices are rarely seen in flat brasses or on effigies but are mainly found on personal seals. The ailette usually sat at an angle so as to protect the neck as well as the shoulder.

Toward the middle of this period the flat top helm was replaced with the *conical helm.* This new defense had for the first time a movable visor that could be raised when not needed. The earlier pot-helm before it had a ventaille (breathing grate) that could only be swung out sideways, if at all.

The crest, while not too different from its initial form of the previous period, displayed better detailing. The fan shape seemed to be the prevalent style, but a new feature entered the scene. This was a decorative

narrow ribbon attached to the point where the crest joined the helm—perhaps to hide an unsightly or crude welding at that juncture. This was the forerunner of the mantling and torse, two future accessories of the crest.

The short period of armor (1325–1335) that next followed was again named for the tunic of its time. This vestment was the *cyclas,* a shorter, more form-fitting covering than the surcoat. It was a unique garment, sleeveless like the surcoat, but with a short, apron-like front well above the knees and then sharply cut downward to fall below the knees in the rear. This

De Bacon. Note leather genouillière of transitional period. Ailettes are also in evidence

odd appearance was heightened by the fact that a multitude of newly combined body defenses awkwardly showed below this short front in layers of varied lengths.

The closest to the body of all these protective sheaths was one called the *haqueton*. It was a stuffed three-quarter length covering, which aside from its defensive role eased the pressure of the armor against the body. While mail was able to resist the actual penetration of a weapon, this defense was meant to lessen the bone or tissue bruise from a heavy blow.

The *hauberk* was usually the next defense donned after the haqueton. It was a jacket of leather strips to which overlapping metal rings or discs were attached. This jacket extended to a length just above the knees with the sleeves ending a little below the elbow.

The breastplate (*plastron-de-fer*) was a third defense of the Cyclas Period. This steel plate, which may have had a companion back piece, was worn over the above-mentioned hauberk. Over the breastplate still another stuffed body covering called the *gambeson* was affixed. It slightly exceeded the length of the hauberk, including sleeve length. The gambeson fitted closely at the neck.

The next period of armor change (1335–1360) was called the "Studded and Splinted Armor Period," a time when no specific image or look prevailed. The main reason for this nondescript appearance was the fact that frequent changes in body defenses were made at this time and none seemed to be satisfactory for very long.

The one constant element of this era was the tunic which was called the *skirted jupon*. It was sleeveless and tight in the waist, but flared out from there into deep folds that ended at the top of the knee. All in all, this tunic was shorter than the cyclas that preceded it. It had the same feature as the cyclas of being longer in the rear but the front-to-back-length difference in this case was very slight.

Three forms of defense shared favor throughout the studded and splinted period: boiled leather, chain mail, and plate. The boiled leather advocates reinforced this defense with an under-layer of banded mail. Others reverted entirely to the early chain mail. The final group experimented with plate armor, which was awkward in this experimental stage but nevertheless laid the groundwork for the more effective plate armor of the later periods.

During this period, attempts were made to improve the defenses of the limbs and feet. This is where the studded and splinted armor was used. Broad strips of leather were used for the arms, elbows, knees, and shins, which were either wholly plated or studded with metal. The term *vambrance* described the studded forearm collar; *cuissarts*, the upper leg defense; *jambarts*, the lower leg plates; and *sollerets*, the overlapping scales or plates of the foot defense.

The appearance of the *jupon* in the next period of armor (1360–1410) signaled the first degree of uniformity seen in body defense since the origin of heraldry. The jupon, incidentally, like all armor cover-

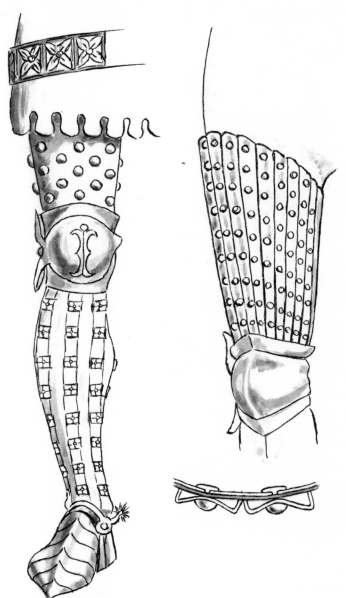

Detail of studded and splinted armor

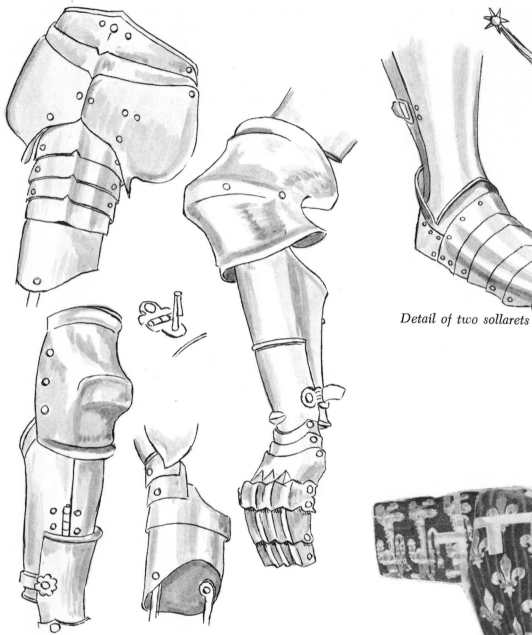

Detail of two sollarets

Details of pauldron, coudière, vambrance, and gauntlet

Jupon of Black Prince

turn freely without drag. The bascinet became rounder at the sides and its near facsimile of the gorget (*the*

French sovereign in Jupon, 15th century

ings before it, was sleeveless but shorter and more body-conforming than ever before. This garment was multi-layered, so as to be fairly stiff, and was usually finished with a rich facing of silk or velvet. In so far as the length was concerned, the jupon ended at the base of the hip and usually was scalloped at the bottom.

The plate metal defenses became dominant and better formed to the body. They also were well coordinated with the portions of chain mail that were still being used between and under these plates. This last matter was especially true in the way the *camail* or mail head covering was linked to the *bascinet* or *barbute*, the pointed headgears of the period.

A relatively brief period of two decades (1410–1430) saw an absence of a cloth covering over armor. This led to the period being dubbed the "Surcoatless" one. Changes in armor were evident, however, and one change was the abandonment of the camail. Another was the simplification of body defenses into one complete plate armor with no more than the padded gambeson underneath to supplement it (circa 1420).

A large neck defense called the *gorget* substituted for the camail's protective function in that body area. This gorget rested on the shoulders rather than on the head as the camail did and thus allowed the head to

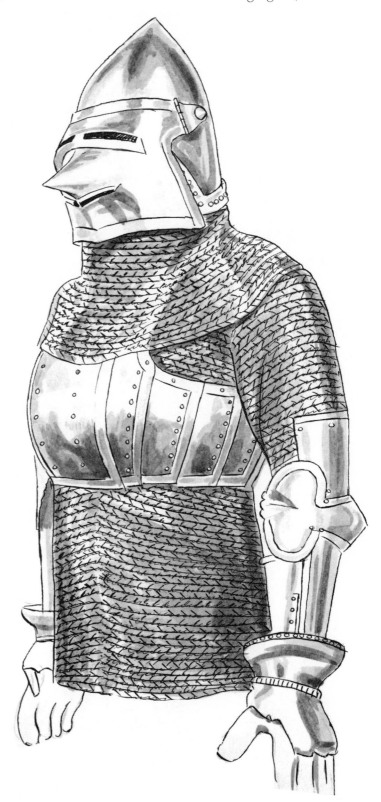

Transitional armor, early Italian breastplate, 1380

Development of armor (left, Chain Mail Period, 1180–1250;
right, Camail and Jupon period, 1360–1410)

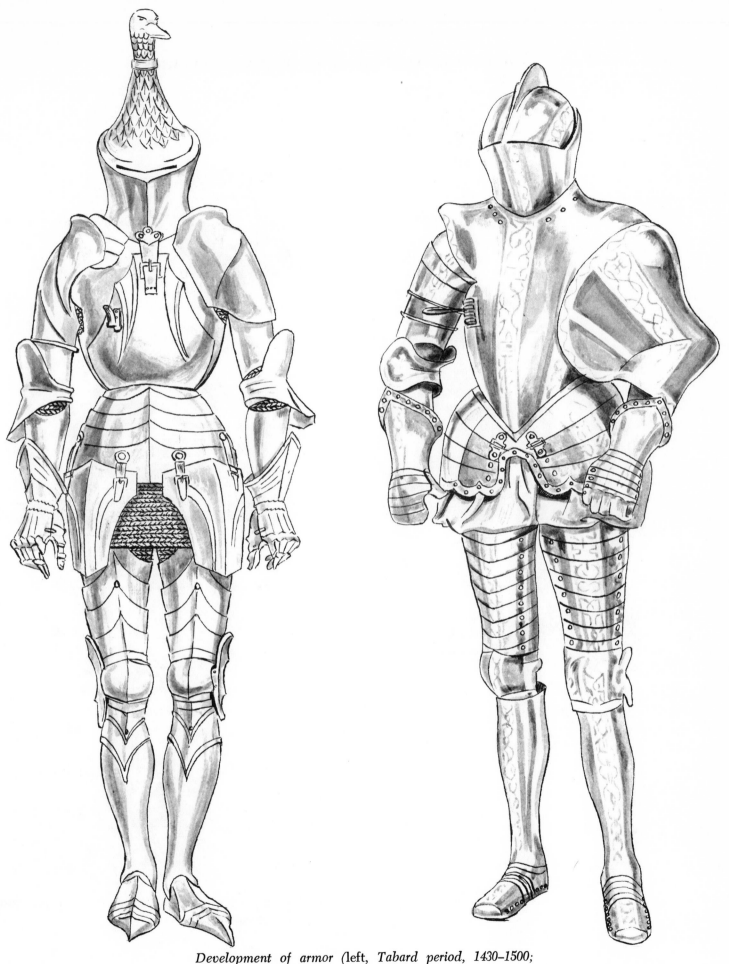

Development of armor (left, Tabard period, 1430–1500; right, Maximilian period, 1525–1600)

Camail attached to bascinet

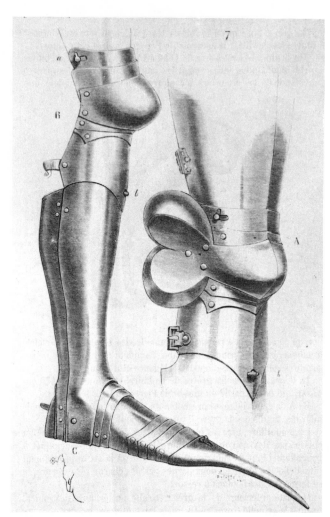

Leg armor. Note fastening points on genouillière

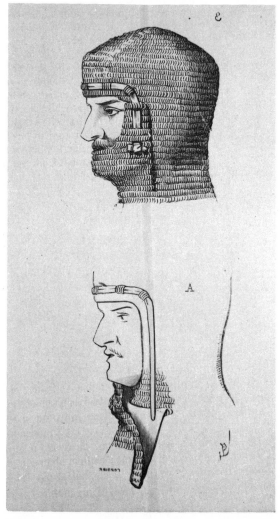

Camail displaying gastening lace (same principle used to attach it to bascinet)

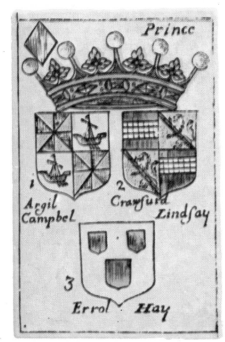

Scottish Playing Cards, 1693. The blazoning of the ensigns armorial of the kingdoms of Scotland, England, France, and Ireland, and of the coats of arms of the nobility of Scotland. (Courtesy the John Omwake Playing Card Collection on permanent loan to the Cincinnati Art Museum from the United States Playing Card Company)

The Tournament

Gothic armor, mid-15th century. This suit features the salade and mentonnière. Also shown is a two-handed sword

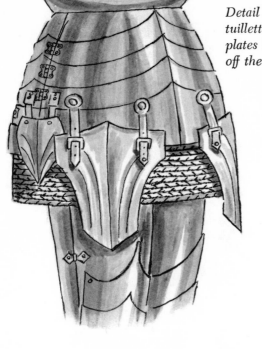

Detail of Tabard period armor showing taces, tuilles, and tuillettes. Taces are the narrow lames, tuilles are the larger plates below taces, and tuillettes are somewhat smaller and off the hip

Puffed and slashed armor, early 16th century. This armor, as the lamboyed of Henry VIII, imitates the dress of the time

Fluted armor, Italian (circa 1480). This armor was eventually discarded because it drew the tournament lance toward vulnerable areas on the body

Etched armor, Milan, 15th century

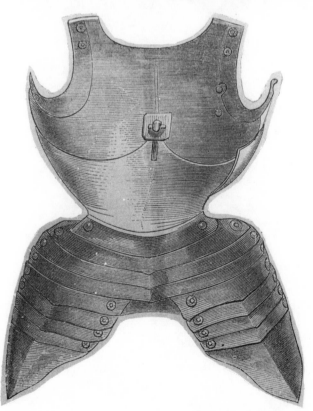

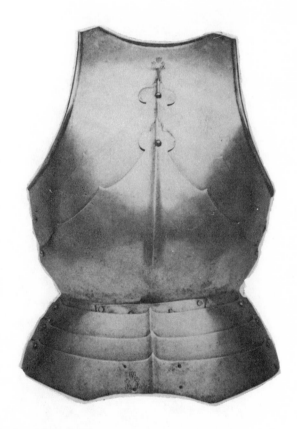

*A demi-placcate, late 15th century. On interior view (left)
note almayne rivet, which allowed the laminated plates
(goussets) to move independently of one another*

Repoussé (hammered) armor, late 16th century

baviere) was pivoted at the temples rather than supported by the shoulders.

The breastplate was further developed and with it the appendages from the waist. The strips or lames of metal suspended thusly were called "taces," and in some suits of armor figured more prominently than the *tuilles* or thigh plates. The coudieres became more intricate.

The general lamination of metal plates became improved and some of these larger plates took on an ornamentation called *fluting*. These were decorative ridges that were embossed into the metal. Armor reached its perfection stage when it also evidenced intricate scroll work etched upon its surface. Some of the vital body defenses were reinforced or enlarged, such as the coudieres.

The narrow overlapping horizontal metal bands called *taces* were gradually reduced in number as they hung between the breastplate and tuilles, while the tuilles, in turn, lengthened to protect the newly exposed thigh area. Spikes were added to the genoullieres and *sabbatons* replaced sollarets. The leg defenses remained about the same but the breastplate developed into a two-part device, the second part of which was called a *demi placcate*.

This two-plate system was ingeniously riveted so that the two parts could move sufficiently apart or together to coincide with the movements of the wearer. The method of riveting throughout was the key to whatever success the Tabard Period had. It gave maximum flexibility and consequently maximum mobility to this picturesque armor.

The "Tabard Period" was the most productive and advanced period of armor thus far in the Middle Ages. The function and strength of body defenses was such that opposing weaponry was hard pressed to cope with

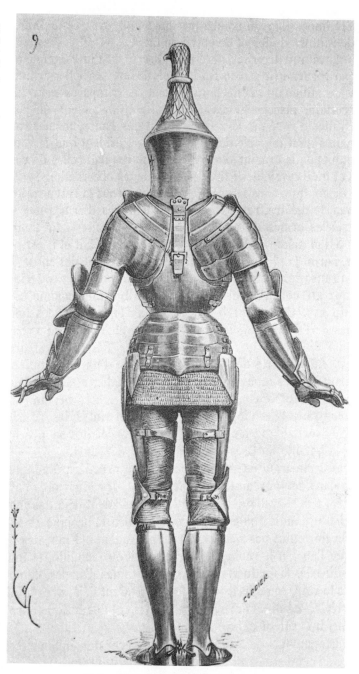

Tabard period armor (rear view)

it. In the next century, when offensive arms improved, armor began its unending decline.

Coats of arms reached their final image in the *tabard*. This jacket was the first to have sleeves, which, while they were only to the elbows, were very loose fitting to accommodate the extensive elbow and shoulder defenses of the next period (1430–1500). The sides of

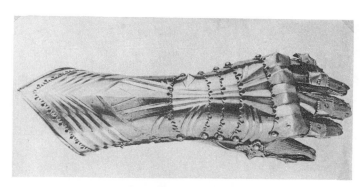

Gauntlet (circa 1480)

Tabard

Salade (circa 1470)

Coats of Arms as seen in monuments (left, Jupon; center,
Tabard; right, Skirted Jupon)

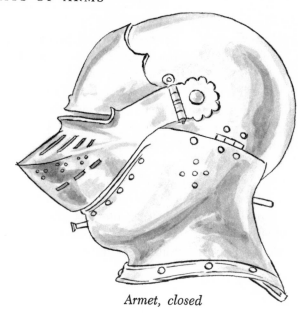

Armet, closed

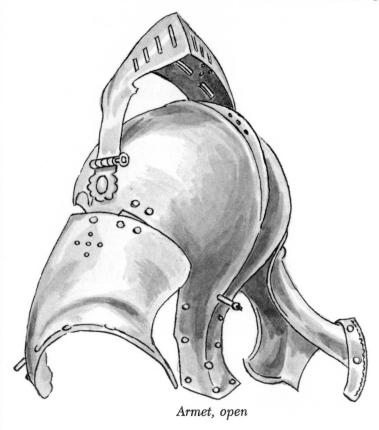

Armet, open

Morion (circa 1570–1580)

Sallet

the tabard were also slit at the sides, probably as an accommodation to the large suspended plates called *tuilles*, which protected the fronts of the upper thigh. The tabard was generally cut short enough to expose the lower half of these tuilles and was fastened by laces to a desirable width at its slit sides.

In the Tabard Period, helmets in particular underwent changes and additions. The orle or decorative wreath appeared on the bascinet, giving it the look of an inverted acorn. The *salade* was introduced from Italy and Germany. This was a distinctive helmet, elongated and pointed in the rear and was usually worn in conjunction with a neck and face defense called a *mentonniere*. This mentonniere's lower section was

fastened to the breastplate and protected the neck while the hinged upper part cupped itself high around the chin so as to protect the nose and cheekbones somewhat.

Another helmet modification occurred in this period. Heretofore helmets had to be made somewhat wider than desired because they were put on by being brought down over the head and so did not fit snugly about the neck. The *armet* was a smaller, specially hinged helmet that could temporarily be widened at the neck for entry and then drawn tight. Its design also allowed the reduced weight to be transferred from the top of the head to the shoulders.

Armor for house pet, 16th century. Note coat of arms near dog's tail

Armor of Henry VIII, presented to him by Emperor Maximilian I. The steel skirt is called a lamboy. It imitates the drapery worn below armor at that time.

German armor of the Maximilian Period (1600s)

30

Weapons

Many of the weapons of the Middle Ages were poled or long-shafted arms. Unlike the ancient spear or javelin, however, they were not intended to be thrown. Some were devices with simple single- or double-edged blades and nothing more, while others combined the pick, spear, and hammer or axe all in one weapon.

Among the simpler poled arms was the *guisarme*, or as it was later called the *fauchard*. This is generally a long, straight, double-edged weapon with a very strong and sharp point. Its edges were also honed so razor-sharp that it inflicted horrible wounds. In time its abolishment was sought. It was considered one of the oldest of the weapons still in use during that era.

The guisarme or fauchard took on several other forms. Some of its blades resembled giant versions of the large blade in a pocket knife. In this case, only one edge was a cutting edge, although the blade was still sharply pointed. In other instances, the blade possessed hooks or spikes to perform other duties for its bearer. As the likeness to a pocket knife blade would indicate, the blade of the guisarme at times curved more sharply than the double-edged form first mentioned.

The *glaive* was a weapon similar to the curved version of the guisarme. It too featured a cutting edge on the convex side of the blade and also displayed hooks and spurs at its base in the manner of the latter arm. The French and Germans used this weapon more than the English.

In some of its forms the *bill* resembled the guisarme, and in some others, the glaive. Its chief difference was that its inner or concave side was the cutting edge. Its origin was a farming scythe that served as a weapon in its basic form during the ninth century. During the ensuing years, it took on modifications but retained its distinctive crescent throughout its development.

The bill remained in use until replaced by the pike in the 15th century. There is a bill of this same century that is much broader in its blade than the usual bill and is straight for most of its length until it curves abruptly at a right angle near its point. This form resembles the linoleum knife used at the present time. The Italian bill also possesses a long S-curving upward hook on its dull side.

The *partisan* is a double-edged weapon of many varieties. Its distinctive feature, whatever its type, is its symmetry both in the blade and the projections that issue from it. Its straight edges taper slowly to a long point in most of its forms. Its hooks or spurs may point either up or down with each type. There are modified partisans called the *ranseur* and the *spetum* that join with the *spontoon, corseque,* and *ox-tongue partisan* to give wide range to this weapon.

The *fork*, like the bill, was derived from a farming implement. It was a two- or three-pronged weapon supplemented with barbs or hooks at the base for added effectiveness. Its first value was to unseat a horseman

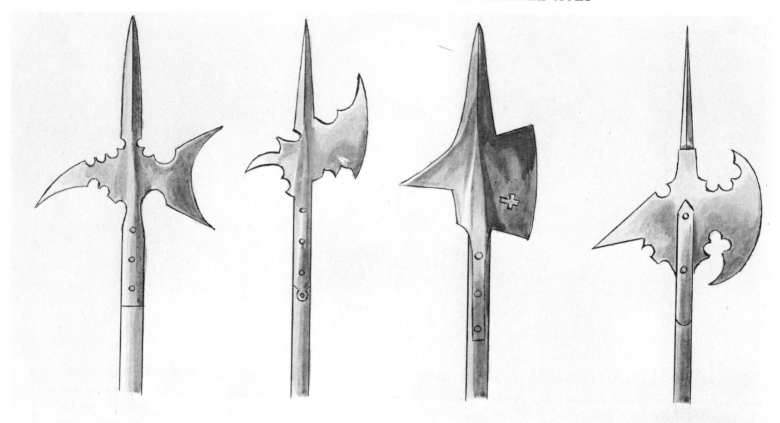

Halberds

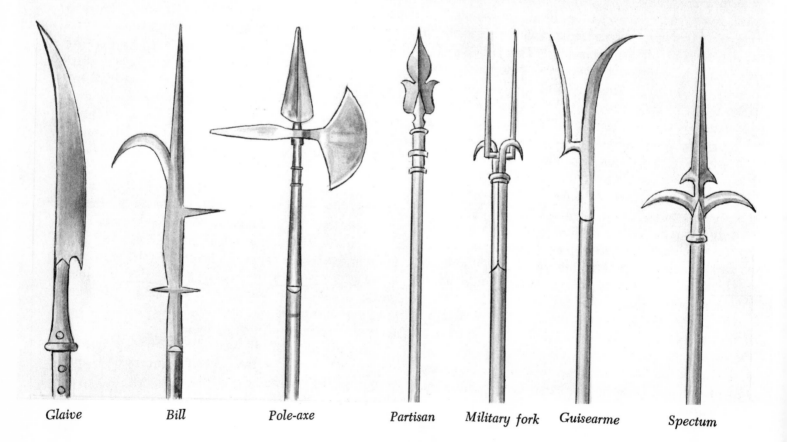

Glaive   *Bill*   *Pole-axe*   *Partisan*   *Military fork*   *Guisearme*   *Spectum*

Weapons

Mace   Bec de Corbin   War hammer   Battle-axe   Mace

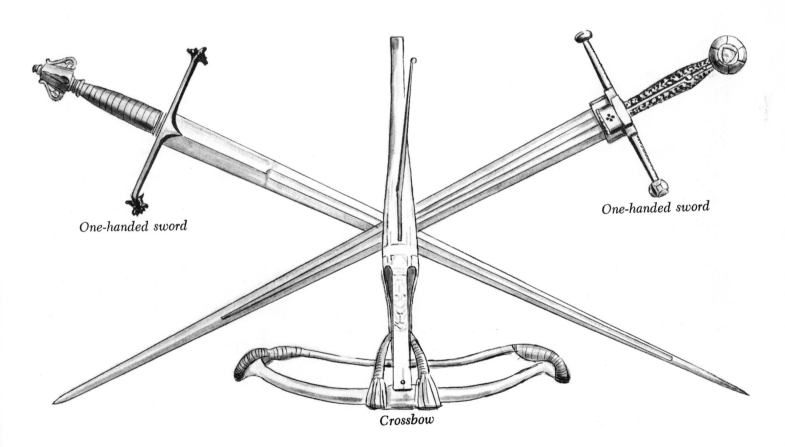

One-handed sword   One-handed sword

Crossbow

Weapons

but later it also served to pull a defender off a battlement. Its main use came during the 14th century but it lasted from the 11th to the 17th.

The *pike* was the predecessor of the modern bayonet. It too was a long, narrow steel lance head. The pole itself was reinforced along a good portion of its length to protect it from sword blows. The pole was generally about ten feet long but some ran as much as 20 feet.

The pike, independent of its shaft, was used in the manner of caltraps to resist cavalry charges. The pike base would be implanted into the ground and anchored by a metal weight. A short pike called a *spontoon* was carried by infantry sergeants during the 18th century. It was distinguished by the metal crossguard at the base.

The *pole-axe* was a combination axe and pick. Its ancestor was the flint-axe of the Stone Age. The pick originally had a straight spike in the Saxon and early Norman period. The spike eventually became fashioned into a bird beak contour in the 14th century while in the same period the blade became longer, wider, and flatter. Between this century and the next, a short double-edge sword blade or spike was added to the head of the shaft.

The *halberd* is perhaps a modification of the basic pole-axe, the most noticeable difference between the two being the numerous notches found on the halberd that served to snare a weapon from the hands of an enemy. Similar to the pole-axe, the halberd contained a pick, a spike, and the axe-head itself. It had an ornamental appearance and when further adorned at the base with gold fringes and tassels it often found use in pageants. This weapon and the bill were both replaced by the pike.

The *lance* was found in two forms. One was the tournament lance of some 12 feet in length and the other was the combat lance five feet in length that was used for fighting on foot. The latter weapon usually had a diamond (lozenge) shape tip and was of uniform thickness from this point to the other end of the shaft.

The tournament lance was normally dulled by a blunted tip called a coronal. These tips were designed to hold fast to the armor but not pierce it. Two types of tournament lances existed. One was a hollow variety that was further reduced in strength by holes periodically placed along its length. Such holes and hollowness would serve to dramatically shatter the lance if well-struck against the opponent's armor. The second

lance was made more solidly with the primary aim being to unseat the opponent with its forceful application.

Several short-shafted weapons were used in the centuries following the Norman Conquest. The *battle-axe* was probably the most common. It was of the same character as the longer shafted pole-axe except that like the other arms that follow it was considered a one-handed weapon. This type of axe had other forms called the *Danish* axe and the *Lochaber* axe. The Danish axe was, in some cases, possessed of a double-axe head, while the Lochaber axe had a hook in the shaft head in place of the spike found in the common battle-axe.

The short-shafted *mace* was a weapon of a more ancient derivation than the poled guisarme. It took on innumerable forms, a shaft with the spiked metal ball being the popular image of the mace. Many of these weapons also had a longer spike continuing from the shaft as did most of the poled arms. Aside from the type with the spikes issuing from an oval or ball shape, there were those maces that contained straight or serrated flanges radiating out from the shaft itself or from a rectangular head.

The mace became a symbol of authority among law officers from the 14th century on. The ornamentation in the lower grip included the Royal Arms as a sign of delegated office and hence more attention was gradually given to the enhancement of this end of the weapon than to the club head. The mace is now a corporate symbol with the arms now appearing in the upper part of the shaft.

The *flail* is another weapon with striking surfaces or parts somewhat like the mace. The important difference is that these parts are not directly joined to the shaft.

Detailing of mace and partisans

Instead they are chained by two or more links to a staple bonded to the shaft. This loose-hanging connection allowed the head of the weapon to build up extra force in being whipped out as it was.

The *Holy Water Sprinkler* is a type of flail that was often used in battle. The name, of course, is a humorous reference to the religious device that is swung in a similar manner. This flail has more than one head form, one being a ball with spikes and the other being without spikes. The head that holds the metal spikes is sometimes made of wood instead of the usual iron.

Another type of flail is called simply the *military flail*. It is a hanging iron shaft with three bands of radiating spikes issuing from it at equal intervals. The French versions of the flail are similar but contain more links between the head and the shaft. Terms for these flails in French are *le godendac, le goupillon,* and *le plommee.*

A type of weapon somewhat related to the mace but decidedly different in contour is the *war-hammer.* Forms of the war-hammer are called the *bec de corbin* and the *martel-de-fer.* These two weapons have a serrated hammer head balanced by a pick or blade on the other side of the shaft head. Some have the spike in the shaft head as well, but these are in the minority. Early martel-de-fers were either short-handled single picks without a hammer or else they were double picks (bisacutas).

Swords appearing in Europe from the 12th to 15th century were mainly of Scandinavian styling. The *broadsword,* a straight wide-bodied, double-edged sword, was the chief weapon seen during this period. Some of these swords lacked cross guards (quillons), which protected the hand from a counter blow. The "tang" or dulled top extension of the blade served as a grip.

Other swords of this era had the same blade characteristics but also possessed the quillons to protect the hand. A third type of sword was one displaying a slightly curved blade.

The grips on these swords were wood covered with skin or occasionally of bone. The pommel, a projection at the end of the grip, was found in triangular, round, and leaf shapes (trefoil or quatrefoil). It was not uncommon for the arms of the bearer to be inscribed in some of these pommels. The cross guards or quillons were plain at first, but they became increasingly ornate as time went by. These quillons were either straight

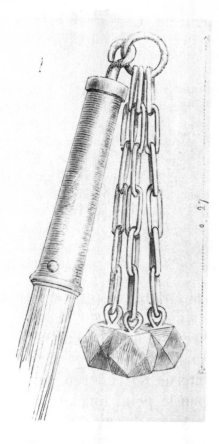
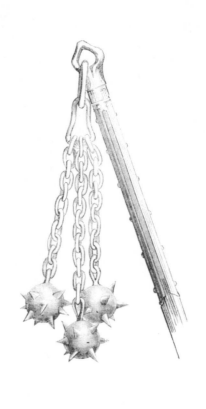
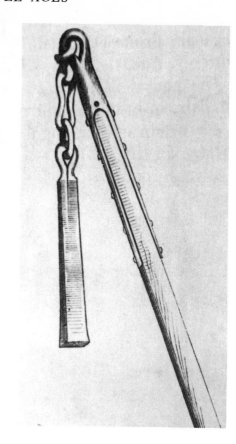

Three types of military flails

or slightly arched downward to deflect an opposing sword.

The blades on these swords all ran about 40 inches in length but the long hilts on some increased the overall height to as much as six feet. These longer swords of the 14th century were called two-handed swords and the hilt length was increased accordingly. The grip was usually more than twice the width of both hands, so that the sword wielder could re-position them for better leverage.

From this extended hilt length, some swords of the one-handed type were so short and wide in the grip as to seem unusable. There was also an in-between hilt length on a sword called the *hand-and-half*. The grip was just long enough to employ a second hand near the pommel, if extra force was needed. This latter sword came into use near the close of the 15th century.

Swords were, of course, individually selected for particular service. The two-handed sword of the 14th century was a foot soldier's weapon, but only effective where enough room (open order) existed between troops to make wide-sweeping blows with it. Not popular in England, it mainly served as a reserve

weapon for a tournament knight who found himself suddenly dismounted. The wavy-bladed "flamberge," circa 1630, is an offshoot of the earlier two-handed sword.

The *falchion* was more the sword used by men-at-arms and archers. Its blade was wide at the point and the edged side was convex with the back concave. In contrast to the two-handed sword, which required swinging room, the *cultellus* was a short sword employed by foot soldiers for close-in fighting. It was used by foot troops to attack knights who had been unseated from their horses, possibly by one of the poled weapons.

An accessory weapon was the *anelace* or *cinquedea*, the Italian dagger from which the former was derived. It possessed a tapered, double-edge blade that was wider at the hilt than most swords. The quillons on this weapon always arched downward. These longer-than-average daggers ran from 18 to 20 inches in length.

The *misericorde* was a dagger more closely proportioned to a triangle than the cingueda. This weapon was used in the latter half of the 14th and early part of the 15th century while the cingueda follows in the middle part of the 15th. A left-handed dagger called

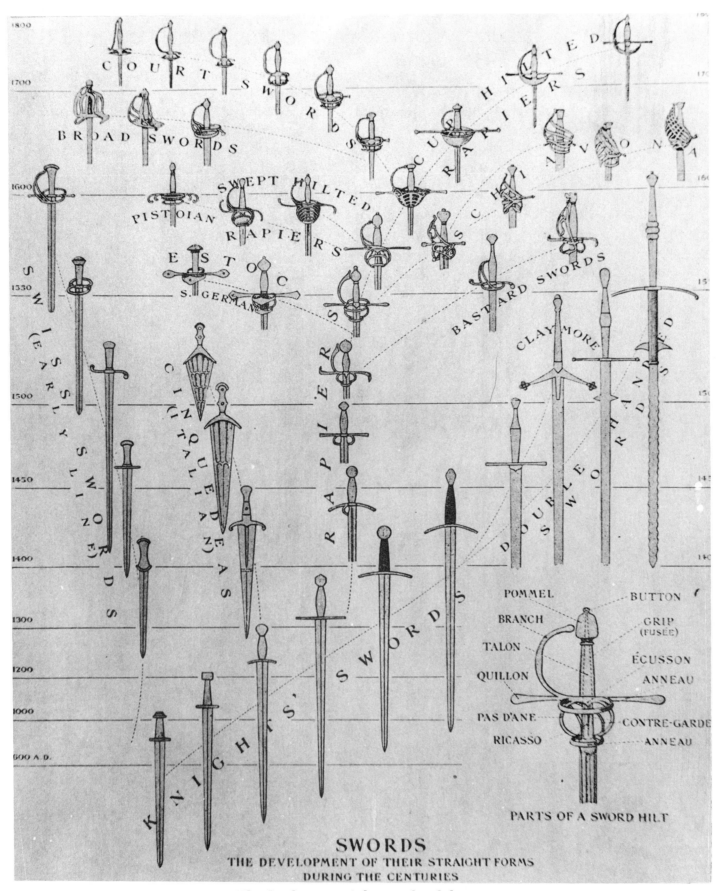

SWORDS
THE DEVELOPMENT OF THEIR STRAIGHT FORMS
DURING THE CENTURIES

The development of the sword and dagger

the *main-gauche* appeared in the 16th century to be used in consort with the right-handed rapier (light, one-handed sword). The main-gauche served the double purpose of parrying blows and also ensnaring the weapon of the foe.

The *scimitar*, which was the forebear of the saber, was introduced toward the middle of the 15th century. It featured a blade sharply curved near the point and a finger guard that was created by the arched extension of one quillon up to the pommel. After 1500,

Hand-and-half and one-handed swords

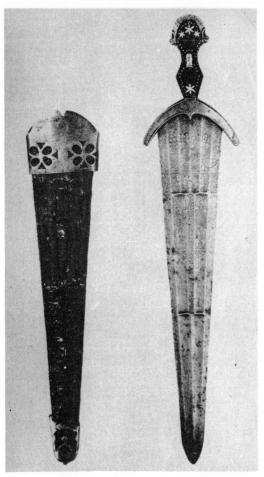

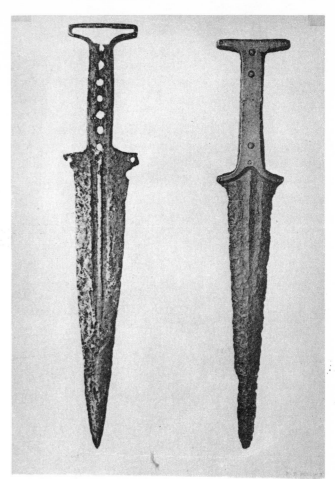

*Cinquedea with tooled leather sheaf, 1490 (left); and
Basilards (right)*

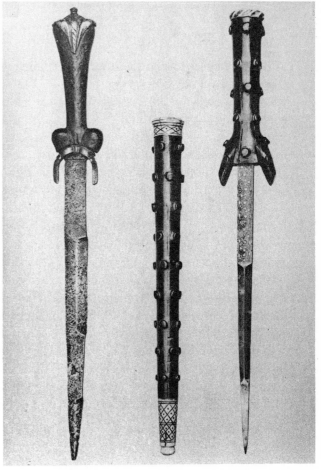

Types of cinquedas (left); types of kidney daggers (right)

Rapiers, 16th century. These swords featured the first finger guards

armorers began to elaborate on these finger guards in the hilt. Knuckle bows were added to the quillon to guard the back of the hand and rings were placed on each of the blades as it met the cross piece. These additions not only protected the hand, but could either break or ensnare an opposing blade.

The *crossbow* is perhaps the most intricate and widely styled hand weapon of the period in question. The first crossbows were drawn by hand, aided by an iron foot *stirrup* at the end of the stock that provided leverage to draw against. This is termed the hand crossbow and originated in the early 14th century.

The *goat's foot crossbow* of the 15th century employed a double lever. The larger of these double levers drew the string back while the smaller arm raised multiple catches that held the string once it was drawn. The bows on these weapons were heavily reinforced with layers of cane, whalebone, and hide. These goat's foot crossbows continued in use into the 16th century.

The *winder* or *wheel and ratchet* crossbow of the 16th century was one involving a separate mechanism fastened to the stock by a strong cord. It was composed of three major parts: a toothed wheel housed in a circular iron case, a long handle to turn the wheel, and a straight ratchet with teeth on one side.

The cogged wheel, when turned by the handle, would enmesh the teeth of the ratchet and draw it through the casing. The ratchet, possessing claws at its far end, would take the bowstring with it as it was drawn into the housing. When fully drawn, the string would be engaged by a catch as in the other crossbows. The winder was then removed until needed again.

The *windlass or pulleys crossbow* was a crossbow drawn by a series of fixed and free-moving pulleys worked by two handles. A foot stirrup was again an aid in obtaining leverage while drawing the bow back. This pulley apparatus, like the winder mechanism, could be removed when not needed. The missiles used for crossbows were called quarrels or bolts.

The *plain bow* and the *long bow* were used suc-

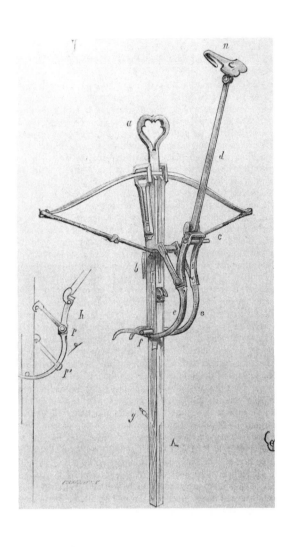

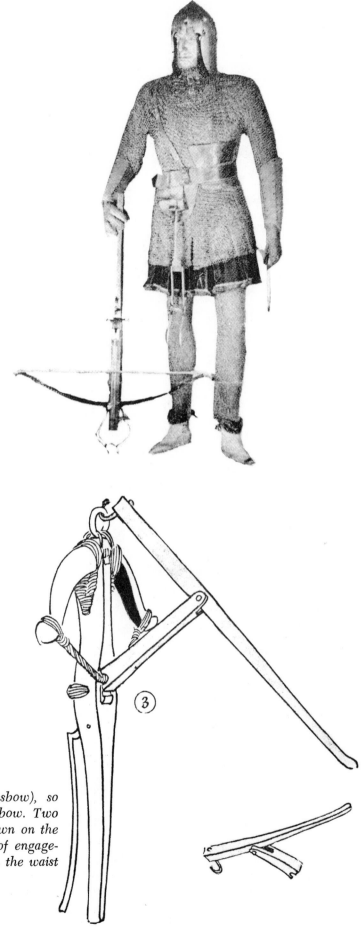

Steel-bow crossbow (or goat's foot lever crossbow), so named because of the device that draws the bow. Two types are shown (above and right). Pressing down on the lever in each case forces string back to point of engagement. The lever when not in use was carried on the waist belt as seen on figure in upper right

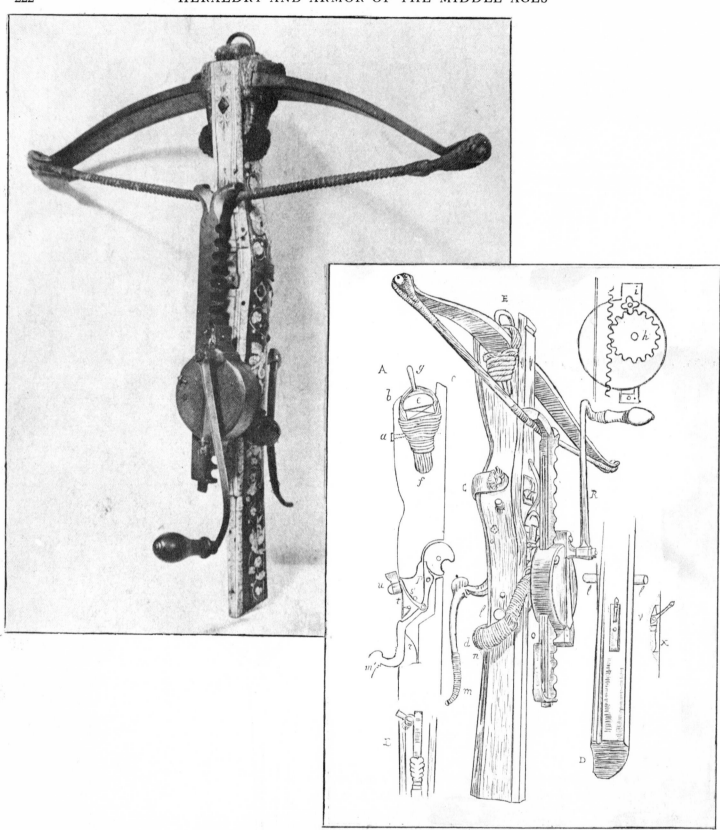

Winder crossbow. The bow is drawn by a toothed ratchet engaged by a toothed wheel that is hand turned by means of a long handle. The mechanism that draws the bow is attached to the stock by a stout cord. When not in use, the winder is kept on the bowman's belt, just as the other crossbow devices

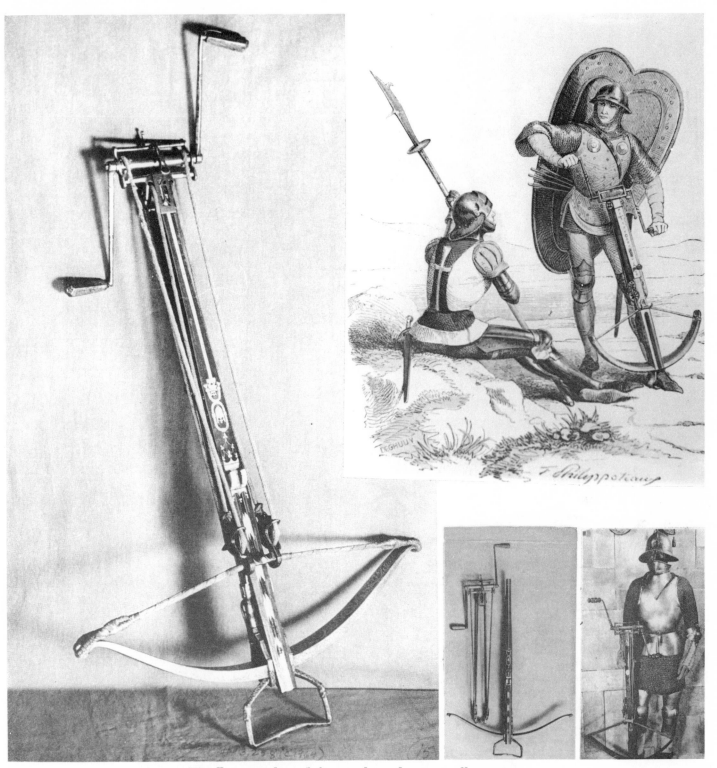

*Windlass crossbow (left, crossbow showing pulley system;
upper right, bowman drawing crossbow string; lower inside
right, winding mechanism before attachment to crossbow;
lower right, armor of crossbowman)*

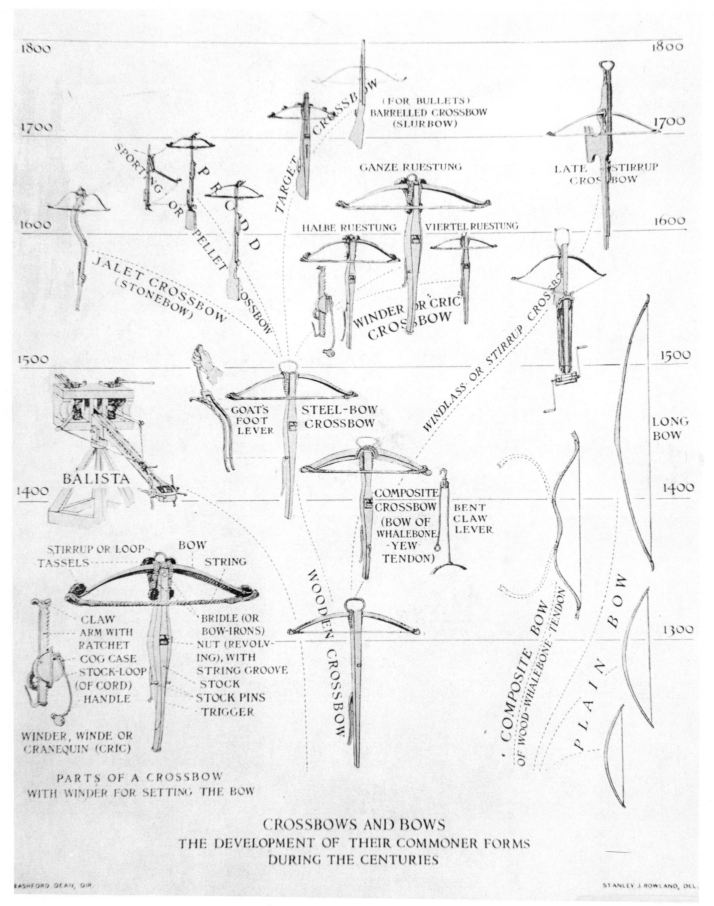

1800

1700

TARGET CROSSBOW

(FOR BULLETS)
BARRELLED CROSSBOW
(SLURBOW)

1800

1700

SPORTING OR PELLET CROSSBOW

P R O D D

GANZE RUESTUNG

LATE STIRRUP
CROSSBOW

1600

1600

JALET CROSSBOW
(STONEBOW)

HALBE RUESTUNG   VIERTEL RUESTUNG

WINDER OR CRIC
CROSSBOW

WINDLASS OR STIRRUP CROSSBOW

1500

1500

BALISTA

GOAT'S
FOOT
LEVER

STEEL-BOW
CROSSBOW

LONG
BOW

1400

COMPOSITE
CROSSBOW
(BOW OF
WHALEBONE
YEW
TENDON)

BENT
CLAW
LEVER

1400

STIRRUP OR LOOP
TASSELS

BOW

STRING

WOODEN CROSSBOW

COMPOSITE BOW OF WOOD-WHALEBONE-TENDON

P L A I N   B O W

CLAW
ARM WITH
RATCHET
COG CASE
STOCK-LOOP
(OF CORD)
HANDLE

BRIDLE (OR
BOW-IRONS)
NUT (REVOLV-
ING), WITH
STRING GROOVE
STOCK
STOCK PINS
TRIGGER

1300

WINDER, WINDE OR
CRANEQUIN (CRIC)

PARTS OF A CROSSBOW
WITH WINDER FOR SETTING THE BOW

CROSSBOWS AND BOWS
THE DEVELOPMENT OF THEIR COMMONER FORMS
DURING THE CENTURIES

BASHFORD DEAN, DIR

STANLEY J. ROWLAND, DEL.

Development of the bow and crossbow

cessively until the middle of the 16th century. During this period they supplemented the various crossbows just described.

The catapult of the Middle Ages was adapted from two projectile throwing machines created by the Romans. These were the *tormentum* and the *balista*. In the medieval device, the lever principle of the Roman catapults was supplemented with a giant slingshot that brought added yardage to the flight of the projectile.

The workings of the catapult were relatively simple.

Roman ballista (reconstructed)

Siege weapons (catapult, top; battering ram, bottom)

Ship-borne battering ram

A large lever elevated on a frame was created with heavy weights on the end that pointed to the direction that the projectile was to travel. On the other end of the lever, pulleys drew the lever down and consequently the weights up. The weights were held in check while the projectile was loaded in the sling at the end of the lever.

When the time was right, the pulley ropes were released and the counter weights threw the sling end of the lever upward as the weights quickly fell downward. At the top of the arc made by the sling, the projectile was flung clear, traveling in some cases seven or eight hundred yards. These catapults could either throw heavy rocks or *fireballs*.

Roman soldiers applying tension to catapult lever

Seal of Peter Stuyvesant

Seal of Benjamin Franklin

Arms of George Washington

Stained-glass windows from a French church (Church of the Convent of Brou, near Bourg-en-Bresse). Depicted are the arms of various towns of France, Italy, and Austria, as well as those of the rulers of the countries

Arms of William Penn and family

Coat of Arms designed for John Paul Jones

Arms of Canada

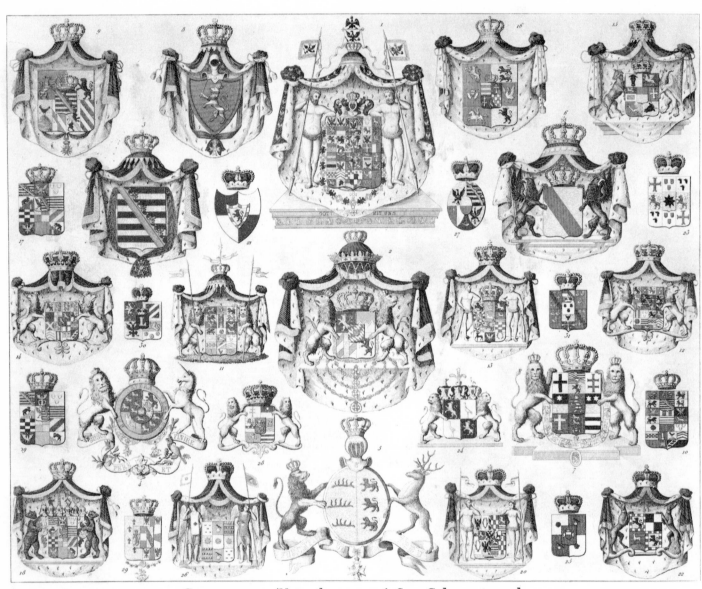

German arms. (Note the arms of Saxe-Coburg, toward upper left.)

World heraldry in the early 20th century

1. Argentina	9. Italy	17. Great Britain
2. Netherlands	10. Portugal	18. Norway
3. Spain	11. Belgium	19. Sweden
4. Brazil	12. Russia	20. Greece
5. Costa Rica	13. France	21. Persia
6. Nicaragua	14. Chile	22. Prussia
7. United States	15. Austria-Hungary	23. Germany
8. Mexico	16. Denmark	

Glossary

ABASED — Lowered (opposite of ENHANCED or raised).

ABATEMENT — A symbolism denoting illegitimacy. A term once applied to each of nine marks of dishonor that were supposedly created but never actually found in arms.

ABEYANCE — The state of a peerage under equal claim by two or more heirs or heiresses. In such cases, the title remains suspended until only one claimant survives to assume it.

À BOUCHE — Term applied to a jousting shield that has a notch in the dexter chief for a lance rest.

ABOUTÉ — Connected end to end.

ACCESSORIES — The heraldic elements placed outside the shield proper that form the total achievement of arms. These include the helm, crest, mantling, supporters, motto, etc.

ACCOLLÉ — Side by side. Usually describing shields so placed.

ACCOMPAGNÉ — Accompanied by. Used to describe a charge placed between two others.

ACCOSTED — Side by side.

ACHIEVEMENT — The total display of armorial bearings (accessories in addition to shield).

ACORNÉ — Having attires (horns). Commonly describing members of the deer family.

ACORNED — Descriptive of an oak tree bearing acorns. An exception to usual term of "fructed," which describes trees bearing fruit.

ADDORSED — Back to back. Opposite of combatant when describing beasts in their attitudes. Also describes a position of bird wings.

ADDUMBRATION — The shadow of a charge placed upon the field in a darker color than the latter, the intention being to create a feeling of depth between the charge and the field.

ADORNED — Decorated or ornamented.

AFFRONTÉ — Said of a beast whose whole body is squarely facing the viewer. The beast whose head alone faces the viewer is described as GUARDANT.

AIGUILETTES — Laces used to join armor plating. Usually found with a bone needle at one end to facilitate threading.

AILETTES — Small square shoulder plates used to protect against sweeping cuts from bladed weapons. These metal plates displayed the arms of the wearer in the same manner as the shield.

À LA CUISSE — At the thigh. The point where a leg is couped or erased.

ALLERION — A mutilated eagle without beak or legs. In French blazonry it is said to symbolize a vanquished empire.

ALLUME — Said of a beast's eyes when tinctured.

ALLUSIVE ARMS — Arms that refer to or play upon the name or property of the bearer.

ANGELS — Appear as supporters.

ANNULET — A small ring appearing either as a common charge or a mark of cadency denoting the fifth son. It appears in units of two or more when used as a common charge. Two annulets touching each other are said to be CONJUNCT. When linked together they are called EMBRACED, and when three annulets are so engaged they are termed INTERLACED.

CYCLAS
1325-1335

SKIRTED JUPON
1335-1360

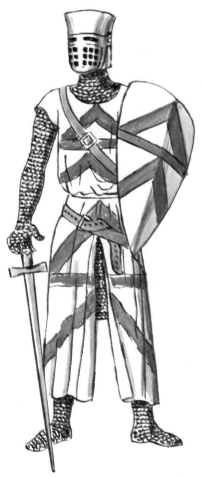

SURCOAT
1180-1250

TABARD
1430-1500

JUPON
1360-1410

Coats of Arms

3rd Infantry Regt.

5th Infantry Regt.

19th Infantry Regt.

103rd Infantry Regt.

7th Infantry Regt.

34th Infantry Regt.

38th Infantry Regt.

196th Infantry Regt.

346th Infantry Regt.

306th Infantry Regt.

35th Infantry Regt.

156th Infantry Regt.

Heraldry of the U.S. Army

ANNULY — Ending in rings as in the cross of the same name.

APPAUMÉ — The position of a hand or gauntlet showing the palm.

ARBALEST, ARBLAST — Alternate terms for crossbow.

ARGENT — The tincture of silver. Often represented by white in emblazoning.

ARMED — A term applied to beasts and birds of prey to describe their possession of teeth, claws, horns, or talons. Also descriptive of arrowheads when of a different tincture than their shafts. Such arrowheads are said to be, as in the case of teeth, claws, etc., "armed" of such tinctures. Applicable also to armored figures and parts of figures.

ARMET — A close fitting helmet that swiveled open at the sides to permit entry.

ARMIGEROUS — Possessing the right to bear arms.

ARMING POINTS — Another name for AIGUILETTES.

ARMORIAL BEARINGS — An alternate term for an achievement of arms.

ARMORY — The branch of heraldry that deals with armorial devices.

ARMS — The heraldic devices found within the shield.

ARMS OF ADOPTION — Arms properly borne by the parent of an adopted child that are assumed by the latter under a special warrant of the King.

ARMS OF ALLIANCE — Arms denoting a union of families through marriage.

ARMS OF ASSUMPTION — Arms assumed in early times by way of the battle conquest of the original bearer. As in the case of the arms of adoption, these arms are subject to sovereign approval.

ARMS OF COMMUNITY — Arms borne by townships, institutions, and corporations.

ARMS OF CONCESSION — Arms bearing an augmentation of honor that was adopted from the Royal Arms.

ARMS OF DESCENT — Arms transmitted through heredity rights.

ARMS OF DOMINION — Arms denoting the realms of the sovereigns who bear such arms. These arms are not the personal ones normally borne by the King.

ARMS OF OFFICE — Arms of an office, sometimes temporary, borne in addition to one's regular arms. Deans of colleges, kings of arms, and bishops impale arms representing their posts along with the hereditary bearings that they already possess.

ARMS OF PRETENSION — Arms denoting a claim to a realm or title not actually possessed or properly recognized.

ARMS OF SUCCESSION — Arms denoting estates or dignities obtained through inheritance.

ARONDIE — Curved or rounded.

ARRANCHÉ — Erased.

ASPECT — Alternate term for *attitude* when referring to a position of an animal.

ASPECTANT — Alternate term for *respecting* (looking at or facing) one another.

ASPERSED — Strewn, scattered (semé).

AT GAZE — Descriptive of a stag in what would normally be termed a guardant attitude (standing with the head turned toward the viewer).

ATTAINDER — Revocation of arms and all civil rights including the right to transmit arms to successors. Mainly associated with treasonable acts.

ATTAINTS — Points scored in jousting that were recorded on top line of *chequé*.

ATTIRES — Antlers of a stag or other deer family member. Mentioned when of a different tincture than head.

AUGMENTATION — Additions to family arms granted as special honor. Often found as an escutcheon lion or rose (symbolic of the royal arms).

AVELLANE CROSS — A cross formed by four filberts placed cross-wise. This device has become stylized so as to resemble sceptres with flory endings.

AVERSANT — showing the rear part.

AXE — Weapon depicted in heraldry. Four principal types of axes used in battle were the battle axe, pole axe, Danish axe, and Lochaber axe.

AZURE — Blue tincture.

BADGE — A mark of distinction worn or borne independently of the shield and its accessories.

BADGER — Animal found in heraldic charges.

BANDED MAIL — A form of body defense that came into being near the end of the 13th century. It consisted of overlapping metal discs with pierced centers through which leather straps were passed to contain and reinforce them.

BANNER — A small square flag carried on the end of a lance in contrast to standard or large flag.

BANNERET KNIGHT — Title given to knight who provided and maintained troops in the service of his sovereign. Distinguished by the banner granted him in recognition of this deed.

BAR — An ordinary derived from the FESS (another ordinary). This charge normally occupies about a fifth of the field unless it is widened to about a third of the field to accommodate a super charge.

BARBUTE — A form of the bascinet (helm) with staples for holding the camail.

BARNACLE — Device used by farriers to curb unruly horses.

BARON — Lowest rank of peerage.

BARON, CORONET — The headpiece granted to lowest rank in peerage. Replaced the red velvet cap originally worn.

BARON AND FEMME — Terms describing those parties sharing impaled arms regardless of their actual rank.

BARONET — A hereditary rank below that of Baron; hence not of the peerage.

BARRY — A field divided horizontally in equal parts. A field composed of bars.

BARRY-BENDY — A field combining both the barry and bendy.

BARRY-PILY — A field divided horizontally into equal pile-shaped pieces.

BARS GEMELLES — Diminutives of bar appearing in pairs.

BASCINET — Open-faced helm with pointed top or apex.

BASE — Bottom edge of shield.

BATON — A bendlet couped.

BATTERING RAM — A siege weapon for battering down the walls or gates of a fortress.

BATTLE AXE — Short-hafted weapon contrasted to the long-hafted pole-axe.

BATTLEMENTS — The interstices atop castle walls or towers. The low apertures were called crenelles and the high positions were called merlons.

BATTLED, BATTLE, EMBATTLED — Line forms used for shield divisions or charge outlines. These lines resemble the castle battlements.

BAVIÈRE — Lower portion of the bascinet that protected the chin and neck.

BEARING — Any device appearing in arms.

BEAVER — Animal figure appearing as a supporter. The heraldic sea-dog may have been an attempt to depict this animal.

BEND — An ordinary in the form of a diagonal device normally occupying one-fifth of the field if uncharged or one-third if charged.

BEHOURD — A term for tournament sword play.

BEZANT — A gold roundle, once gold or silver.

BEZANTY — Scattered, strewn (semé) with bezants.

BI-CORPORATE — Having two bodies. Lion figures that have two bodies but only one head are so termed.

BILL — A farming scythe adopted as a weapon.

BILLET — An oblong charge proportioned like a building brick.

BILLETY — Scattered or strewn with billets (semé of billets).

BLAZON — The heraldic description (oral or written) of arms.

BOAR — An animal seen as a charge, supporter, and crest.

BOMB — A common charge found in arms, it appears as a bursting black ball issuing flames.

BONNET — Red velvet cap with gold tassel worn with the sovereign crown or the coronets of the peerage. Baronets at one time wore only this cap without the coronet.

BOOK — A common charge mainly found in educational arms.

BORDURE — Subordinate charge frequently used for differencing. A small margin around circumference of shield upon which other charges were usually placed.

BOTONNY, CROSS — So named because of clover leaf (trefoil) endings at each limb.

BOUGET, WATER — Hard leather water bags joined by a carrying yoke. Often found as a heraldic charge in various forms.

BOWEN KNOT — Badge of Bowen family.

BRACED — Interlaced.

BRASSARTS — Plate defenses for upper arm.

BRASS — Engraved brass plates found at monuments that depict knights and nobles in their armor and surcoats as well as displaying their armorial bearings. An important source of heraldic information and armor details.

BRETESSÉ — Embattled on both sides (Battle-embattled).

BRISTOL, CITY OF — Civic arms.

BROCK — Another name for badger. As a consequence, this animal served as allusive device for Brock family arms.

BULL — Animal frequently seen as shield device, badge, and supporter.

CABLE — Chain or rope tied to anchor. Not always shown unless specified.

CABOSHED — Said of an animal's head seen affronté when closely severed so that no neck appears.

CADENCY — A system using differencing marks to denote the line of inheritance in relation to the head of an arms-bearing family.

CALTRAP — A balled weapon with spikes in all directions so that one will always stand erect when cast on the ground. Meant to maim the cavalry horses of the enemy attackers.

CAMAIL — Chain mail hood protecting the head, neck, and shoulders.

CANTING ARMS — Allusive arms. Referring to or playing upon the name of the bearer; often a whimsical reference.

CANTON — A subordinate charge usually appearing in the dexter chief and occupying a ninth of the field. A sinister canton may appear in the sinister chief in the same proportions. An early mark for differencing.

CARBUNCLE — A charge said to be adopted from a lady's brooch. Somewhat resembling a rimless wheel. The spoke-like rays that are normally eight in number end in a semi-fleur-de-lis.

CARRICK PURSUIVANT — A Scottish Officer of Arms.

CATHERINE WHEEL — Symbol of the martyrdom of St. Catherine. A wagon-type wheel with blades outside the rim in line with each spoke.

CELESTIAL CROWN — A crown similar to Eastern Crown but with the addition of a star on each point.

CERCELÉ — Curled.

CHALICE — An uncovered cup.

CHALLENGES — System for picking opponents in tournament jousts. Challengers called TENANTS, responders called VENANS.

CHAMFRON — Armor for a horse's head.

CHAPE — The metal tip of a scabbard, also called CRAMPET. Badge of the Earl of De la Warr.

CHAPELLE-DE-FER — Iron skull cap.

CHAUSSÉ — Wearing shoes.

CHAUSSES — Leg defenses in armor.

CHECKY — A varied field consisting of equal squares formed by combining barry and paly fields.

CHEQUES — Scoring tablets used at tournaments.

CHESTER HERALD — An English Officer of Arms.

CHEVALIER — A French word for horseman.

CHEVRON — An ordinary resembling an inverted V that normally occupies one-fifth of the field.

CHEVRONEL — A diminutive of the chevron.

CHEVRONNY — A varied field composed of chevron pieces.

CHEVRONWISE — An alternate term for PER CHEVRON.

CHIEF — An ordinary in the form of a horizontal bar occupying the top third of the field.

CINQUEFOIL — A common charge imitating a five petal flower with a pierced center.

CIVIC CROWN — A wreath of oak leaves and acorns.

CLECHE, CROSS — A cross whose limbs are slightly splayed as well as pointed. Also called CROSS-URDE.

CLOSET — A diminutive of the bar.

COAT OF ARMS — Alternate term for complete achievement of arms. Also literal term for surcoat, cyclas, jupon, or tabard, which displayed bearings in the same manner as a shield.

COCK — An animal encountered in arms as a common charge, supporter, or crest. Equivalent of the farm rooster.

COCKATRICE — A monster having the head, upper body, and feet of a cock and the tail of a dragon.

COGNIZANCE — A device that identifies its bearer. A term especially applied to badges.

COHEIRS — Two men with equal claim to a title or family achievement of arms.

COHEIRESSES — Two women sharing a claim to the family arms.

COJOINED — Joined together.

COIF DE MAILLES — A chain mail hood (camail).

COLLEGE OF ARMS — The office having the authority over all heraldic matters. Composed of Kings of Arms, Heralds, and Pursuivants.

COMBATANT — Two beasts facing each other in rampant attitude are said to be combatant.

COMBAT À OUTRANCE — A joust of war.

COMBED — Said of a cock's crest when of another tincture than the body.

COMPARTMENT — A Scottish heraldic term for the panel below the shield containing the motto.

COMPLEMENT — Descriptive of the moon when full (in her complement).

COMPONY (GOBONY) — A single row of chequers or checks.

COMPOUND QUARTERING — The subdividing of arms already quartered.

COMPOUNDED ARMS — Arms combining two or more sets of bearings to form a new and separate bearing.

CONEY — An old name for a rabbit.

CONFRONTÉ — Facing each other (respectant).

CONTOISE — A scarf twisted in a turban-like fashion about the helm. Also called TORSE.

CONTOURNÉ — Facing to the sinister. Sometimes used in place of REGUARDANT.

CORBIE — Alternate term for crow or raven.

CORNISH CHOUGH — A black bird similar to the raven except for its red beak and feet.

CORONALS — Crown-shaped lance tips that dulled the point for purposes of safety during jousts.

CORONETS — Gold headpieces worn by peerage that, by their individual styling, denote the rank of each wearer.

COTISE — Diminutive of the bar.

COTISED — Condition of an ordinary such as the bar or bend being placed between two or more of their diminutives.

COUCHANT — Said of beast in lying position.

COUDIÈRES — The elbow defenses in armor.

COUNTER-CHANGED — Said of field divided in two equal parts wherein the color or tincture pattern is reversed from one side to the other.

COUNTER-COMPANY — A double row of checks.

COUNTER-GOBONY — A device decorated on both sides with fleur-de-lis. In changing from one side to the other, the petals alternately face in and out. The tressure of the Scottish Royal Arms features this ornamentation.

COUNTER-PASSANT — Walking in opposite directions. Said of two lions so disposed.

COUNTER-POTENT — A variation of the *potent* fur pattern.

COUNTER-RAMPANT — Rampant in opposite directions.

COUNTER-SALIENT — Salient in opposite directions.

COUNTER-SEAL — The reverse or back side of the disc.

COUNTER-VAIR — A form of the *vair* pattern.

COUNTESS — Wife of an Earl.

COUPED — Cut or cut short in a straight line. Applied most often to animal heads. Distinguished from ERASED, which means "roughly torn."

COUPLE-CLOSE — Diminutive of the chevron.

COURANT — Running. Applied to beasts of chase.

COURSE — A term for a single tournament event.

COWARD — Said of an animal with its tail between its legs.

CRAMPET — Metal tip at the end of a scabbard. Badge of Earl of DeLaWarr.

CRANE — Bird mainly found as a supporter or crest.

CRENELLATED — Embattled. The fortress walls that alternated in height for equal short distances so as to provide viewing apertures (*crenelles*) for archers and such between high points (*merlons*).

CRESCENT — A charge having different representations. It is a cadency mark for the second son when its points are placed upwards. When the points are facing to the dexter or sinister it represents phases of the moon.

CREST — Figures above the helm in an achievement.

CRINET — Laminated neck armor for horses.

CRINED — Said of hair or mane when of a different tincture than the rest of the head or body.

CROSIER — The Bishop's staff or rod. Often found in ecclesiastical arms.

CROSS — An *ordinary* possessing dozens of variations and is the most frequently seen charge in heraldry.

CROSS-BOW — A bow with a cross bar through the center to which the drawn string became engaged. This was done manually at first and later by mechanical means.

CRUSADES — A series of seven expeditions embarked upon by Christian forces to recover the Holy Land from the Moslems. First campaign began in 1096 and the last one in 1270.

CRUSILY — A field strewn with crosses.

CUBIT ARM — A hand and arm shown couped at the elbow.

CUFF — Cubit arm may be vested (See *vested*). If cuff displayed on such arm varies in tincture from sleeve, the tincture of the cuff must be stated.

CUIRASS — Breastplate. Basis for later term CUIRASSIER, which described cavalry men who wore this defense.

CUISSES — Thigh plates. Also called CUISSARTS.

CUIR-BOUILLI — Boiled leather that is pounded into desired shape. Basis for early armor.

CUP — A common charge also termed chalice, goblet. It sometimes appears as a covered cup.

CYPHER — Monogram. Sometimes part of a badge and also found on banners.

DAMASKED — Alternate term for DIAPERED.

DANCETTY — A jagged-line form used to outline charges.

DANISH AXE — A battle-axe formed of two similar curved blades on either side of shaft.

DEBRUISED — Said of a common charge over which an ordinary has been placed. A rampant lion crossed by a bend would be an example of this condition.

DECHAUSE — Dismembered (mutilé).

DECKED — Decorated, adorned, ornamented.

DECRESCENT — Said of a crescent whose points or horns face to the sinister.

DEER — Beast of chase found as common charge, supporter, and crest.

DEFAMED — Without tail.

DEMI-LION — Top half of lion appearing as common charge. Usually seen ISSUANT or NAISSANT out of a fess or bar. The top half is always inferred when the term "demi" is used, unless otherwise stated.

DEMI-PLACATE — A secondary breastplate hinged to the original plate by a special sliding rivet that allowed them to spread out or draw together as the body movement dictated.

DEVELOPED — Fully displayed. Term used in describing flag.

DEXTER — The right side of the shield from the viewpoint of the bearer.

DIAPERING — Subtle ornamentation of an otherwise plain surface.

DIFFERENCING — System of arms modifications to distinguish one family from another. Also a series of cadency marks that denotes order of inheritance.

DIMIDIATION — An early form of impalement whereby the dexter half of the husband's arms were joined with the sinister half of the wife's arms.

DIMINUTIVE — A smaller version of a particular ordinary.

DINGWALL PURSUIVANT — Scottish Officer of Arms.

DISARMED — Said of a bird or beast without its natural weapons (teeth, claws, horns, beak, etc.).

DISCLOSED — Said of a bird's wings when opened or displayed. Intended to describe wings of birds other than birds of prey.

DISPLAYED — Same meaning as DISCLOSED. Applicable at present time to all birds.

DORMANT — Asleep. A term applied especially to the lion but common to other beasts as well. Also descriptive of an unclaimed peerage.

DOUBLE ARCHED — A curved line form used to divide fields.

DOUBLE COTISED — Said of the fess or bend when it appears between a double row of its smallest diminutives.

DOUBLE QUATREFOIL — Another name for octofoil; cadency mark for the ninth son.

DOUBLE-QUEUED — Having two tails.

DOUBLE TETE — Having two heads. Found with eagle and lion.

DOUBLE TRESSURE — A narrow double border inset from the edge of the shield.

DOUBLING — The lining of a mantling. When describing the tincture of this lining it is said to be "doubled" of it.

DOVETAILED — A line of partition derived from the carpentry method. A late heraldic development (1720).

DRAGON — Imaginary animal (monster) much spoken of in ancient and medieval legend. The wyvern is a two-legged version of this beast.

DROPS — Gouttes.

DUCAL — Relating to a duke, such as the ducal crown.

EAGLE — A predominant charge also found as a supporter and crest. Symbol of the emperor.

EAGLET — Term applied to each of several small eagle charges necessarily smaller in order to be accommodated on the same shield. Same sort of characterization as given to multiple small lions (lioncels) when placed together on a shield.

EARL — The third highest rank of the peerage (following duke and marquess); equal to the French Count.

EARL MARSHALL — Duke of Norfolk. Hereditary overseer of the College of Arms.

EASTERN CROWN — Crown of eight points. Granted for distinguished service in the East.

EAU, GOUTTE D' — Sprinkled with drops of silver.

ECCLESIASTICAL HERALDRY — That which pertains to the sees and the offices of the prelates.

EGUISCÉ — Pointed, also termed AIGUISE. Later term basis for word AIGUILETTES (arming points).

EIRE, BADGE OF — The harp.

EMBATTLED — A line of partition resembling a castle or tower top.

EMBOWED — Bent or curved as in the couped arm. Also applicable to that attitude of the dolphin. "Flected" or "flexed" are also synonymous of embowed when referring to the arm.

EMBRUED — Blood-stained.

ENDORSE — A diminutive of the pale.

ENFILED — The condition of being pierced by a sword. Term applied to a beast's head or a coronet when an upright sword passes through either.

ENGOULÉ — Pierced through the mouth. A term related to the previous term when describing the condition of a beast's head.

ENGRAILED — A line of partition resembling a series of small waves or a serrated knife edge.

ENHANCED — Raised above usual position. This condition has been primarily applied to the bend or its diminutive.

ENSIGN — A term for a type of flag. Also applied to marks of distinction such as a badge.

ENSIGNED — Said of a charge having a mark of distinction (insignia of office or rank) above it.

EN SOLEIL — Said of the sun when encompassed by its own rays. Said of other charges so encompassed.

ENTIRE — Describing a charge that reaches out to the edges of the shield.

ENTOIRE — One of three terms generally describing the type of charges placed within a shield border. This term describes a border filled with inanimate objects. The term ENALURON describes a border filled with bird charges. The term ENURNEY refers to a border filled with animal charges.

EPAULE DE MOUTON — Plating attached to vambrance to protect inside of forearm. Also called POLDER MITON.

ERADICATED — Uprooted. A term applied to tree trunks appearing as common charges. Such uprooted trees are usually couped as well

ERECT — Standing upright.

ERMINE — A white fur with black tails. Tails of this fur are symbolized in many forms in heraldry as common charges.

ERMINES — A black fur with white spots or tails.

ERMINOIS — A fur denoted by black spots on gold.

ESCALLOP — The scallop shell.

ESCROLL — A term for the elongated parchment scroll below the shield whereon the motto is inscribed. Called the "compartment" in Scottish heraldry. This shield accessory is also intended to uphold the shield supporters.

ESCUTCHEON — A shield. The word for a shield within a shield when used as a mark of honor is called an INESCUTCHEON.

ESQUIRE — Attendant of a knight (ranked just below him), usually selected from the wellborn.

ESTOILE — A star. Distinguished from the molet by its wavy or undulated rays.

FALSE — A term for *voided*. A condition wherein the center of a charge is removed, leaving only a small outer border. Annulets are sometimes referred to as false roundles since they subscribe to the above condition.

FEATHERED — A term used when necessary to describe the separate tincture of the arrow feathers in contrast to the shaft. The term *flighted* is also used in this regard.

FEAT OF ARMS — A tournament term that refers to a series of events between the same two opponents.

FER DE MOLINE — French for mill-iron; a metal piece holding the mill stone in place. It appears in several forms as a common charge.

FESS — A principal charge or ORDINARY. A horizontal device occupying the middle third of the shield. So named because of its placement over the fess point, or center of the shield.

FESS POINT — The center point on a shield.

FESSWISE — Said of a charge running horizontally.

FETTERLOCK — A shackle for birds or animals. Seen as a common charge.

FIELD — A term for the entire surface area of a shield. That area which serves as the background for a primary charge.

FIELD OF THE CLOTH OF GOLD — A tournament at Westminster in the reign of Henry VIII, marked by its great pageantry.

FIGURED — Any charge other than a human depiction bearing a human face. Said of the sun when so represented.

FILLET CROSS — Any very narrow cross. One that sometimes unites the four sections in quartered arms when its limbs are extended to the edges of the shield.

FIMBRIATED — Said of a charge bordered in a different tincture than the rest of it.

FITCHY — Said of a cross whose shaft or lower limb tapers to a point.

FLAIL — A military weapon consisting of a shaft to which a spiked metal ball is chained to swing freely. The spiked object may also be a ball of wood rather than metal or the object may be a spiked shaft of smaller size than the one serving as the handle.

FLEXED — Bent.

FLORY — Said of a cross whose limbs end in a fleur-de-lis. A field scattered with this flower is termed *flory, fleury,* or *floretty.*

FORMY — Said of a cross whose limbs are splayed (curved outwards) and whose ends are straight.

FOURCHÉ — Forked (as in the cross of this type).

FRACTED — Broken.

FRET — A subordinate charge composed of a voided lozenge interlaced with two bendlets in saltire.

FRETTY — A pattern of bendlets (diapered field) continually crossing one another at evenly spaced intervals.

FRUCTED — Bearing fruit. Said of trees ready for harvest.

FUSIL — An elongated lozenge shape. One of the subordinate charges.

FUSILY — A varied field composed of fusil pieces.

FYLFOT — A cross with limbs bent at right angles; a swastika.

GALLEY — A single-masted ship seen as a common charge. Also called lymphad. Sometimes emblazoned as a three-masted galley but always specified when such is the case.

GAMB — The leg of an animal.

GAMBESON — A padded jacket worn as a layer of armor during the transient stage of body defenses (the Cyclas Period).

GARB — A sheaf of wheat or other grain, but mainly associated with wheat.

GARDE-DE-BRAS — An armor defense attached to the left vambrance to protect the inside of the left elbow. This was a special protection against the lance in jousting.

GARDE-DE-REIN — An armor defense attached to the back plate to protect the kidneys.

GARNISHED — Adorned or ornamented.

GARTER — A strap worn at the knee and fastened with a buckle, the strap end left hanging downward. The symbol of the Order of the Garter, a degree of knighthood established in 1348.

GARTER KING OF ARMS — The principal Officer of Arms in England.

GATEHOUSE — A common charge appearing as a single embattled tower. Not to be confused with a multi-towered castle.

GAUNTLET — A metal glove with movable joints.

GEMMELES — A term used to denote twin or duplicate charges such as bars gemelles.

GENOUILLIERES — Armor caps that protected the knee.

GENTLEMAN — The lowest rank of arms bearer found in heraldry.

GLAIVE — A medieval poled weapon that resembled a curved knife mounted on a staff. The cutting edge was on the convex side of the curve. It was distinguished by hooks or projection at the base of the blade intended to catch the weapon of the enemy.

GLISSANT — A sliding movement associated with snakes appearing as common charges.

GLOPÉ — A purple roundle.

GOBONY — A field composed of a row of small squares of alternating tinctures. Two such adjoining rows would be called *counter gobony.* More than two would be called *checky.*

GORGED — Collared. Usually referring to the state of many beasts and birds found as supporters.

GORGET — Neck or throat defense in armor. One of the last pieces of armor to be abandoned. A simple version worn as late as the American Revolutionary War.

GOUTTE — A drop of liquid that appears in one of several tinctures. The term *gutte* denotes a field scattered with drops of one specified tincture, such as *gutte d'or* (A scattered field of gold drops). A single gold drop would be *goutte d'or.*

GRAFTED — Fixed in after insertion.

GRANDE(E) GARD(E) — An armor plate introduced in the 16th century to protect the left side of the chest and the shoulder. It extended from the neck to the waist. Mainly intended as a tilting or jousting defense. Some authorities include the volante piece (neck and chin defense) to which it was attached as part of the grande garde itself.

GRANT OF ARMS — An act of official approval and recording of arms by the proper heraldic officers.

GREYHOUND — A frequently found animal of heraldry. Appears as common charge, badge, or supporter.

GRIFFIN — An imaginary beast with the head of an eagle and the body of a lion.

GUARDANT — Said of an animal whose head is turned to the viewer.

GUIDON — A small flag. Judged by some to be a third smaller than a standard.

GUIGE — A shield belt with which to sling the shield over the shoulder when not in use.

GUISEARME — An ancient poled weapon with a curved and pointed blade honed razor sharp.

Also called the *fauchard* during the Middle Ages.

GULES — Red tincture.

GUTTE — Scattered with gouttes.

GYRON — A subordinate charge formed by the lower half of a diagonally bisected canton or quarter.

GYRONNY — A field composed of gyron pieces. A varied field formed by the combined party per cross and saltire fields.

HABITED — Clothed or vested.

HALBERD — A pole-axe additionally possessing a long spike atop the shaft. More complex in contour than the simpler pole-axe in that it featured more ridges or grooves to snare the enemy's weapons.

HALO — A symbolic ring of light above a divine figure. Also called a GLORY OR NIMBUS.

HAMMER — A tool appearing as a common charge. Varied according to the craft that it was intended to denote (blacksmith, carpenter, etc.).

HAND — The human hand appears as a common charge. It must be blazoned either as dexter or sinister, appaume (open) or closed (perhaps grasping an object).

HARP — A common charge also appearing as the badge of Ireland.

HART — A member of the deer family often found in all components of the total achievement (common charge, crest, and supporter). This animal depicted no differently than the stag is also a badge symbol.

HASTILUDE — A tournament term for spearplay.

HATCHMENTS — Lozenge-shaped boards or panels placed in front of the home of a deceased person at the time of mourning. These hatchments or LOZENGES displayed the bearings in such a prescribed manner as to also denote the bearer's marital status at the time of his or her death.

HAUBERK — Usually a jacket of chain mail, but during the Cyclas Period of armor it was generally made of banded mail.

HAURIANT — Said of a fish erectly rising to the surface as if to draw air.

HAWKS LURE — A decoy used in falconry that appears as a common charge.

HEART — A common charge depicting the human heart. Symbolic of feudal loyalty or religious devotion.

HEAUME — Helmet; from the French word of the same meaning.

HEDGEHOG — An animal appearing occasionally as a common charge.

HENEAGE KNOT — One of several rope designs or entwinements that served as badges.

HERALD — An Officer of Arms of intermediate grade (above the Pursuivant, below the King of Arms).

HERALD'S COLLEGE — Another name for College of Arms.

HERALDRY — See Chapter 1 for several definitions.

HERON — A bird appearing as a charge or supporter.

HILTED — Said of a sword whose grip and crosspiece are of a different tincture than the blade (hilted or).

HIND — A deer without antlers, depicted with ears erect.

HIP BELT — A sword belt of the Middle Ages. Such belts were usually made up of ornate square or oblong brooches linked together. Some were even jeweled.

HIRONDELLE — Another name for the swallow.

HOLY WATER SPRINKLER — A term for one type of military flail. A whimsical comparison to the religious device, which is swung similarly to the hanging spiked ball or shaft of the weapon.

HONOR POINT — A shield location halfway between the fess point (shield center) and the middle chief.

HOOFED — A term used to refer to the tinctures of the hoofs of animals when such hoofs varied from their body tinctures.

HORNED — A term used to refer to the tinctures of the horns of animals when such horns varied from their body tinctures.

HORSESHOE — A charge found in heraldry that sometimes was associated with the ostrich, who is supposed to be able to digest such metallic objects.

HUILLE, GOUTTE D' — Sprinkled with green drops.

HURST — A clump of trees.

HURT — A blue roundle.

HURTE — Scattered or strewn with hurts.

IMBRUED — Stained with blood.

IMPALED — Said of a shield displaying two complete coats of arms. Earliest form of impalement was dimidiation, which showed only the dexter half of one family's arms (the husband's) and sinister half of the other (the wife's).

IMPARTIBLE ARMS — A shield displaying two or more coats of arms that are united by a bordure or fillet cross, etc., so as to make them in-separable or indivisible.

IN BEND — A term to describe two or more charges that conform in their alignment to the diagonal character of this ordinary. The terms *in chevron, in chief, in cross*, etc., may likewise be applied to charges whose mutual placement suggests the nature of any of these other ordinaries.

INCENSED — Having fire issuing from the mouth and ears. The panther is sometimes found in this state.

INCRESCENT — Said of a crescent whose horns are pointed to the dexter.

INDENTED — A jagged or zig-zag line form sometimes used to outline the ordinary charges. Its *teeth* are noticeably smaller than those of the *dancety*, a line form of a similar nature.

INESCUTCHEON — A shield within a shield. Usually associated with an augmentation in this form.

INFULAE — The ribbons pendant from a mitre as seen in ecclesiastical arms.

IN GLORY — Radiating a circle of light and/or heat.

INGRAILED — A line form sometimes used to outline the ordinary charges. Similar in appearance to the edge of a serrated knife blade. Its points turn outward toward the nearest shield edge. When a similar line form has its points turned away or inward from the shield side nearest it, such a line is said to be INVECTED.

IN LURE — Said of a pair of wings tipped downwards as a hawk's lure.

IN PRIDE — State of peacock's tail when spread or displayed.

INSIGNIA OF OFFICE — This temporary bearing often appears impaled with the hereditary or permanent arms of the office-holder.

IN SPLENDOR — Referring to the sun when encompassed by its own rays.

INVECTED — A line form sometimes used to outline the ordinary charges. A series of small connected arches pointed inwardly away from the shield edge nearest it; opposite from ENGRAILED.

IRRADIATED — Issuing or encompassed by rays of light.

ISSUANT — Rising out of. A term often applied to a demi-lion rising out of or appearing on the top of an ordinary such as a bar or fess. The word NAISSANT also implies the same meaning.

JAMB — The leg of a beast. Also GAMB.

JAMBARTS — Armor defenses for the legs or shins.

JELOPPED — Describing the wattles of a cock when of a different tincture than the body. Said to be "jelopped" of such tincture.

JESSANT — Shooting forth (sprouting) as plants from the earth.

JESSANT-DE-LIS — Possessed of a sprouting fleur-de-lis. Applicable to the leopard head from whose mouth a fleur-de-lis appears to be shooting forth.

JESSED — Said of a hawk or falcon whose legs are tied with leather thongs.

JEZERAINT — Studded armor that utilizes very small and thin iron plates overlayed with canvas in the varied construction.

JOUST — A contest associated with the tournament but also run independently of it. Usually a contest on horseback between two opponents armed with lances. The term TILTING is also used to describe the joust.

JOUSTS OF COURTESY — An event wherein no intent to do serious bodily harm was intended. As a consequence, the lances that were used were blunted.

JOUSTS OF PEACE — Same meaning as JOUSTS OF COURTESY.

JOUSTS OF WAR — A contest between hostile opponents wherein sharp or pointed weapons are used.

JOUTES à OUTRANCE — French phrase implying the preceding definition.

JUDICIAL COMBAT — Duels whose outcome alone decided the guilt or innocence of the defendant in a civil or criminal charge. They were often a part of a tournament and subject to its same rules. They could be fought on foot or horseback.

JUPON — A short, sleeveless, and tight-fitting tunic of the 1360–1410 period.

KING OF ARMS — Senior Officer of Arms in England. The Garter King of Arms is the principal Officer of Arms while the Norroy and Clarenceux Kings rank just below him.

KING OF HERALDS — An early term for the above Officer of Arms.

KNIGHT BACHELOR — The lowest degree of knighthood wherein the knight only supplies his own services in combat to his king or feudal lord for a prescribed period.

KNIGHT BANNERET — A high degree of knighthood wherein the knight provides troops and their supplies to his sovereign or feudal lord. He is thus entitled to carry the small personal banner (banneret) in evidence of this service.

KNIGHTHOOD — A degree of rank originally associated with feudal service or duty to the king in times of war. Presently awarded to English subjects who have distinguished themselves in other ways.

KNOTS — A series of distinctive and varied rope entwinements that served as badges of recognition for a sovereign or feudal lord and the adherents and retainers in each case.

LABEL — A cadency mark for the oldest son of a family. Originally a subordinate charge.

LAMBREQUIN — Mantling placed over a helmet supposed to keep the sun from hitting the metal. This mantling became an accessory in the total achievement of arms.

LAMES — Small metal armor plates that overlapped for flexibility where it was especially needed.

LAMINATED — Said of armor plates that overlapped.

LANCASTER HERALD — An English Officer of Arms.

LANCE — A long pointed weapon associated with the joust. This weapon with its distinctive vamplate (hand guard) ran from ten to twelve feet and some inches long.

LANCE, REBATED — A lance whose point was dulled to prevent injury. The coronal was the dull, three-pointed tip that was eventually developed for this purpose.

LANCE REST — A bracket attached to the breastplate of jousting armor to steady and support the lance.

LANGUED — A term used to describe the tincture of a beast's tongue when it varied in color from the rest of its body. The tongue is said to be *langued* of such tincture.

LARMES, GOUTTE DE — Sprinkled with blue drops.

LATIN CROSS — The plain long cross.

LATTICED — Said of a diapered field composed of dexter and sinister bendlets in which the dexter bendlets are superimposed over the sinister ones. An early variant of the fretty in which the bendlets interlace.

LAUREL — A plant whose leaves are used to form the wreath granted in reward of distinguished military service.

LEGGED — Birds are said to be *legged* of a tincture when their legs are colored differently than the rest of their bodies.

LINED — A term usually applied to mantlings with an inside lining. Also descriptive of the cord or chain attached to the collars of beasts seen as supporters.

LISTS — The enclosures in which tournaments were held.

LOCKING GAUNTLET — A closed metal glove that gripped the weapon so it could not be knocked loose.

LODGED — Said of a beast of chase when at rest.

LONG BOW — The word *long* applied to the name of this weapon to distinguish it from the shorter cross-bow.

LOZENGE — A subordinate charge in the shape of a diamond. The shape of a panel upon which armigerous single women and widows normally displayed their arms. Also the shape of the panel upon which funeral hatchments were displayed in front of a building during mourning.

LOZENGY — A varied field made up of connected lozenges.

LUCE — Another name for the fish called pike. One of several fish depicted in common charges.

MACE — A heavy metal club with spikes. Also a scepter of authority.

MAIN — A word for hand.

MAINFARE, MANIFER — A stiff heavy jousting gauntlet for the bridle hand and forearm.

MALLET — A mason's hammer. One of several hammer types seen as common charges.

MALTESE CROSS — A type of cross that is both splayed and forked.

MANCHE — Also manch or maunch. A lady's sleeve that had a long appendage (lappet) hanging from the cuff. Depicted in many forms as a common charge.

MANED — A term of reference to the manes of beasts such as the lion or horse when such manes are of a different tincture than the rest of the body.

MANTEAU D'ARMES — Concave shield attached to left shoulder of jousting armor. The surface of this shield was embossed with lattice strips to catch the point of the lance and thus prevent it from flancing up into the helmet.

MANTLES — The robes of state worn by peers are of crimson velvet trimmed with miniver fur bars on the cape. The number of bars that start at two for barons increase by half bars accordingly to each successively higher rank of nobility. Dukes who rank highest wear four bars.

MANTLING — An accessory of the crest. The covering above the helmet to lessen the effect of the sun and rain.

MARSHALLING — The combining of two or more coats of arms into a single heraldic field. Dimidiation, impalement, and quartering are three forms of marshalling.

MARTEL — A term for hammer.

MARTLET — A heraldic swallow depicted without feet. The mark of cadency for the fourth son of a family.

MASCLE — A subordinate charge in the form of a pierced lozenge.

MASCULY — A field composed of mascles.

MASONED — A term to describe the cemented or otherwise-bound joints between bricks; as in a castle wall.

MATRICULATION OF ARMS — A re-recording of family arms by the oldest son after the death of the father so as to properly inherit such arms.

MEMBERED — A bird whose beak, talons, and legs are of a different color than his body is said to be "membered" of that tincture.

MENTONNIERE — A two-part armor defense for the neck and lower face. Usually worn in supplement to the salade; a helmet that left that part of the face and body otherwise exposed. A defense somewhat similar to the volante piece.

MERLON — A part of the crenellated battlements atop a castle wall or tower. That part that alternately rises.

MERMAID — An imaginary half-woman, half-fish figure often found as shield supporters.

MILL-IRON — A pierced metal piece fixed to the center of a millstone. Found in several variations as a common charge and the basis for the cross moline.

MISERICORDE — A short dagger carried on the right side of the waist.

MITRE — A bishop's cap.

MOLET — A pierced, star-like charge that is the mark of cadency for the third son.

MOLINE CROSS — That cross whose limbs are shaped in the manner of a millstone (fer-de-moline).

MONOGRAM — Also called cypher. The E R of Queen Elizabeth and the H R of Henry the Eighth are two good examples.

MONSTERS — Imaginary animals whose hybrid form combines, as an example, faces of a bird with the body of a beast. The griffin is such a creature, the dragon, wyvern, cockatrice are other monsters all com-bining the body features of two animals.

MOON — A common charge classified under natural objects. It may appear FIGURED (with a human face). A full moon is described as "in her plentitude" or "in her complement."

MOTON — An armor defense covering the armpits.

MOTTO — A phrase normally appearing on the scroll below the shield. It expressed a sentiment of loyalty or morality in some cases and in others a religious thought.

MOUND — A ball or globe form symbolizing the world. A fixture atop the Royal Crown surmounted by a cross formy.

MOUNTED — Said of a horse bearing a rider.

MOURNED — Blunted or without teeth or claws as the lion is occasionally found.

MURAILLE — Masoned.

MURAL CROWN — A crown styled in the manner of castle battlements.

MURREY — Sanguine. A reddish purple (plum) tincture rarely seen. Said to be a livery color.

MUTILE — Mutilated or dismembered. Animal charges so depicted show their parts couped but left closely spaced to each other.

NAIANT — Said of a fish in an attitude of swimming.

NAISSANT — A term usually applied to a living creature rising from the center or top of an ordinary. A demi-lion issuing from a fess is a classic example.

NAVEL POINT — That location on a shield's surface halfway between the fess point and the base. Also called NOMBRIL POINT.

NEBULY — A cloud-like or mushrooming partition line sometimes used to outline ordinary charges.

NIMBUS — A halo.

NORFOLK, DUKE OF — Hereditary Earl Marshall of the College of Arms.

NORROY KING OF ARMS — Senior Officer of Arms north of the Trent River.

NOWED — Knotted, as in a lion's tail.

NOWY — A rarely seen line form used as a partition or outline for a common charge. It is basically a straight line with a single arch, perhaps symbolic of a knot.

OAK — A tree commonly depicted in arms.

OCCULARIUM — Eye slits in a helmet.

OCTOFOIL — An eight-leafed flower used as a mark of cadency for the ninth son.

OFFICERS OF ARMS — In England these are the members of the College of Arms; namely the Pursuivants, Heralds, and Kings of Arms.

OGRESS — A black roundle that is also called a PELLET.

OLIVE, GOUTTE D' — Sprinkled with green drops.

OPINICUS — A rarely used monster charge somewhat akin to a griffin, except for the former's bear tail.

OR — Gold tincture, often substituted with yellow.

ORDINARIES — The principal charges such as the fess, chief, bend, etc.

ORDINARY OF ARMS — A listing of arms grouped accordingly to the principal charge that distinguishes each one.

ORLE — A subordinate charge in the form of an inset bordure. Also a wreath around the bascinet originally placed there to hold the jousting helm snugly over it. Later retained in a more elaborate form for its own decorative value.

OSTRICH — A bird found as a shield supporter. Its feathers have appeared as crests, common charges, and badges.

OVERT — Open. A term usually applied to bird wings when found in this attitude.

OWL — A bird found as a badge or supporter.

PALE — An ordinary charge vertically occupying the middle third of the field.

PALEWISE — A reference to the placement of a charge that occupies the position of a pale.

PALL — An ordinary resembling the religious vestment, the pallium. This Y shaped charge when couped short of the edges of the shield is termed a *shakefork*.

PALLET — A diminutive of the pale.

PALLIUM — A mantle worn by bishops.

PALY — A varied field of palewise lines.

PALY-BENDY — A varied field combining palewise and bendwise lines.

PANACHE — A cluster of feathers which formed a crest on a helmet.

PARTED — A term describing the basic heraldic field. Also termed *party* or *party field*.

PARTED and FRETTY — A type of cross where the limbs are parted or sub-divided and interlaced where they cross at right angles.

PARTITION LINES — Those straight, zig-zag, arched, undulating, or cloudlike lines that can be used to outline an ordinary.

PASCHAL LAMB — The lamb found in a passant attitude with its head encircled with a halo and supporting a pennon between its paw

and dexter shoulder. The flag bears a cross gules. A charge found in ecclesiastical arms.

PAS D'ARMES — A passage of arms. A series of events between the same two opponents in a tournament. This series would usually include jousting as well as several contests on foot. The weapons used would change with each dismounted contest in which the two opponents were engaged. Such weapons would be the axe, sword, dagger, etc.

PATRIARCHAL CROSS — A long cross whose vertical limb is re-crossed near the top.

PATY — An alternate term for the cross called formy.

PAULDRON — An armor plate protecting the shoulder. This defense was introduced in England about 1430. Normally a large single plate but sometimes found in a laminated form.

PAVON — A flag about four or five yards long. Starting with a width of a half yard and tapering to a point. It is further distinguished by its lower side running exactly at right angle to the staff.

PEACOCK — A bird found as a charge, crest, or supporter. Uniquely described as being "in his pride" rather than "displayed" when its tail is spread.

PEAN — From the French word (pannes) for fur. A fur having gold spots on a black field.

PEER — The term describing any member of the nobility of Great Britain regardless of rank.

PEERESS — A lady who inherits her father's peerage by surviving all male heirs, if any, in her family.

PEERS' CORONETS — The crowns of nobility that vary in ornamentation according to rank.

PELICAN — A bird found in arms, depicted "in her piety" (feeding her young with her own blood).

PELLET — A black roundle. Also termed OGRESS.

PENNON — A flag resembling the guidon but only half the size of the latter. Also called PENNANT.

PENNONCELLE — A streamer (diminutive of the pennon) that was carried by the esquire to signify his aspiration toward knighthood. Also called a PENSIL.

PER — By way of or by means of.

PER BEND — By means of the bend—the manner in

which this line divides the shield. Per chevron, per cross, per fess, per pale, per pall, and per saltire are other means of partitioning the shield. Such partitions were the basis for the ordinary charges that came after them.

PIERCED — Voided through the center to show the field through the opening.

PIKE — A fish sometimes termed LUCY. One of the common charges and also a poled weapon.

PILE — One of the ordinaries. A wedgelike charge.

PILLOW — Also cushion. A common charge.

PILY — A field of pile-shaped pieces.

PILY-BENDY — A field of piles running bendwise.

PLANTA GENISTA — The plant whose pods were the badge symbol of the House of Plantagenet.

PLATE — A silver roundle.

PLATY — Strewn or scattered with plates.

PLUME — One of the forms of the crest.

POINTED, CROSS — A cross whose limbs end in points.

POIX, GOUTTE DE — Sprinkled with black drops.

POLE-AXE — A weapon combining a pick and a broad curved blade affixed to a long shaft. This weapon differs only from the battle-axe in the length of the shaft. The pole-axe, being longer, required both hands.

POMME — A green roundle.

POMME, CROSS — That cross whose limbs each end in a ball. In the manner of the Cross Annuletty whose limbs end in rings.

POMMEL — That ball or projection above the grip on a sword hilt. Often displaying the arms cognizance of the owner.

POMMETTY — Sprinkled with green drops.

POPINJAY — Another name for a parrot. A common charge found in arms and a figure found as a supporter.

PORTICULLIS — The iron grill protecting a gateway. Raised by chained pulleys and having spikes holding the ground at the base to help resist battering. A common charge that became the Royal Badge of the Tudors.

POT-DE-FER — An iron skull cap worn in the early part of the Middle Ages, often under the camail.

POTENT, CROSS — So named because of the crutch-like T endings of the limbs (potent being an old term for crutch). Also referred to as the Jerusalem cross.

POTENTY — A line of partition in the manner of

connected T's (alternately inverted). A design apparently adopted from earlier Roman ornamentation.

POWDERED — Said of any field with small repeated charges that appear to be strewn or scattered upon the field. This effect is heightened by their reaching the edges of the shield in various stages of completion. The French word "poudre" is an alternate term to describe this field.

PREYING — Said of a beast in the act of devouring its catch.

PRENOMINAL COAT — That portion of the quartered shield that displays the arms inherited from the father.

PROPER — In normal or natural colors. The letters Ppr. are sometimes used in blazoning to denote this condition of tincture.

PURFLED — Lined or bordered with fur (such as a crown or coronet). The term also applies to armor that is ornately garnished (such as with gold). This armor was common in the Maximillian period (1525–1600). Also termed *purflewed*.

PURPURE — The purple tincture.

PURSUIVANT — A junior Officer of Arms. Four Pursuivants presently exist in the College of Arms: the Rouge Dragon, Rough Croix, Porticullis, and Bluemantle.

QUADRATE, CROSS — That cross whose limbs extend from a square (quadrate) in its center.

QUARTER — That portion of the shield that occupies a fourth of its entire surface. An area that bears a portion of multiple arms united through marriage.

QUARTERED — Said of a shield divided into four parts for the purpose of displaying paternal and maternal arms.

QUATREFOIL — A four-petal flower appearing as a common charge. A double quatrefoil or octofoil is the mark of cadency for the ninth son.

QUEUE — An animal's tail. Also the term for the bar affixed to the breastplate of jousting armor to rest the lance grip.

QUINTAIN — Originally a post from which a suspended shield served as a target for mounted lancers to direct their aim. This was meant to develop skill in combat or tournaments.

QUINTFOIL — A five petal leaf more often termed cinquefoil. A common charge.

RABBIT — An animal found as a charge but usually

blazoned as a *coney*.

RADIANT — Encompassed, encircled or surrounded by rays. Also termed *rayonne*.

RAGGED STAFF — This symbol combined with a standing bear was the badge of the Earl of Warwick.

RAGULE — A line of partition suggesting a ragged staff or pruned tree limb. This line is one of those that are sometimes used to outline ordinaries.

RAINBOW — A natural object sometimes appearing as a charge (usually with clouds).

RAM — An animal found in heraldry as a common charge, crest, or supporter.

RAMPANT — An attitude of beasts when erect and supported solely by one foot on the ground. A position that suggested hostility. In this rampant attitude, the animal can be looking to his front, side, or rear (rampant, rampant guardant, or rampant reguardant).

RAPIER — A long, thin, tapering bladed sword. This trusting sword was developed in the 16th century. The single-edge version was carried at parades and the double-edge type was for combat.

RAVEN — A bird that is a member of the crow family. In heraldry, black birds are all depicted in this crow form whether they are termed crow, raven, rook, or corbie. The Cornish chough is also similar except that he is possessed of a red beak and legs and is so depicted in arms.

RAYS — Light beams as found in the sun "in its splendor" or in a *nimbus* (halo).

REBATED — Cut short or recessed. In tournament weaponry, this term meant blunted or dulled.

REBUS — A figure or object whose name suggests the name of the bearer. There is supposed to be a subtle difference between a rebus and allusive arms. Perhaps this is only that allusive arms constitute a complete shield bearing, whereas a rebus is only a component of such arms.

RECERCELE — Curled, as the *cross recercele*.

REFLECTED — Bent or curved backwards. Usually applied to chains attached to collared beasts.

REGUARDANT — Said of a beast whose head is turned to the viewer.

REINDEER — A beast of chase found in arms along with other members of the deer family.

These include the hind, buck, elk, stag, hart, antelope, and springbok. The stag, hart, buck, and hind are the earliest charges most commonly seen.

RESPECTANT — Facing one another. Also termed respecting.

RIBAND — A diminutive of the bend.

RISING — Said of a bird about to take wing.

ROACH — A fish found as a common charge.

ROLL OF ARMS — A term applied to any index of arms compiled in the Middle Ages. Many were actually vellum skin rolls upon which the arms were emblazoned. Others were manuscripts whereon the various arms were described rather than painted. Common participation in a battle was a basis for such groupings. Others recorded the contestants of a major tournament. Still others were the results of surveys or visitations conducted from time to time.

ROMPU — Broken or interrupted. An example of this term is the *chevron rompu*, a chevron that is interrupted halfway toward its point by an elevated positioning of the remainder of the charge.

ROOK — A type of crow depicted in arms in the same form as the raven and corbie. Not to be confused with the chessrook.

ROSE — The mark of cadency of the seventh son. The gold rose was the badge of Edward I and the Tudor (red and white) rose the badge of Henry VIII. The War of Roses was symbolized by the white Yorkist rose and the red Lancastrian rose.

ROUGE CROIX — An intermediate Office of Arms in England.

ROUGE DRAGON — An intermediate Office of Arms in England.

ROUND TABLE — A gathering of contestants to select specific opponents to a tournament.

ROUNDLES — Circular objects depicted in all of the tinctures. All but two of the nine roundles may be shown as balls. The remaining two, the bezant and the plate, are depicted as gold and silver discs respectively.

ROUSANT — An alternate term for rising as applied to the attitude of a bird.

ROWEL — A small wheel with star-like points attached to the spur. Said to be the basis for the molet charge.

RUNNING AT THE TINE — A later form of the quintain wherein the charging horseman attempts to snare a metal ring with his lance. This exercise was a preparation for the joust as were other forms of the quintain.

RUSTRE — A subordinate charge in the form of a pierced lozenge.

SABBATON — Broad-toed foot defenses. Successors to the sollarets (pointed and laminated foot coverings).

SABLE — The black tincture.

SALADE — A light-weight helmet introduced into England about 1450. This helmet rested entirely on the head and tapered to a distinctive point in the rear. Because it left the lower face exposed, it was usually worn with the mentonniere (a neck and cheek defense).

SALIENT — Springing or leaping. Said of a beast in this attitude.

SALLET — A form of the bascinet distinguished by its smaller T-shape opening in the front to make the face less vulnerable.

SALMON — A fish depicted in arms.

SALTIRE — One of the ordinaries. A diagonal cross.

SALTIREWISE — Said of a series of charges following the direction of the saltire. Also a substitute term for PER SALTIRE.

SANGUINE — Reddish purple tincture.

SARACEN'S HEAD — A common charge.

SARCELLE — Cut or voided through the middle as seen in the Cross Sarcelle.

SAVAGE — Wildman or men of the forest. Usually seen as a supporter.

SCALING LADDER — A siege device possessing hooks at the top to secure the ladder to the top of a beleaguered castle wall. A common charge.

SCARP — A bendlet sinister.

SCROLL — The device below the shield that displays the motto. Also called escroll.

SCRUTTLE — A winnowing fan seen as a common charge.

SEA-DOG — An imaginary animal resembling a talbot hound with webbed feet and a beaver tail. Possibly an attempt to depict the beaver from memory.

SEAGRANT — A term applied to griffins or dragons in describing their being in a rampant attitude.

SEA-HORSE — An imaginary creature combining the upper part of a horse and the lower part of a fish.

SEA-LION — Depicted both as a natural creature and an imaginary one. The imaginary or heraldic sea-lion is one with a lion's head and forepaws and a fish's body.

SEALS — The personal cognizances that leaders imprinted in wax to authenticate documents and messages.

SEAX — A notched and curved sword found as a common charge.

SECRETUM — A private seal in addition to the official seal of sovereigns, which mark more confidential papers.

SEEDED — A reference to the vessels of flowers such as the rose when of a different tincture than the petals.

SEJANT — Sitting. A term usually applied to the lion in this attitude.

SEMÉ — Scattered or strewn with a charge. Powdered or poudre are alternate terms meaning the same thing.

SERPENT — Snake. Found in a *nowed* (knotted) or *glissant* (sliding) attitude. It may also be found coiled with its head erect.

SHAFTED — A term used when necessary to describe the tincture of an arrow shaft.

SHAKEFORK — A principal charge in the form of a pall with the limbs couped.

SHEAF OF ARROWS — A common charge normally displaying three arrows with one erect and the other two crossing it in saltire.

SINISTER — The left side of the shield from the viewpoint of someone positioned behind it. More commonly considered the right side as seen from the front.

SIREN — Another term for mermaid; a figure appearing as a shield supporter.

SLIP — A leafed twig.

SLIPPED — Said of a flower or leaf when it carries the stem that attached it to the plant or tree of its origin.

SOARING — The attitude of a bird in flight.

SOLLARETS — Foot armor in the form of several laminated plates generally coming to a point after reaching the toes. Predecessors of the sabbatons, a broad-toed metal shoe.

SPEAR — A common charge generally appearing as a tilting lance. A general term for an ancient poled weapon that was replaced by the many long-shafted weapons of the Middle Ages. These included the pole-axe, bell, glaive, halberd fauchard (guisarme), and partisan.

SPLINTED ARMOR — The body defenses of the transitional period of armor (1335–1360). A type of armor that featured hard leather strips (splints) over which either metal strips or studs were fastened. The aim was to obtain maximum freedom of movement. This period introduced the skirted jupon as the surcoat that bore the arms of the wearer.

SPRINGING — An attitude associated with the deer, an animal of chase, in preference to *salient*, a springing attitude of the beasts of prey.

SQUIRREL — An animal infrequently found as a common charge.

STAFFORD KNOT — One of a great number of badges variously employed by the Stafford family as personal cognizances.

STALL-PLATE — A gilt copper plate affixed to the church stalls of Knights of the Garter, Bath, and Thistle. These plates of a square or oblong shape displayed the arms of each knight.

STANDARD — A long or large swallow-tailed flag. In the Middle Ages, each sovereign, nobleman, and knight banneret was said to carry one of a size in keeping with his rank.

STAR — Called an *estoile*. A common charge adopted from the natural object. It displayed six wavy rays and differed from the molet, which had only five straight rays and a pierced center.

STATANT — Standing or stationary. In describing the attitude of beasts this term is sometimes followed by terms such as *guardant* or *reguardant* to define the head position when faced other than to the dexter.

STOCK — A tree stump. Usually blazoned *couped* and *eradicated* (uprooted).

STORK — A bird usually found as a shield supporter.

STRINGED — A term used in describing strings of an arrow, bugle horn, or musical instrument when such strings are of a different tincture than the object itself.

SUFFLUE — Clarion. An odd looking wind instrument with a series of pipes apparently played like a harmonica. This instrument was depicted in several forms as a common charge. At one time it was wrongly interpreted as a lance rest.

SUN — A natural object that appeared as a common charge. When surrounded by its own rays, it is termed "in its splendor." When displaying a human face, it is termed *figured*.

SUNBURST — A device that was the basis for certain badges. A military cap ornament in modern times as well.

SUPER CHARGE — A charge placed on top of another charge.

SUPPORTERS — Animal or human figures that uphold the shield on each side.

SURCOAT — Any tunic worn over armor. Such tunics normally displayed the arms of the wearer, although their original purpose was to protect the armor and the wearer from the weather. The expression, "coat of arms" is an outgrowth of the display of arms upon these tunics.

SURMOUNTED — Said of a charge overlayed (supercharged) by another.

SWALLOW — A bird frequently seen as a common charge. The martlet is a heraldic swallow depicted without legs in support of the belief that this bird is incapable of perching on the ground.

SWAN — A bird found as a common charge, supporter, and crest.

SWASTIKA — Called *fylfot*; also *cross potent rebated*. A cross whose limbs are bent back at right angles at their halfway points.

SWORD — A common charge. Usually *hilted* of a different tincture than the blade.

SWORD, REBATED — A sword whose point is blunted or broken off and whose edge is dulled. A tournament sword so fixed as to minimize the chance of injury from it.

SWORD, THRUSTING — The rapier; a narrow-bladed sword.

SWORD, TWO HANDED — A sword with a very long hilt and a double-edge blade meant for sweeping cuts.

TABARD — A tunic worn over armor. The last tunic style to be introduced following the long surcoat, cyclas, skirted jupon, and jupon.

TACES — Laminated armor plates or hoops protecting the hops. Also called tasses or tassets.

TALBOT — A hound appearing as a common charge and supporter.

TAU CROSS — A cross so named for its resemblance to the Greek T.

TENANS — Also *Tenants*. Challengers at a tournament. Their respondents were called *venans*, a term in French heraldry that meant human-figured shield supporters. The latter use of this term is apparently in some way connected with its tournament meaning. An example of this is the fact that French knights representing their country or *supporting* its honor would offer challenges to their English counterparts.

TENNE — Orange tincture.

THISTLE — The flower that was the Royal Badge of Scotland. Still a part of the present badge representing the United Kingdom (England, Scotland, and Ireland).

THUNDERBOLT — A common charge depicted as a bolt of flame between two conjoined wings.

TIGER — An animal depicted in a natural and heraldic form. Most frequently found as a supporter.

TINCTURE — A word for color.

TORCH — A common charge depicted as a burning shaft of wood.

TORQUED — Wreathed.

TORSE — Originally a simple ribbon placed at the juncture of the tournament helmet and its crest presumably to conceal an awkward fastening at that point. Later this ribbon was replaced with a scarf or contoise (the latter term being the word from which *torse* was derived). This scarf eventually ceased to hang in a free-flowing manner and was deliberately twisted about the helm in a turban-like form. It became a permanent crest accessory in this form. Such scarfs and ribbons were said to have been provided by ladies as tokens of favor.

TORTEAU — A red roundle.

TOURNAMENT — A series of armed contests or war games between individual opponents and/or two groups of mounted troops.

TOWER — Gatetower. A single tower not to be confused with a castle with two or more towers.

TOWERED — A term reference regarding castle towers.

TRAPPER — The horse blanket usually ornamented with the arms of the rider.

TREES — The oak tree is the most common of the trees found in arms. It is said to be *acorned* when such growths are displayed upon its branches. Other trees that bear fruit (always shown in an ex-

aggerated size) are said to be *fructed*.

TREFLE — Scattered or adorned with trefoils.

TREFOIL — A three-leaf flower that is a common charge.

TRELLIS — Latticed. Similar to fretty except that trellis does not interlace. It is merely an *overlapping* of bendlets upon bendlets sinister.

TRESSURE — A subordinate charge. An inset border in the manner of the orle but about half its width. This charge generally appears double as seen in the Royal Arms of Scotland.

TRICKED — Sketched. Said of a coat of arms that has been drawn in outline and whose colors have been indicated by notations placed near the areas involved with a line leading thereto. The substitute system of line hatchings is also a method of denoting colors when the hatching is placed *within* each appropriate area. When arms have the same charge repeated, only one charge is sketched and is designated number one, while the remainder are only indicated by successive numbers in the area in which they would normally lie.

TRI-CORPORATE — Having three bodies joined to one head. Said of the lion charge possessed of three bodies.

TRIDENT — The three-pronged spear associated with Neptune, the sea god, and also linked with lesser mermen.

TRI-PARTED — Divided into three parts.

TRIPPANT — said of a stag (or other deer) when passant.

TRONCONE — Cut into pieces but left closely spaced in their normal alignment. Descriptive of the lion mutile (dechaussé).

TROUT — A type of fish found as a common charge.

TRUMPET — A common charge found in more than one form.

TRUSSED — Said of a bird whose wings are closed.

TRUSSING — Devouring prey. The equivalent of vorant in other beasts.

TUDOR ROSE — The red and white flower that became the Royal Badge of Henry VIII.

TUILLES — Large armor plates hanging from the taces or tassets that protected the upper thigh.

TYGER — Intended to indicate the heraldic tiger rather than the natural one by the manner in which it is spelled.

TYNES — The points of a stag, or other deer's antlers (attires).

ULSTER KING OF ARMS — The principal Officer of Arms of Northern Ireland.

UNDY — An alternative for *wavy*. The undulating line of partition also used to outline charges.

UNGULED — Hoofed. A term introduced in blazoning when describing an animal's hoofs being of a different tincture than its body.

UNICORN — An imaginary animal appearing in heraldry. Essentially a horse form mainly distinguished by a long horn issuing from its forehead. The unicorn appears as a charge as well as a supporter.

UNION FLAG — The national flag of England, combining the Crosses of St. George, St. Andrew, and St. Patrick.

UNITED KINGDOM BADGE — The Royal Badge combining the Tudor rose, the Irish harp, and the Scottish thistle.

URDY — A line of partition made up of a connected series of roof-shaped (gabled) points alternately facing upward and downward. The Cross Urdy has limb endings whose points are of this same character.

URIANT — Diving. A term to describe fish appearing as a common charge when palewise with their heads downwards. *Urinant* is an alternate term to describe the aforementioned attitude.

VAIR — A type of fur. It is distinguished by the repeated wavy blue pieces of its original form and by the urdy and potent blue pieces of its variant forms (*counter-vair, vair en point, potent,* and *counter potent*).

VALLARY CROWN — A crown whose styling is derived from the form of defensive works (angled wooden spikes) meant to deter cavalry charges. The Palisado crown is similarly associated with this defense.

VAMBRANCE — An armor defense for the forearm. Later supplemented by the *epaule de mouton,* (Polder miton) which was attached to the vambrance to protect the inside of the right elbow. A similar attachment to the left elbow was called the *garde-de-bras.*

VAMPLATE — The metal plate around the grip of the jousting lance that protected the hand and arm.

VARIED FIELD — A field created in two ways:
1. By repeating several times a basic line of partition (such as *per bend*) to obtain a *bendy field*.
2. By combining two fields, each derived from repeated partition line (such as *bendy, barry,* or *paly*) to obtain an even more complex varied field. A third variation may be derived by a line of partition dividing the first, or less complex, of the above mentioned fields so as to necessitate an adjustment of the tinctures. This is a varied field called *counter-changed.*

VERDE — Strewn (semé) with leaves or plants.

VERT — Green tincture.

VERVELS — The rings attached to the restraining thongs on falcons.

VESTED — Clothed. Said of couped arms that display sleeves when appearing as common charges. Described as being *vested* of a specific tincture.

VISCOUNT — That rank of nobility below earl and above baron.

VISITATION — A periodic survey of arms conducted by the heralds on the commission of the king. Such visitations determined the validity of existing arms and recorded those deemed properly borne.

VOIDED — Said of a charge whose greater central area is removed so as to leave only a shell or near outline of the original. An annulet (ring) might be described as a *voided roundle*. The term *false* also implies *voided.*

VOL — Said of two wings cojoined and tipped upwards.

VOLANT — Flying. Said of a bird in this attitude.

VOLANTE PIECE — A lower face and neck guard attached to the breastplate. Similar to the *mentonniere.*

VORANT — Devouring. A reference to beasts and birds of prey.

VULNED — Wounded and showing blood. Said of the pelican feeding her young from a self-inflicted wound in her breast.

WAKE KNOT — One of several different rope entwinements that served as badges. In this case, it was the personal cognizance of the Wake family.

WATER — Depicted naturally or heraldically represented by barry wavy azure and argent.

WATER BOUGET — Two water bags cojoined by a carrying yoke. Depicted in several abstract forms.

WATTLED — A term referring to a cock's comb and wattles when of a different tincture than the body.

WAVY — A line of partition also used to outline charges. An undulating form suggestive of the character of sea water. This form can be used to suggest sea water in heraldry or it can be depicted in a natural form.

WHEAT — Depicted in a cluster called a *garb*. The term *garb*, when blazoned alone, is always meant to imply a wheat sheaf. If sheaf of another grain is intended, the name of the grain must be stated.

WHEEL — Found as a common charge in the form of the usual wagon wheel.

WHEEL, CATHERINE — A common charge symbolic of the martyrdom of St. Catherine. A wheel similar to a wagon wheel to which curved blades have been affixed outside the rim in line with the spokes.

WHELK-SHELL — An occasional common charge.

WHITE — A substitute tincture for silver.

WILD MAN — Savage. Figure seen as a supporter with a wreath about the head and loins. Usually further distinguished by the wooden club that he bore.

WINNOWING FAN — Called a scruttle; a common charge.

WOLF — An animal seen as a common charge and supporter.

WREATH — A circle of entwined leaves granted as a special honor, the laurel and oak being the most common types.

WYVERN — A type of dragon with only two legs.

YALE — A monster of rare heraldic usage. A sort of goat-horned and hoofed animal with a talbot's (dog) face.

YORK HERALD — One of the intermediate Officers of Arms in England.

YORK, HOUSE OF — The family whose cognizance was the white rose. One of the two participants in the War of the Roses.

Selective Heraldic Bibliography

Barron, Oswald. *Encyclopaedia Britannica*. 11th ed. (Heraldry Section). Cambridge: University Press, 1910.

Bolton, Charles K. *Bolton's American Armory*. Boston: T. W. Faxon Co., 1927.

Boutell, Charles. *Boutell's Heraldry*. several revised eds. Revised by J. P. Brooke-Little. London, New York: F. Warne, 1970.

Burke, Sir Bernard. *General Armory*. London: Harrison, 1883.

——. *Peerage and Baronetage*. London: Hurst and Blackett, 1853.

Carr, H. Gresham. *Flags of the World*. London, New York: F. Warne, 1953.

Davis, Cecil. *Monumental Brasses of Gloucestershire*. London: Phillimore & Co., 1899.

Denholm-Young, Noel. *History and Heraldry 1254–1310: A Study of the Rolls of Arms*. Oxford: Clarendon Press, 1965.

De Walden, H. *Banners, Standards and Badges: From a Tudor Manuscript in the College of Arms*. London: DeWalden Library, 1904.

Ellis, W. S. *Antiquities of Heraldry*. London: J. R. Smith, 1869.

Eve, G. W. *Decorative Heraldry*. London, New York: G. Bell & Sons, 1897.

——. *Heraldry as an Art*. London: B. T. Batsford. New York: C. Scribner's Sons, 1907.

Fairbairn, G. W. *Book of Crests*. rev. ed. Edinburgh: T. C. & E. C. Jack, 1892.

Fox-Davis, A. C. *The Right to Bear Arms*. 2d ed., rev. & enl. London: E. Stock, 1899.

——. *The Art of Heraldry*. London: E. C. Jack, 1904.

——. *Heraldic Badges*. London and New York: J. Lane, 1907.

——. *The Book of Public Arms*. London: T. C. & E. C. Jack, 1915.

——. *Complete Guide to Heraldry*. London: T. C. & E. C. Jack, 1929.

Franklyn, Charles A. H. *The Bearing of Coat Armour by Ladies*. London: J. Murray, n. d.

Gatfield, George. *Guide to Printed Books and Manuscripts Relating to English and Foreign Heraldry and Genealogy*. London: Mitchell & Hughes, 1892.

Gayre, Robert. *Heraldic Standards and Other Ensigns*. Edinburgh: Oliver & Boyd, 1959.

Gough, Henry. *Glossary of Terms Used in Heraldry*. Rutland, Vt.: E. C. Tuttle Co., 1970.

Grant, F. J. *Manual of Heraldry*. Edinburgh: J. Grant, 1914.

Harleian Society. *Heralds' Visitations*. vols. 1–89. London: Harleian Society Publications. 1869–1952.

Heraldry Society. *The Coat of Arms* (quarterly). East Knoyle, Wiltshire.

Hope, Sir W. H. St. John. *Grammar of English Heraldry*. 2d ed., rev. Anthony R. Wagner. Cambridge: University Press, 1953.

——. *Heraldry for Craftsmen and Designers*. London: J. Hogg, 1913.

Innes, Thomas. *Scots Heraldry*. 2d ed. Edinburgh: Oliver & Boyd, 1956.

Lawrence, Henry. *Heraldry from Military Monuments Before 1350 in England and Wales*. Harleian Society Quarterly 96 (London) (1946).

London, H. Stanford. *Royal Beasts*. East Knoyle, Wiltshire: Heraldry Society, 1956.

Lynch-Robinson, Adrian, and Sir Christopher. *Intelligible Heraldry*. London: Macdonald, 1949.

Metzig, W. V. N. *Heraldry for the Designer*. New York, Cincinnati, Melbourne: Reinhold Co., 1970.

Messenger, A. W. B. *Heraldry of Canterbury Cathedral.* Canterbury: Office of the Friends, 1947.

Montague, J. A. *A Guide to the Study of Heraldry.* 1840.

Moule, Thomas. *Heraldry of Fish.* London: J. Van Voorst, 1842.

Rapworth, J. W. *Ordinary of Arms*: reproduced from 1874 edition. London: Tabard Publications, 1961.

Paul, Sir James B. *Ordinary of Scottish Arms.* Edinburgh: W. Green and Sons, 1903.

————. *Heraldry in Relation to Scottish History and Art.* Edinburgh: D. Douglas, 1900.

Pine, L. G. *The Story of Heraldry.* London: Country Life, 1953.

Planche, J. R. *The Pursuivant of Arms.* London: R. Hardwick, 1859.

Reitstap, J. B. *Armorial General.* 2d ed. Lyon, France: Sauvegarde Historique, 1884.

Scott-Giles, C. W. *The Romance of Heraldry.* 1st ed. New York: E. P. Dutton & Co., 1929; 3d ed., 1950.

————. *Civic Heraldry of England and Wales.* 2d ed. London: J. M. Dent & Sons, 1953.

————. *Shakespeare's Heraldry.* London: J. M. Dent & Sons, 1950.

Seton, G. S. *The Law and Practice of Heraldry in Scotland.* rev. by J. H. Stevenson. Glasgow: J. Maclehose & Sons, 1914.

Squibb, G. D. *The Law of Arms in England.* rev. ed. East Knoyle, Wiltshire: Heraldry Society, 1953.

————. *The High Court of Chivalry*: A Study of the Civil Law. Oxford: Clarendon Press, 1959.

Victoria and Albert Museum: National Art Library. *Classified Catalogue of Printed Books of Heraldry.* London: Wyman & Sons, 1901.

Wagner, Sir Anthony R. *Historic Heraldry of Britain.* London, New York: Oxford University Press, 1939.

————. *Heralds and Heraldry in the Middle Ages.* London: H. Milford, Oxford University Press, 1939, 1956.

————. *Heraldry in England.* Harmondsworth: Penguin Books, 1949.

————. *A Catalogue of English Medieval Rolls of Arms.* vol. 100. London: Harleian Society, 1950.

————. *The Records and Collections of the College of Arms.* London: Burkes Peerage, 1952.

————. *Heralds of England.* London: Her Majesty's Stationery Office, 1967.

Woodward, John. *Ecclesiastical Heraldry.* Edinburgh, 1894.

————, and Burnett, G. *Heraldry, British and Foreign.* Edinburgh and London: W. & A. K. Johnston, 1892.

Early Heraldic Bibliography

Berry, William. *Encyclopedia Heraldica.* vol. 1. London: Sherwood, Gilbert and Piper, 1828.

Betham, Sir William. *Baronetage of England.* 5 vols. London: E. Lloyd, 1801–1805.

Bossewell, John. *Works of Armorie.* London: Richard Tottell, 1572.

Camden, William. *Britain, or a Chorographical Description of the Most Flourishing Kingdom of England, Scotland and Ireland, etc.* Trans. and rev. by Philemon Holland. London: G. Bishop & I. Norton, 1610.

Dallaway, James. *Science of Heraldry In England.* Gloucester: R. Raikes for T. Cadell, London, 1793.

DeBara, Hierome. *Le Blason des Armories.* France, 1581.

Edmondson, Joseph. *Complete Body of Heraldry.* 2 vols. London: T. Spilsburg, 1780.

Ferne, Sir John. *Blazon of Gentry.* London: J. V. Vindet for A. Maunsell, 1586.

Godwin. *Peerage of England.* (2 vols.) London, 1790.

Guillim, John. *Display of Heraldry.* London: William Hall, 1610.

Leigh, Gerard. *Accidens of Armorie.* London: Richard Tottell, 1591.

Morgan, Sylvanus. *Sphere of Gentry.* London: W. Leybourne, 1661.

Menestrier, C. F. *La Methode du Blason.* Lyon, 1688.

———. *La Nouvelle Methode Raisonnee du Blason, etc.* Lyon: T. Amaulrys, 1696.

Miller. *Catalogue of Honour.* London, 1610.

Nesbit, Alexander. *Ancient and Armories.* Edinburgh: J. Mack Euen, 1718.

Philipot, Thomas. *Origin and Growth of Heraldry.* 8 vols. London: E. Tyler & R. Holt, 1672.

Robson. *British Herald* (Supplement). *Symbol Heroica or Mottoes of Nobility and Baronets of Great Britain and Ireland.* London, 1736.

Siebmacher, J. B. *Wappenbuch; 1655.* Reprint 1856. Nurnberg: Verlag Von Bauer und Raspe, 1898.

Tournament Bibliography

Aikman, James. *The Tournament at Eglington*. Edinburgh: H. Paton, 1839.

Archeologia. Published by the Society of Antiquaries of London. London: Printed by J. Nichols, 1773–1970.

Archeology Journals. Published by Cambridge Antiquarian Society. Cambridge and London, 1897–1905.

Ashmolean MSS. British Museum.

Catalogues:
> *Catalogo Real Armeria de Madrid.*
> *Musee d'Artillerie, Paris.*
> *Guida Officiale della Reale Armeria.*
> *di Torino, Turin.*
> *Porte de Hal Collection, Brussels.*
> *National Museum, Munich.*
> *Wallace Collection, London.*
> *The Armouries of the Tower of London.*

Chaucer, G. *Knights' Tale*. London: G. S. Harrap, 1954.

Clark. *History of Knighthood*. England, n. p., n. d.

Clephan, R. Cottman. *The Tournament: Its Periods and Phases*. New York: Frederick Unger, 1967.

Cottonian MSS. British Museum, London.

Cripps-Day, Francis H. *The History of the Tournament in England and France*. London: B. Quaritch, 1918.

Dugdale, Sir William. *Origines Judiciales*.

———. *Pageants of Richard Beauchamp, Earl of Warwick*. Oxford: Private printing, Roxburgh Club, 1908.

Favine, Andre. *Honour and Knighthood*. London: W. Laggard, 1623.

ffoulkes, Charles. *The Armourer and His Craft*. London, Methuen & Co. Ltd., 1912.

Froissart. *Late 15th Century Illustrated Chronicle*. British Museum, Harl MS 4379.

Harleian MSS. British Museum.

La Colombière—*Theatre d' Hon and de Chivalarie*.

Lacroix, Paul. *Military and Religious Life in the Middle Ages*. Trans. from the 1874 French ed. New York: Frederick Ungar Co., 1964.

Luard, Lt. Col. John. *History of the Dress of the British Soldier*. London: W. Clowes & Son, 1852.

Mann, Sir James. *European Arms and Armour*. London: W. Clowes & Son, 1962.

Martin, Paul. *Arms and Armour: From the 9th to the 17th Century*. Rutland, Vt.: Mombray Co., 1968.

Menestrier, C. F. *Traite des Tournois, Justs Carrousels, etc*. Lyon: Chez Iaques Muguet, 1669.

Meyrick, Sir Samuel R. *A Critical Inquiry Into Ancient Armour, etc*. London: H. Bohn, 1842.

Mowbray, E. Andrew. *Arms-Armour: From the Atelier of Ernst Schmidt, Munich*. Rutland, Vt.: Mombray Co., 1969.

Oakeshott, R. Ewart. *Archeology of Weapons*. New York: Praeger, 1960.

———. *The Sword in the Age of Chivalry*. London: Lutterworth Press, 1964.

Oxford University Press. *Great Tournament Rolls of Westminster*. Oxford, 1970.

Rous, Francis. *Life of the Earl of Warwick: Cott MS*. Julius, E. IV.

Schwenk, Hans. *Wappenmeisterbuch: Jousts of Duke William of Bavaria*.

Spelman, Sir Henry. *Spelman's Glossary*. London: Thomas Braddyll, 1687.

Stone, George Cameron. *A Glossary of the Construction, Decoration and Use of Arms and Armor in All Countries and in All Times*. Portland, Me.: Southwest Press, 1934.

Armor Bibliography

Ashdown, Charles H. *Armor and Weapons in the Middle Ages.* London: G. G. Harrap, 1925.

Boutell, C. *Monumental Brasses and Slabs.* London: G. Bell, 1947.

Dufty, Arthur R. *European Armor in the Tower of London.* London: Her Majesty's Stationery Office, 1968.

ffoulkes, Charles. *The Armourer and His Craft.* London: Methuen & Co. Ltd., 1912.

Grancsay, Stephen V. *Catalogue of Armour: From the Higgins Armory, Mass.* Worcester, Mass.: 1961.

Hayward, J. F. *Swords and Daggers: Of Victoria and Albert Museum.* London: Her Majesty's Stationery Office, 1951.

Holmes, M. R. *Arms and Armour in Tudor and Stuart London.* London: Her Majesty's Stationery Office, 1951.

Luard, Lt. Col. John. *History of the Dress of the British Soldier.* London: William Clowes & Sons, 1852.

Mann, Sir James G. *European Arms and Armour.* London: William Clowes, 1962.

Meyrick, Sir Samuel. *A Critical Inquiry into Ancient Armour, etc.* London: H. G. Bohn, 1842.

Mowbray, E. Andrew. *Arms-Armour: From the Atelier of Ernst Schmidt, Munich.* Providence, R.I.: Mowbray Co., 1967.

Oakeshott, R. Ewart. *Archeology of Weapons.* New York: Praeger, 1960.

———. *The Sword in the Age of Chivalry.* London: Lutterworth Press, 1964.

Stone, George Cameron. *A Glossary of the Construction, Decoration and Use of Arms and Armor in All Countries in all Times.* Portland, Me.: Southwest Press, 1934.

Thomas, B., Gamber, O., and Schedelman, H. *European Arms and Armor.* New York: McGraw-Hill, 1964.

Viollet-le-Duc, E. E. *Dictionnaire Raisonne du Mobilier Français.* (6. vols.). Paris: Bance & Co., 1858–1875.

Index

257